Creative Reconstructions

A volume in the series

Cornell Studies in Political Economy

Edited by Peter J. Katzenstein

A list of titles in this series is available at www.cornellpress.cornell.edu.

Creative Reconstructions

*Multilateralism and European
Varieties of Capitalism after 1950*

Orfeo Fioretos

Cornell University Press
Ithaca and London

First published 2011 by Cornell University Press

Printed in the United States of America

Library of Congress Cataloging-in-Publication Data

Fioretos, Karl Orfeo, 1966–
    Creative reconstructions : multilateralism and European varieties of capitalism after 1950 / Orfeo Fioretos.
        p. cm. — (Cornell studies in political economy)
    Includes bibliographical references and index.
    ISBN 978-0-8014-4969-7 (cloth : alk. paper)
    1. Europe—Economic policy.   2. Europe—Foreign economic relations.   3. Capitalism—Europe.   4. International trade agencies—Europe.   5. European cooperation.   I. Title.
    II. Series: Cornell studies in political economy.
    HC240.F457   2011
    330.94—dc22   2011000864

Cloth printing   10 9 8 7 6 5 4 3 2 1

For Priya

Contents

Preface   ix

1. Capitalist Diversity in Open Economies   1

2. Governments, Business, and the Design Problem   16

3. Three Models of Open Governance   44

4. Britain: From Replacing to Reinforcing a Liberal Market Economy   68

5. France: The Centralized Market Economy and Its Alternatives   99

6. Germany: Stability and Redesign in a Coordinated Market Economy   136

7. Lessons from Capitalist Diversity and Open Governance   172

Appendix   185

Notes   193

References   211

Index   239

Preface

Joseph A. Schumpeter, the Austrian economist whose concept of creative destruction received so much new attention in the last decade of the twentieth century, remarked that "capitalism not only never is but never can be stationary" (1942, 82). He argued that the corporate sector stood to lose more from choosing the status quo than from reform when it faced greater competition. Schumpeter's notion of creative destruction became a leitmotif in the debate over the consequences of globalization. Policymakers used the term to underscore that in the age of globalization, it was important to embrace the new and shed the old. Scholars attributed changes in economic governance to creative destruction—and instances of limited change to political inefficiencies. But in linking economic globalization so closely to processes of creative destruction, scholars often overlooked other creative responses to greater competition, including the innovative ways in which governments and the corporate sector sought to *preserve* historic designs.

This book explores the creative ways in which governments and the corporate sector destroyed and preserved integral features of national economic systems through periods of profound change in Europe's advanced market economies. Reforms in economic systems are often about dismantling past designs, but equally if not more often in some periods, they are about protecting designs that are deemed integral to success in the face of technological revolutions, economic crises, and the integration of international markets. After World War II, however, the politics of institutional destruction and preservation went beyond national borders and entailed a significant and evolving commitment to international cooperation and the institution of multilateralism. This book finds that the manner in which governments reconciled their domestic reform agendas with their multilateral commitments profoundly shaped the institutional evolution of Europe's largest market economies.

Western Europe was a veritable laboratory of institutional innovation after 1950. Governments actively and frequently engaged in extensive reforms that aimed to alter the structure of their economies. With a debt to the varieties of capitalism tradition pioneered by Peter A. Hall and David Soskice (2001), this book examines the distributional conflicts associated with economic reform and explores how these conflicts affected the sustainability of a diverse set of economic models. It explains the role that historic designs and the politics of the moment played, and it documents what effects national and international politics jointly had in shaping reforms across multiple economic domains, countries, and distinct periods.

The domestic consequences of greater reliance on multilateralism were not one-sided. As Alan Milward (1992) noted in an early study of the relationship between domestic reform and international cooperation, multilateral initiatives often helped "rescue" core features of national economic models after 1945. But multilateral designs may also threaten to undermine important features of national economic models. For these reasons, European governments have persistently devoted great attention to what form multilateral rules will take, what norms will guide economic governance, and how these multilateral rules and norms will shape their ability to achieve domestic goals.

In post-war Europe, the European Union and its predecessors would acquire particular significance for governments seeking to sustain or transform national economic models. Alongside the strong material interests that governments and the corporate sector had in European multilateralism—a matter comprehensively documented by Andrew Moravcsik (1998) and Barry Eichengreen (2007)—governments and the business sector expended much effort and political capital in securing particular forms for multilateral institutions. The outcomes of such attempts were key to the successes of governments in sustaining domestic reform. These reforms were typically sustainable when governments secured multilateral designs that were compatible with national economic designs, but tended to be undermined when they were unable to ensure compatible multilateral designs or when the latter drifted out of alignment with domestic ones.

This book examines how European governments managed the integration of domestic and multilateral institutions at various moments after 1950 across a range of areas of economic governance. Its substantive scope and analytical and methodological profiles are informed by practices in the disciplines of comparative and international political economy. To ensure a relatively large set of empirical cases on which assessments can be made about the sources of varied patterns of institutional reform, the book focuses on three paradigmatic cases of post-war capitalism (Britain, France, and Germany); on four economic areas that are commonly considered integral to advanced capitalism; and on the most consequential international organizations and multilateral institutions. The empirical sections are structured as a set of analytical narratives, an approach that places specific political governance problems at the center and that examines historic material through the lens of how those particular problems are resolved (Bates et al. 1998). More specifically, the volume's analytical focus falls on institutional alternatives to coordination between governments and the business community, and the conditions under which members of the latter supported the reforms championed by the former as international economic and institutional contexts evolved.

To avoid drawbacks associated with analytical narratives, the book introduces procedures associated with systematic process analysis (Hall 2003). It examines the claims of three approaches to institutional analysis—rational choice, historical, and behavioral—and documents how effectively each accounts for a broad set of empirical cases. This research design helps identify which theoretical tradition does a better job of accounting for empirical patterns. The book concludes that a historical institutional approach supplemented with behavioral economics facilitates nuanced answers to why European economies experienced varied patterns of reform across time and issue areas.

The book answers a set of analytical questions that have bearing on the causes behind consequential, long-term processes of institutional development in advanced market economies. It is not designed to account for all details of reform and is therefore not invested in claims of primary research originality. Primary material citations are selective, focused on key cases, and placed in the general reference section. When primary research was corroborated in the secondary literature, the latter is typically cited to facilitate access for readers. A list of the archives that were used appears in the section on sources. Also detailed are semi-structured interviews that were conducted over a decade.

The 2008 global financial crisis serves as the bookend to this volume. Like earlier crises, the 2008 one has generated intense debates about alternative models of capitalism. Also like earlier ones, this crisis will usher institutional innovations in modern capitalism, a significant portion being incremental rather than radical. If this book has an implication for what advanced capitalist systems may look like in the future, it is that the institution of multilateralism will become more important both in shaping relations between states and in managing economic affairs within states. This has been a pattern for decades, and economic crises of national, regional, and global nature have featured prominently in spurring innovations in multilateralism. For all its purported inflexibility, European multilateralism has been an adaptable device that has allowed countries both to jettison and to protect key features of historic models of advanced capitalism through economic crises and booms alike. Though governments were not always successful in designing multilateral institutions in ways that strengthened the prospects for domestic reform, they were frequently able to avoid designs that would have had immediate and politically problematic consequences.

The finding that multilateralism served periodically to recreate European capitalism ought not to be controversial. There is a broad consensus that the European Union is a multilateral organization that significantly affects economic management within states. Yet the role of the EU in shaping national forms of capitalism over time is a theme often addressed in select pieces or with a broad brush, rather than in the context of sustained contextualized and controlled comparisons across multiple time periods and issue areas. To wit, studies of the relationship between national economies and the EU have tended to focus either on the domestic effects of the same multilateral design at a specific moment in time or on the economic reasons that states have promoted international cooperation. The political story of how the interplay between domestic and multilateral institutions constrained and facilitated particular national strategies of economic reform, across a variety of issue areas and time periods remains an open area for research. This volume fills particular lacunae in this area and identifies the conditions under which post-war European governments succeeded in sustaining and transforming distinct economic models over time.

Multilateralism today is a widely and deeply employed institutional form to create and regulate markets. The concluding chapter addresses lessons that post-war Europe holds beyond its borders and for the study of fundamental questions in comparative and international political economy. It notes that although there is little reason to expect that the European examples will be emulated elsewhere, the particular ways in which Europe's diverse economies reconciled the expansion of economic multilateralism with diverse domestic reforms entails valuable lessons for economic management outside Europe.

I have incurred much personal debt in completing this book during relatively distinct periods. At Columbia University, Helen Milner inspired my interest in the relationship between domestic and international politics; Charles Tilly helped me explore the consequences of international competition in historical perspective; Richard Nelson taught me about business and mixed economies; and Hendrik Spruyt and Arvid Lukauskas guided my early inquiries into the relationship between national economies and international economic organizations. I am also grateful to Robert Jervis for his guidance when exploring the promise and pitfalls of interdisciplinarity, especially at the intersections of international relations, history, and psychology.

I thank the Department of Political Science at the University of California, Berkeley, and those who gave me an opportunity to test out new ideas. I thank Richard Abrams, Richard Buxbaum, Robert Price, Michael Rogin, Pablo Spiller, Oliver Williamson, Jonah Levy, Michael Watts, Nick Ziegler, and in particular Steve Weber who shared his interdisciplinary perspective on the effects of competition and economic organization with the greatest generosity. Washington University in Saint Louis also hosted me for a year, and I owe a great deal to Jack Knight, Sunita Parikh, and Andrew Sobel. At Georgetown University, Gregory Flynn, Samuel Barnes, and Jeffrey Anderson were terrific hosts and interlocutors when I was a fellow at the Center for German and European Studies.

The University of Wisconsin-Madison was a wonderful place to deepen the project over a longer period. The Department of Political Science and the International Institute were intellectually vital places to work, and I thank Mark Beissinger, Dennis Dresang, Kathy Kramer-Walsh, Bert Kritzer, David Leheny, Jon Pevehouse, Tamir Moustafa, Leigh Payne, Joe Soss, David Trubek, Erik Olin Wright,

Jonathan Zeitlin, and especially Michael Barnett and Mark Pollack. Unfortunately, my time in Madison was also marked by injury, and I am grateful to those who got me back to a vertical state. In particular, I thank my physicians Thomas Zdeblick, Jo Ann Anderson, and Anthony Margarita who together with teams of physical therapists were genuine miracle workers.

The book was completed in Philadelphia, and I am endlessly grateful to my colleagues at Temple University for putting an end to many years of commuting that a transcontinental marriage had entailed. They have offered an inspiring place to work, and special thanks are due to David Adamany, Kevin Arceneaux, Richard Deeg, Gary Mucciaroni, Joseph Schwartz, Sandra Suarez, Chris Wlezien, and more than anyone, to Mark Pollack whom I have had the very distinct honor to work with both in Madison and Philadelphia and whose professionalism and friendship are examples beyond compare.

In early and late stages of my work, and in many cases throughout, I benefited greatly from discussions with and feedback from Steve Casper, Pepper Culpepper, Keith Darden, Dan Kelemen, Bob Hancké, Julie Lynch, Isabela Mares, Sophie Meunier, Kathleen McNamara, Abraham Newman, Sigurt Vitols, Jonas Tallberg, and Gunnar Trumbull. I owe very special thanks to Peter Hall whose engagement with my work has done so much to improve it. I am likewise indebted to David Soskice for his many generosities. To Peter Katzenstein, who offered fresh and constructive suggestions that improved virtually all parts that follow, I owe gratitude that is hard to convey.

Many other institutions have offered support in the course of this project. I am grateful to the British Council, the European Institute at the London School of Economics, the Vilas Foundation, World Affairs and Global Economy Center, and the European Union Center at the University of Wisconsin-Madison, United States Institute of Peace, the Wissenschaftszentrum in Berlin, and the Research Council of the College of Liberal Arts at Temple University.

The staff at university libraries in New York, Berkeley, Madison, Washington, and Philadelphia, and those at archives in Britain, Germany, Belgium, and Italy offered extraordinary assistance as I worked with primary sources. I also owe much to the women and men at national ministries and other public bodies, offices of the European Union, and business associations who helped me gain finer insights to the years following the early 1990s.

My thanks to Roger Haydon for his stewardship at Cornell, to the Press's thorough and deeply constructive reviewers, to Karen Laun and Irina Burns for their miracle work, and to its production team.

The research assistance of Michelle Atherton, David Kennedy, Josh Leon, Moira Nelson, Louise Rothschild, Pooja Shah, and Timo Weishaupt was indispensable.

Babis Sadarmis found my family a home away from home; Nikos Moraitis helped me travel; Johnny Zanakis opened windows; the friendship of Joan and Rachel Porter and the thoughtfulness of Kusum Joshi nurtured me; Manlio Narici's music distracted me; and Arthur van der Beek's garden has been a source of immense rejuvenation and reflection.

My family in Europe offered places of joyous escape. From my parents Michael and Linde, whose joint lives spanned three countries and six decades, I had a steady diet of love and happily consumed their perspectives of the challenges and opportunities that dynamic histories entail. From my siblings and their families, I enjoyed regular doses of amusement and thoughtfulness. And in the United States, I am ever grateful for the unceasing joyfulness of the Nanavati and Joshi families.

Only Priya has lived this project and me through all its phases. With her daily smile, humor, and beauty, my eyes rise and set. The birth of our little boy Nestor made me look beyond the pages that follow and those that did not. This book is dedicated to Priya for her laughter and love, and for making us possible.

Creative Reconstructions

Chapter 1

Capitalist Diversity in Open Economies

Openness to international markets, technological revolutions, and the booms and busts that accompany capitalism periodically ignite debates across Europe over what economic system is best suited for achieving broad economic goals such as structural reform, growth, and social equality. At the core of these debates are alternative answers to the question of what economic model is best placed to help a country modernize its industrial structure as technologies and markets inevitably change. Answers have entailed different prescriptions to what should be the division of labor among public authorities, markets, and organized social groups in harnessing a country's financial, material, and human resources. Though some economic models have been more popular in some periods—centralized ones in the 1950s and 1960s, coordinated models in the 1970s and 1980s, and the liberal market economy during the 1990s and much of the 2000s—there has been no point since 1950 when governments in the major industrial economies of Europe successfully sustained the same type of market economy. Europe's market economies, in fact, were intense laboratories of institutional innovation and reform.

Why are some national economic models sustainable over time while others disintegrate? What explains the fact that some countries are able to transform their economic institutions successfully when others fail? These are important questions with many domestic and international implications. Economic models that are stable often aid governments in implementing structural reforms, securing economic growth, and promoting social progress. Stability in national designs also frequently helps to ensure that governments' commitments to international agreements remain credible over time and may enhance the prospects for international cooperation. Yet too much stability can be a source of concern if a country is unable to adapt to new circumstances such as major shifts in international markets. The ability of countries to reform successfully and at times to *trans*form a model of economic governance is, therefore, imperative if they are to secure domestic goals and meet international obligations over time.

Governments often stake much political capital on protecting valued historic designs and transforming those they deem inimical to their economic agendas. Yet, historically, their ability to successfully implement reforms to the basic institutions of advanced capitalism has been mixed across countries, time periods, and areas of economic governance.

This book examines the political origins of diversity in national patterns of institutional reform. It finds that the ability of governments to variously sustain and transform core designs of a diverse set of economic models depended on how successfully they built and maintained support among domestic economic groups, especially within the business community. The degree to which that community supported government reforms was important because the reverse—active opposition—tended to stymie reforms and make transformative agendas unsustainable over time. Moreover, support from the business sector was key, for without it the very capacities and competencies that governments sought to create within that sector as a means of spurring economic growth—competitive innovation practices, new skills, advanced knowledge, and more—would fail to materialize and thus decrease the chances that economic reform agendas would deliver intended results.

In building support for their economic reform programs, governments participate in what Joseph A. Schumpeter (1942) described as a process of "creative destruction" in which institutions inimical to capitalist innovation are jettisoned to enhance the performance of the corporate sector. Their political ambitions served by economic growth, governments have incentives to dismantle or displace economic institutions that constitute comparative disadvantages for sectors targeted for modernization as a means of promoting economic expansion. But governments also frequently aim to protect historic designs that are highly valued by domestic constituencies for the purposes of staying competitive and guarding against the risks of greater competition. Indeed, in a global economy where competitive pressures are great and where international agreements may undermine the ability of governments to sustain historic designs, the protection of national designs has itself become a creative process. Governments embrace a variety of subtle and incremental reforms and often attempt to ensure that domestic designs are legally protected through international agreements.

The cumulative effects of patterns of institutional destruction and protection, a process in which the nature of modern market economies can be said to be creatively reconstructed has been a persistent feature of post-war Europe. Often misrepresented as a stable region where advanced capitalism was firmly grounded, Western Europe was a place of relentless institutional innovation after 1950. The consolidation of advanced capitalism after World War II was not inevitable (Maier 1987; Mazower 2000; Tilly 2009). Nor was its later development a linear process. Variations in national reforms, evident both in moments of comprehensive and transformative reforms and in periods of relative calm—the periods that Schumpeter (1942) described as economic revolutions and their absorption—were nowhere more apparent than in programs associated with changes to the structural composition of the industrial sector in Europe's largest economies.

After 1950 governments regularly sought to modernize national manufacturing and financial services industries by reforming the institutional building blocks of the modern market economy, including national financial, corporate governance, industrial relations, and innovation systems. They sought to rebuild national industry and move toward peace-time production with a particular focus on consumer goods and heavy machinery (Shonfield 1965; Eichengreen 2007). This entailed a transition from large agricultural sectors and an often-fragmented industrial landscape that was undercapitalized into economies defined by large advanced manufacturing firms oriented toward mass production. In the mid-1970s, governments sought to bring about a transition to more flexible and more specialized forms of production in higher value-added product markets and expanded the service sectors (Piore and Sabel 1984; Streeck 1992). In most countries, this transition involved a move from highly labor-intensive industries to ones characterized by greater levels of human capital and technological intensity. Finally, with the 1990s digital revolution, governments sought to compel firms to pursue more knowledge-intensive product markets and actively targeted the expansion of the information and financial services industries (Hall and Soskice 2001a; Zysman and Newman 2006).

Table 1.1 summarizes the aggregate outcome of domestic reforms in Europe's largest economies from 1950 to 2008. During the 1950s and 1960s, France and Germany undertook reforms in major supply-side domains and successfully sustained centralized and coordinated market economies. They rebuilt their systems of industrial relations, corporate governance, and finance, as well as promoted distinct arrangements for industrial innovation. Although Britain also undertook comprehensive reforms and attempted to transform core designs in these domains in ways more similar to a centralized economic model, reforms were not sustainable in that country.

During the 1970s and 1980s Germany's institutional trajectory was characterized by greater specialization of established designs through the extension of core features of the post-war coordinated market economy. However, France's and Britain's trajectories took different routes. Britain rejected its earlier experiments with alternative forms of governance and gradually consolidated a liberal market economy after 1979. Reforms were comprehensive and covered important areas: the industrial relation and financial systems were deregulated, an active market for corporate governance was encouraged, and governments took a less active part in shaping institutions for innovation. In France, where institutional experimentation was particularly extensive, neither efforts to introduce a limited set of liberal reforms in the 1970s nor efforts to extend post-war centralized designs in the early 1980s were successful. Attempts to emulate features of the coordinated market economy appeared sustainable in the latter part of the 1980s, but many of these did not prove lasting.

The trajectory of the three industrialized economies again varied from 1992 to 2008. With greater levels of economic globalization, many countries placed a stronger emphasis on market-oriented reforms in national financial, corporate

TABLE 1.1
Summary of cases

	1950–1973	1974–1991	1992–2008
Britain	Failed transformation to centralized designs (1960s)	Successful transformation to liberal model after 1979	Successful specialization on liberal model after mid-1990s
France	Consolidation of centralized market economy	Failed attempts to introduce liberal designs (1970s) Failed specialization on centralized model (early 1980s) Temporary consolidation of coordinated economy designs (late 1980s)	Recombination and emergence of hybrid system (mid-1990s)
Germany	Consolidation of coordinated market economy	Successful specialization on coordinated model	Recombination and emergence of hybrid system (late 1990s/early 2000s)

governance, and industrial relations systems. It was widely asserted that these innovations would maximize countries' chances of benefiting from globalization because they aligned national incentives of reform to global conditions and would help economic groups adapt autonomously and quickly to increases in international market integration (e.g., Barro 1996; Alesina and Giavazzi 2006). Meanwhile, in an argument reminiscent of Mancur Olson's (1982) classic study of the long-term effects of organized interests on the evolution of societies, coordinated economy models were said to stymie institutional innovation because they enabled economic groups to prevent major reforms (e.g., Shlaes 1994; Phelps 2007; Sinn 2007). Centralized forms of governance were also widely rejected for representing an anachronistic form of economic governance under globalization. Among many other voices, the editorial team of the *Financial Times* (8 April 1998) concluded during new heights of globalization: "What is left is Anglo-Saxon capitalism. It is becoming a global standard."[1]

Yet, for all the promised rewards from adopting the new "global standard," patterns of reform did not converge in Britain, France, and Germany. Although the movement toward liberal *policies* was a significant trend across these economies, the adoption of the panoply of *institutions* that are associated with the liberal market economy was more limited and differentiated. Britain sustained a strategy where the internal coherence of the liberal market economy increased during the 1990s and 2000s, but France and Germany experienced patterns of institutional recombination that generated distinct hybrid systems of governance. Both countries saw fundamental change in some designs, principally in financial and corporate governance institutions, but there were also important continuities, especially in their industrial relations and innovation systems.

Outline

The chapters in this volume offer new answers to why specific outcomes prevailed in distinct economic domains and why the aggregate trajectory of national reforms took their particular shape in Europe's largest economies after 1950. They bridge the substantive concerns of the comparative and international political economy disciplines and document how the manner in which governments reconciled domestic reforms with their foreign economic policies, in particular their multilateral commitments, shaped the outcome of domestic reforms in Britain, France, and Germany.

Drawing on complementary approaches to political economy, including the varieties of capitalism, historical institutionalism, and behavioral economics traditions, this book revisits academic debates about the sources of institutional development in advanced industrialized countries. It introduces nuance to when and how historical legacies matter and when governments were able to sustain valued national designs and when they were able to transform others in lasting fashion. It also underscores the crucial impact institutional innovations beyond national borders had in shaping domestic developments. The book concludes that how governments mediated the domestic effects of international markets through an evolving set of multilateral designs, shaped with variable success, had profound consequences for the evolution of Europe's modern varieties of capitalism.

Capitalist Diversity in Theoretical Perspective

There is no shortage of academic texts on why governments have recorded varied success in sustaining and transforming the institutional architecture of national economies. Scholarly attention has typically peaked following major changes in the nature and composition of markets for industrial goods and services. In the aftermath of World War II and the international economic crises of the 1970s, scholars studying industrial modernization and economic management were preoccupied with the question of why governments promoted alternative models of capitalism (e.g., Shonfield 1965; Katzenstein 1978; Zysman 1983; Hall 1986). These studies showed that historical legacies, often dating to the early period of industrialization, played major roles in determining why governments promoted a diverse set of market economies. Scholarly debate was reignited in the 1990s as researchers argued over whether one or more models of advanced capitalism was sustainable in a globalized world economy and sought answers to whether high levels of economic openness would eclipse the role of historical legacies (e.g., Zysman 1994; Berger and Dore 1996; Hall and Soskice 2001a; Baumol, Litan and Schramm 2007; Rodrik 2007).[2]

The role of historical legacies also featured prominently in explanations of why national variations persisted during the 2000s. Frequently invoking logics of path-dependence and positive feedback effects that have been a major part of historically oriented studies of the evolution of capitalism (North 1990; Pierson 2004), studies of capitalist diversity often suggest that historical legacies make radical changes in modes of economic governance all but impossible. Long-established and deeply entrenched designs that shape the organizational resources of governments, the capacity of economic groups to resolve coordination problems, the manner in which domestic markets have traditionally been regulated, and political institutions that give some societal groups extensive powers to veto change are common obstacles to radical reform. Rather than finding support for the thesis that economies are converging on a single model of capitalism, studies find support for anything from two to five distinct models (e.g., Doremus et al. 1998; Hall and Soskice 2001b; Schmidt 2002; Amable 2003; Pontusson 2005).

The persistence of institutional differences across countries in multiple discrete periods must not obscure the possibility that the nature and sources of these differences themselves may have varied across time. The following chapters illustrate the importance of historical legacies in shaping the evolution of national economic models during periods of greater international economic integration. However, they underscore that studies of historical legacies often overstate the degree of continuity in national systems. Although institutional differences across countries have been present over time, the nature of these differences has varied. There have been major synchronic variations across countries in all post-war periods, but greater similarities in some periods and areas than others. Diachronic differences in national economic designs have also been significant. To wit, the version of liberal capitalism that characterized Britain during the 1980s differed from that of the 2000s; the centralized market economy France employed in the early 1960s differed from that promoted two decades later; and Germany's coordinated market economy that governments championed in the 2000s differed from the model that characterized earlier decades. Moreover, when the most recent period is compared to earlier ones, it is apparent that patterns of cross-national differences, including the direction, timing, and scope of reform, and thus aggregate patterns, varied significantly across distinct post-war periods.

If studies in the historical institutionalist vein tend to *over*estimate the long-term effects of historical legacies, explanations based in the rational choice institutionalist tradition tend to *under*estimate such effects. The latter tradition expects changes in national economic designs to be relatively rapid when international conditions alter the balance of costs and benefits that key domestic groups associate with retaining or transforming extant domestic designs. Regardless of whether the empirical focus is placed on early or late post-war periods, it cannot be said that the evolution of European varieties of capitalism was the product of a process in which governments ensured that designs optimal for a particular form of industrial production were quickly and successfully implemented. Although some specific institutions may appear to have been designed in ways that nearly perfectly reflected the preferences of some constituencies, such conclusions cannot be drawn when the totality of reform programs are examined either in a single period or when the post-war period is viewed in its full.

Past reforms have legacies that alter the distributional consequences of new reforms. Such legacies may not be as enduring as some historical institutionalist accounts may suggest, but they often alter the political realities that governments confront and thus the ease with which they build support for comprehensive and radical reforms. Moreover, many reform programs take place against the backdrop of unintended consequences and situations where earlier reforms created new constituencies with stakes in preserving designs.[3] Depending on the constellations of these factors, governments have varied in their embrace of comprehensive and transformative reform agendas. They have variously promoted encompassing reform agendas and engaged in a variety of incremental reform strategies that sought to downgrade the importance of historic designs, promoted others by infusing them with new mandates, and introduced new designs.[4] However, the outcome of these efforts have varied significantly across time and countries, ranging from successful and failed efforts to consolidate complex models of governance, to sustainable agendas of institutional specialization and transformation, to partial transformations that brought new hybrid systems of advanced capitalism (see table 1.1). To account for these variations, this book revisits methodological, empirical, and theoretical features of the debate on the nature of capitalist diversity.

Why Europe after 1950?

A focus on Europe's largest economies has distinct methodological advantages when assessing alternative explanations for why national patterns of institutional development vary. Because Britain, France, and Germany industrialized relatively early and are often associated with diverse traditions of capitalism, they represent an appropriate set of cases for testing arguments about historical legacies. They also offer a good foundation for examining arguments about the role of international forces in potentially trumping national factors in determining the institutional trajectory of countries. It has been suggested in recent contributions to international and comparative political economy that high levels of market integration and dense forms of multilateralism are associated with a convergence in national institutions. If that is the case, then there should be no better place to observe such a trend than among Europe's most industrialized economies. Since the 1950s these economies have been a great deal more exposed to international markets than other large economies and have over time become governed by a significant and growing number of multilateral rules, especially in the context of the European Union and its precursors.[5]

Two features of this volume's research design help revisit debates about capitalist diversity. First, it goes beyond the narrow focus on developments after the early 1990s, which characterized the most recent installment of the debate about the sources of capitalist diversity to placing at the center synchronic and diachronic variations in the institutional structure of national varieties of capitalism. Extending the historical scope to include two other periods after 1950 offers a larger foundation for identifying the general conditions under which international factors such as market integration and international cooperation affect national trajectories.[6]

Second, the volume examines the evolution of institutions in four separate economic areas. Disaggregating national economic models gives greater room to draw conclusions about the type of aggregate outcomes highlighted in table 1.1 and a foundation on which to identify general conditions under which governments have been successful in sustaining or transforming specific institutions. It is common in comparative capitalisms debates that scholars adopt a dichotomous dependent variable and compare national trajectories to determine whether they remain distinct or have become more alike (diversity vs. convergence, stasis vs. change). Instead, the chapters in this book distinguish four different patterns of institutional development in which economic systems are characterized either by patterns of consolidation, specialization, systemic transformation, or by patterns of recombination that lead to hybrid systems of governance. This disaggregated approach makes possible controlled and contextual comparisons that facilitate answers to questions concerning the relationship between domain-specific and systemic changes, the direction of reform, as well as areas of synchronic and diachronic variation.[7]

Multilateralism Matters

This book revisits the debate about the sources of capitalist diversity by moving beyond the narrow focus that characterizes much of the comparative political economy literature in which the institutional environment shaping the behavior of governments and domestic groups is construed as strictly national in character. An important key to explaining why national trajectories varied in Europe's largest economies after 1950 is to explicitly recognize how governments mediated the effects of multilateral institutions at the domestic level. The large majority of studies on the topic of capitalist diversity examines national responses to economic globalization in isolation from changes in the international institutional environment. Rather than asking whether and how shifts in that environment affected the ability of governments to sustain or transform specific national designs, it has been more typical to engage in a maneuver similar to Andrew Shonfield's classic study of post-war capitalism. In *Modern Capitalism* (1965), Shonfield quickly explained the omission of considering the role of international institutions in shaping answers to the cardinal question. Hidden in a footnote in a book that was to define several generations of political economy studies, Shonfield wrote:

There are, of course, other types of machinery, international in character, which have developed since the war . . . [*Modern Capitalism*] is, however, concerned with an analysis of national institutions of capitalism; the role of new international institutions (EEC, GATT, IMF, and others) . . . is a large topic that deserves treatment on its own. (1965, 230, n. 16)

Shonfield would later devote attention to addressing the lacuna in *Modern Capitalism* (e.g., Shonfield 1972, 1976), but those following in his footsteps have tended to persist in omitting sustained attention to multilateralism. Scholars have explored the role of the EU in shaping economic governance in the recent period, among long-standing members and newer ones (e.g., Schmidt 2002; Menz 2005; Jacoby 2006; Epstein 2008; Höpner and Schäfer 2010). But the comparative capitalism literature, which remains most deeply invested in the study of national economies, devotes little attention to how the institution of multilateralism has affected domestic economic institutions over time. As Gregory Jackson and Richard Deeg conclude in an exhaustive review of the comparative capitalism literature, extant studies of the modern market economy have "rested on the assumption that capitalism is most usefully segmented for analytical purposes into distinct economies bounded by the borders of nation states" (2006, 38). Others charge the discipline with "methodological nationalism" (Callaghan 2008).

A growing literature on the "Europeanization" of the EU's member-states has done much to fill voids in the comparative capitalism literature by examining how countries have responded to common EU rules (e.g., Cowles, Caporaso, and Risse 2001; Featherstone and Radelli 2003; Kohler-Koch 2003; Falkner et al. 2005). However, it has been organized around synchronous comparisons of national institutional variations or changes in the recent and relatively short time period and has thus left open the question of what accounts for variations over longer periods. Moreover, because this literature is mostly concerned with domestic responses to common rules, the national and international political processes through which governments and domestic groups have sought to shape the very multilateral designs that would later constrain their behavior have not been a dominant area of inquiry. As such, the creative aspects of institutional reform that are so central to the evolution of capitalism are overlooked in this literature, especially the manner in which governments alternatively sought to undermine and destroy or reinforce and protect domestic designs by securing particular forms of multilateralism within the EU.

The following chapters examine how the manner in which governments embedded national programs in multilateral contexts shaped their ability to implement domestic economic reforms. The multilateral institutions that governments established after 1950 altered the nature of markets and the terms of government intervention. These included what constraints governments could use to shape domestic financial institutions, what constituted permissible forms of direct support for industry, the manner in which governments shaped markets for corporate control, the level of guaranteed benefits for workers, and other aspects of employment contracts. The effect of multilateral institutions has varied historically and may be weak in some cases, but with time they have become more plentiful and cover a broader scope with far-reaching consequences for the relationship among public authorities, markets, and economic groups.[8] Acknowledging the centrality and evolving character of multilateral institutions in shaping constraints on government action is therefore critical to a nuanced understanding of why national trajectories took their particular form and why these varied over time.

In analytical terms, bridging the comparative and international political economy subfields involves a transition from conceptualizing national economies as closed systems of governance to treating them as open systems of governance. Such a transition is at the center of this book, which focuses on how the manner in which governments resolve what is known as the design problem affects their ability to build support for domestic reform agendas. The design problem is a governance dilemma that concerns how governments and other economic actors reconcile the internal integration of institutions with their integration into the external environment (Goodin 1996; Roberts 2004, 19–22; see also chapter 2). How governments resolve the design problem is material for the sustainability of domestic reforms, because their solutions may serve to either reinforce or undermine support for national reforms. For example, the construction of Europe's internal market in the late 1980s strengthened support within the British manufacturing and financial sectors for changes to national financial and corporate governance institutions at the time. Yet the same multilateral project gradually undermined support for historic designs among such constituencies in both France and Germany.

Because neither national nor multilateral designs are constant in their form over time, the analytical transition to open systems analysis involves a move from a focus on partial equilibrium analysis to engaging in general equilibrium analysis.[9] Jeffry A. Frieden and Lisa Martin (2002, 120) describe this shift as an "ultimate goal" in achieving a nuanced understanding of the relationship between domestic and international politics. Consonant with such a shift, this volume's objective is not to provide a general theory of institutional development in advanced market economies. Rather, it is to identify the mechanisms through which and conditions under which governments in diverse national and temporal settings are successful in sustaining or transforming specific economic designs under diverse forms of multilateralism and what implications their record have for aggregate patterns of institutional development in national market economies.

The manner in which governments integrated national reform programs with multilateral institutions had major consequences for institutional reform agendas at the domestic level. Multilateral commitments had an impact on all major domestic constituencies on which governments relied when implementing reform agendas. However, they had particularly strong consequences for the nature of support governments enjoyed within the business sector. Beyond shaping long-term investment horizons and product market strategies of companies by altering firms' exposure to international markets, multilateral designs altered the ability of governments to influence in direct and indirect fashion the profile of domestic industry. Membership in international trade and monetary organizations, especially the European Union and its precursors, directly impacted the incentives of the business community to support domestic reform agendas.[10] By focusing on how governments resolved the design problem, the following chapters show when multilateral designs served to undermine the ability of governments to sustain domestic support for long-standing national practices and when multilateral institutions had the opposite effect and instead served to reinforce existing forms of economic governance within states.

Theoretical Traditions and Behavioral (Historical) Institutionalism

Most studies of why national patterns of reform vary have focused on the choices that governments make. They often foreground the role played by constitutive or principled norms in shaping how political elites arrive at what is the appropriate or superior model of economic development. Constructivist studies explore the role of such norms in shaping economic choices across Europe, including in advanced industrialized and transition economies (e.g., Abdelal 2001; Blyth 2001; Schmidt 2002; Darden 2007). These studies offer sophisticated answers to how governments arrive at a particular mix of economic reforms and provide particularly persuasive answers to what informs the choice of governments after major crises. They also document the role played by historical events such as economic recessions, the ascendance of new economic thinking, and the priorities of historically important political leaders (e.g., Hall 1989; McNamara 1998; C. Parsons 2005).

The question at the center of constructivist studies is analytically distinct from the one in the present study. This volume's primary focus is not why governments chose to promote a particular reform agenda, but rather the conditions under which they were successful in sustaining their agendas over time. It emphasizes that governments' success in implementing reforms over time cannot be reduced to their intentions or choices alone. For governments to successfully implement economic reform programs, they need to secure support from domestic constituencies with stakes in reforms (e.g., Gourevitch 1986; Hall and Soskice 2001a).[11] Like a large political economy literature, it addresses this issue with attention to the nature of key interest groups' institutional preferences. Variations in preferences hold particular importance in accounting for patterns of institutional stability and change when the political institutions that shape the process by which societal preferences are aggregated remain relatively constant.[12]

A comparative historical and institutional literature underscores that many interest groups have stakes in the structure of economic institutions, but it often foregrounds the role played by business groups in shaping developments in the modern market economy (e.g., Hall and Soskice 2001a; Swenson 2002; Mares 2003; Thelen

2004; Greif 2006). There is broad agreement within the political economy literature on the primacy of business in shaping the evolution of the modern market economy's institutional architecture.[13] However, because scholarly traditions make different assumptions about what motivates firms and how these respond to changes in their economic environments, they reach different conclusions about how and the conditions under which firms impact patterns of institutional development. Such differences have characterized many exchanges in the social sciences about the relationship between governments and business, including the contemporary "new institutionalisms debate" that has revolved extensively around the relative merits of the rational choice and historical institutionalism traditions (e.g., Bates et al. 1998; Katznelson and Weingast 2005a). These traditions offer alternative understandings of social actors' institutional preferences, which in turn lead to different conclusions about the conditions under which actors like firms will support or oppose the reform agendas that governments champion.

Both rational choice institutionalism and historical institutionalism offer relatively crude views on the structure of firms' preferences that lead to overly broad conclusions about when they will support a particular design. Theories based in the former tradition rely on global rationality models that see firms as actors who seek to eliminate the opportunity costs of operating in institutional contexts that are less attractive than alternatives. This leads to the overestimation of the frequency of preference transformations among firms with implications for what patterns of institutional development scholars expect to emerge, including expectations that radical transformations will be common and stability quickly (re)established. By contrast, historical institutionalism employs embedded rationality models that represent firms' preferences as heavily shaped by their investments in past institutions. Such models lead to the underestimation of the frequency of preference transformations and to expectations that incremental change will be the defining feature of institutional development in advanced market economies.[14]

This book draws on a third tradition, behavioral economics, to introduce more nuance to the conditions under which firms will support or oppose the reform agendas promoted by governments. A behavioral theory of firms helps overcome both tendencies to over- and underestimate the frequency of preference transformations. The basic finding of behavioral economics, in particular a subset known as prospect theory, is that economic actors respond differently to prospective changes depending on whether they frame departures from the status quo or other reference points as entailing losses or gains. It thus underscores that historical legacies matter not because they lock governments into a steady reform path, but because they have an impact on whether domestic constituencies frame the consequences of present and prospective reforms as advantageous or disadvantageous with respect to achieving their particularistic goals.

The situational framing effects to which behavioral economics point have implications for the study of institutional development, including the resources actors willingly devote to achieving particular outcomes, the type of incentives governments that seek their support must provide to ensure loyalty, and the circumstances under which firms' commitments to incremental or radical reforms are credible. A behavioral theory suggests that social actors willingly devote more resources to protecting institutional advantages than jettisoning correspondingly sized disadvantages and that the intensity of preferences will decline over time as new realities are normalized. Because it expects that opportunity costs are underweighted, societal support for potentially promising reforms is expected to emerge more slowly than expected by a global rationality model if the status quo is framed as an advantage (e.g., Kahneman and Tversky 1979; Thaler 1980). However, if existing designs are framed as disadvantages, political actors are expected to be risk acceptant and to become strong supporters of radical reform (Kahneman, Knetsch, and Thaler 1991; Weyland 2008). A behavioral theory thus expects that radical reforms are more frequent and become sustainable more quickly than do theories employing embedded rationality models.

Behavioral theories of human action have a long lineage (e.g., Simon 1955; Kahneman and Tversky 2000) and inform areas of political science, notably international relations (see Levy 1992, 1997; McDermott 2004; Mercer 2005). They have been explored in the context of political economy where the focus is mostly on how policymakers evaluate the gains and losses associated with alternative economic policies (Weyland 1996, 2002; Elms 2004).[15] In this book, their potential contributions are explored for the study of economic groups and economic institutions. More specifically, the insights of behavioral economics are used to complement contributions to historical institutionalism. Especially when informed by the varieties of capitalism literature, historical institutionalism offers insights into why firms situated in diverse contexts hold particular preferences over the design of institutions. But it offers few details on the conditions under which such preferences will intensify or be transformed and thus how different types of changes in firms' environment will affect the credibility of their commitments to the reform agendas governments champion. What is here termed behavioral institutionalism aims to address this lacuna and is thus best understood as a variety of historical institutionalism.[16]

Because the behavioral, global, and embedded rationality models may generate observationally equivalent inferences, the following chapters employ a research strategy that is informed by systematic process analysis (Hall 2003, 2008). This strategy of inquiry is a theory-oriented comparative approach to process tracing that aims to assess the validity of scientific inferences based in diverse traditions. It shares some features with the analytical narratives tradition (Bates et al. 1998) in that it encourages a focus on specific political governance dilemmas when examining the historical archive. Where it departs from the standard approach to analytical narratives is in its commitment to extend the study of governance dilemmas beyond a single theoretical approach and beyond a narrow type of outcome. When these principles of systematic process analysis are observed it is possible to establish whether a particular tradition is appropriate or superior in accounting for sets of outcomes and the foundation exists for making generalizable claims with greater confidence.

Conclusion

The evolution of modern capitalism in Europe was closely connected to institutional innovations at the multilateral level. The following chapters underscore that multilateralism in Europe did not simply serve to "rescue" historic national designs in the early post-war period (Milward 1992), nor did it only serve to undermine nationally distinct designs in more recent times.[17] Multilateralism has had both effects—often simultaneously in different domains of the same economy, frequently sequentially in the same domain over time, and typically in varied ways across countries. By identifying when specific patterns were apparent across time, domains, and countries, the book shows the conditional, yet often integral, role that multilateralism has played in the periodic reconstruction of national varieties of capitalism in Europe's largest economies.

A modified historical institutional approach informed by behavioral economics helps isolate how the advantages and disadvantages firms attach to historic designs and multilateral innovations that affect such designs impact government-sponsored reform programs. This behavioral institutionalism approach explains why governments, when they promoted economic designs that delivered tangible comparative benefits to domestic constituencies and ensured that these designs were incentive compatible with the external institutional environment, were successful in creating domestic coalitions that could sustain reform programs. This approach also assists in accounting for why, when domestic and international designs were incentive compatible and the value of domestic designs increased relative to alternatives, governments were able to implement strategies of institutional specialization. Finally, behavioral institutionalism offers answers to why governments often failed to ensure stability in national designs or successfully transform targeted institutions in a lasting fashion when multilateral designs threatened historical investments that pivotal parts of the business community had in national designs.

The remaining chapters present the analytical and empirical foundations for the book's findings. Chapter 2 explains the rationale for the book's firm-centric approach to accounting for variations in institutional development and for behavioral institutionalism. Chapter 3 examines the core hypotheses of three models of firm behavior based in global, embedded, and behavioral rationality models. It details what form business coalitions take and identifies how, under conditions of economic openness, the interaction of different national and multilateral designs affects the credibility of firms' commitments to the institutional designs championed by governments when different assumptions are made about what informs the utility functions of firms.

Chapters 4–6 entail case studies of economic reform programs in Europe's three largest industrial economies: Britain, France, and Germany. These chapters examine instances in which governments succeeded and failed in sustaining or transforming national designs in the face of significant pressures for reform. They show that the outcomes that characterized these processes were often heavily impacted by how governments managed both sides of the design problem.

Although the experiences of European countries after World War II have been described as specific to that continent, the conditions under which individual countries were able to sustain and transform economic designs have theoretical and empirical implications beyond Europe. Identifying these conditions promises to strengthen integrated research agendas in comparative and international political economy. The concluding chapter outlines partial lessons for other parts of the world that are contending with how national economic reforms can be implemented under growing levels of global market integration and dense forms of multilateralism.

Chapter 2

Governments, Business, and the Design Problem

The modern market economy is the composite of a large number of institutions that regulate markets, define the role of public authorities, and incentivize economic groups to make particular kinds of social and material investments. In the course of the twentieth century, European governments engaged in a great deal of innovation in these institutions to achieve specific economic goals, including structural reform in the industrial sector. Institutional innovation was not limited to the domestic sphere, however. Governments came to rely to an unprecedented extent on innovations in the international sphere through a major expansion in the use of multilateralism. Multilateralism served many and often interrelated purposes in post-war Europe, ranging from broad goals like establishing the conditions for peaceful relations among former adversaries to more specific ones associated with the creation of stable access to international markets, the regulation of these markets, and the enforcement of a non-discrimination regime.[1]

In the process of adding a layer of multilateral institutions to existing national ones, the modern market economy became an open system of governance. As an open system of governance, the parameters that affected the conditions under which governments were able to implement domestic reform programs included the manner in which national designs were integrated with multilateral ones. Multilateralism, depending on its form, can both serve to reinforce and to undermine national reform agendas. This chapter explains how the integration of national and multilateral institutions shaped patterns of institutional development by focusing on how the manner in which governments resolved the so-called design problem had an impact on their ability to sustain particular domestic economic reform agendas.

Disaggregating Market Economies

To harness a country's material, financial and human resources for the purposes of achieving specific economic, social, and political goals, governments employ and promote a multitude of economic institutions. One area that has had implications for all types of goals championed by governments has been structural reform in the manufacturing, financial services, and technology industries (e.g., Porter 1990; Hall and Soskice 2001a; Steil, Victor, and Nelson 2002). Structural reform focuses on helping firms modernize their production processes, develop new markets, and enhance competitiveness. Debates over what is the best model to implement structural reform have historically revolved around the scope and nature of market competition, the tasks of and resources given to public authorities, and the role of institutionalized coordination among organized economic groups. It has, in short, been about which variety of capitalism—the liberal, centralized, or coordinated market economy model—is the best means of implementing structural reform.

Table 2.1 captures the basic differences in the three models of economic governance by comparing ideal-type variations in their constituitive institutions. All advanced industrialized states employ some type of financial, corporate governance, industrial relations, and innovation systems. These systems may be disaggregated into distinct economic domains as follows: (a) those in the financial system that define the structure of the banking system, the control of credit, and access to risk capital; (b) areas of corporate governance systems that pertain to management autonomy, shareholder arrangements, and constraints on the market for corporate control; (c) features of national industrial relations systems such as the nature of social partner autonomy, collective bargaining, and the flexibility of employment contracts; and (d) aspects of innovation systems such as those shaping the nature of direct government support of firms, public support through the funding of research institutes, and the nature of inter-firm relations in innovation chains.[2] Finally, the twelve domains in the table may be disaggregated further into a set of core institutions that may be understood as "sets of regularized practices with a rule-like quality in the sense that the actors expect the practices to be observed" (Hall and Thelen 2009, 9).[3]

Four Patterns of Institutional Development

Depending on whether the institutions highlighted in Table 2.1 remain relatively intact over time or change radically and become more similar to those associated with alternative models determines which of four patterns of institutional development characterizes an economy in a given historical period. When the institutional designs of most economic domains remain structurally intact over time, economic systems are characterized by patterns of institutional consolidation. This is a process in which policymakers and interest groups successfully protect or adapt existing designs in incremental ways that preserve the status quo in the mode of economic governance. To be a sustainable pattern, institutions must be self-enforcing, which means that pivotal social groups must agree that no feasible alternative is more attractive than extant arrangements.[4]

Patterns of consolidation are qualitatively different from instances where an economic model undergoes a process of institutional specialization. In the latter, an

TABLE 2.1
Dimensions of varieties of capitalism

| | | Institutions | | |
| | | Variety of capitalism | | |
Systems	Domains	Liberal	Centralized	Coordinated
Financial	a. Bank structure	Private, investment-oriented	Public ownership high	Private and public
	b. Credit control	Private	Public	Private
	c. Risk capital	Large equity markets	Limited, public funds	Limited, public and private
Corporate governance	a. Corporate boards	High management autonomy	Low management autonomy (government control)	Codetermination
	b. Shareholding arrangements	Diffuse	Blockholding (public)	Blockholding (private)
	c. Market for corporate control	Limited constraints	Heavy constraints	Significant constraints
Industrial relations	a. Social partners autonomy (wage setting)	High (uncoordinated)	Low (state-directed)	High (coordinated)
	b. Collective bargaining	Low (firm level)	Low (industry level)	Extensive (industry level)
	c. Employment contracts	High flexibility	Low flexibility	Low flexibility
Innovation	a. Public subsidies for firms	Limited	Extensive, direct and discriminatory	Limited, indirect and non-discriminatory
	b. Inter-firm relations	Competitive	Cooperative, state directed	Cooperative, private
	c. Public support for research institutes	Low with emphasis on non-discrimination	High with discriminatory rationale	Low with emphasis on non-discrimination

economic model moves closer to the ideal-type, which may result from reforms that remove constraints or add new ones depending on the model in question. Historic examples from Europe include the successful efforts by governments in Germany during the 1970s and Britain in the 1990s to promote the coordinated and liberal market economies, respectively. Though both consolidation and specialization cases are instances of systemic continuity in the broad sense, they represent distinct trajectories because the nature of reform is different (relative stasis versus incremental changes in the direction of an ideal-type). They are also associated with diverse adjustment patterns and different conditions under which they are sustainable over time. By contrast to consolidation, which occurs when institutions are self-enforcing for pivotal social groups, patterns of specialization are sustainable when designs are self-*re*inforcing.[5]

Scenarios where institutions associated with one economic model become more similar to an alternative represent instances of radical change.[6] An economic model undergoes fundamental transformation when a majority of institutions across most domains is replaced by alternatives more closely aligned with a different model. This standard is frequently employed in convergence debates where the central issue is whether countries are becoming more or less alike over time.[7] In these debates, transformative change so that two or more economies are institutionally more similar to each other than their own past constitutes confirmation of the hypotheses that economic globalization or common international designs cause convergence in economic models.

Though regularly attempted, there are few historical examples of successful transformations of economic models. A rare exception is the post-war British model of governance, which had introduced a significant number of designs associated with both centralized and coordinated market economies in the 1960s and 1970s, but which after 1979 embarked on a radical reform agenda centered around a liberal model of capitalism. More typically, institutional transformation is limited to some domains or even to some institutions within specific domains. Such cases are distinct in the aggregate from systemic transformations for they represent processes of recombination in which designs associated with diverse models are integrated into potentially new hybrid systems of governance (Crouch 2005; Campbell and Pederson 2007; Callaghan 2007). Examples include the French and German cases in the late 1990s and 2000s, respectively, when radical shifts in financial and corporate governance systems co-existed with more limited changes in the industrial relations and innovation systems.

Governments, Business, and Institutional Reform

Patterns of institutional development may be understood as the outcome of coordination games that involve governments and the social groups that are most integral to sustaining particular designs over time (e.g., Greif 2000; Hall and Soskice 2001a;

Thelen and Kume 2005). Institutions are characterized by stability or continuity in form when pivotal social groups behave in ways that reproduce particular designs instead of promoting feasible alternatives (Bates et al. 1998; Hall and Thelen 2009).[8] Analytically, then, what is required to identify the conditions under which governments are successful in securing support for the institutional designs they champion is not a theory of what informs their choices of institutional designs. It is a theory of when governments are able to generate sufficient domestic support among those economic groups whose backing is necessary to reproduce specific design over time. In Albert Hirschman's (1971) terminology, this is a question of when governments ensure that groups are "loyal" to the designs they promote rather than "exit." In the language of contemporary institutional theory, what Hirschman terms loyalty are situations when governments are able to get those groups whose participation is pivotal to ensuring stable designs to credibly commit to behave in ways that reproduce particular institutions.[9]

Pivotal Firms and Business Coalitions

Governments engaged in structural reform have historically placed great significance on gaining support from the corporate sector. The success of firms is key to employment and economic growth and the extent to which they are willing and able to support the designs is critical for producing the results sought by governments. In more analytical terms, the behavior of firms is key to the institutional trajectory of market economies because they occupy pivotal positions in each of the core domains that define market economies. If institutions are "regularized practices" (Hall and Thelen 2009, 9), then they may be understood as the outcome of formal or informal contracts among social groups that agree to be bound by particular sets of constraints (see also North 1990; Bates et al. 1998; Hall and Soskice 2001a). Those groups that are in a position to sustain an institution play pivotal roles for if they are unable or decide to no longer abide by the social contracts that underpin institutions, the latter are undermined. In the modern market economy, the corporate sector occupies such positions in several key settings.

Though with some important variations across models of governance, a distinct part of the business community plays the role of a pivot in the social contracts that sustain the core institutions across the major supply-side domains of advanced market economies. In the financial system, banks and in some cases shareholders hold pivotal positions as their decisions to lend capital and invest in companies are key in shaping the type of product market strategy the latter will adopt (Deeg 1999; Vitols 2001a; Goyer 2003). If the financial institutions promoted by governments fail to push banks and investors to extend capital to firms in ways that allow the latter to make the type of investments sought by governments, the designs favored by governments will not be sustainable over time. Similarly, in the corporate governance domain, especially when defined by an insider system based on blockholding arrangements, the basic structure of an extant system is not sustainable if major shareholders divest themselves (Culpepper 2005; O'Sullivan 2005).

In the industrial relations system, employers coordinate, respectively, with organized employees and individuals. Should employers opt to defect from an existing contract with the latter, the institutional equilibrium in these domains may, despite legal constraints, become self-undermining over time and bring fundamental changes in the structure of national industrial relations systems (Pontusson and Swenson 1996; Thelen 2000). Firms are also pivotal actors in the innovation system, which is a product of social contracts between large firms and suppliers, firms of different sizes (including lenders), and between firms and public research bodies. If the firms targeted for growth by governments are unwilling or unable to credibly commit to a particular type of innovation—for example, by failing to make significant investments in research and development or collaborative partnerships—they will be unable to fully exploit the institutional advantages associated with a particular innovation system (e.g., Soskice 1994; Hancké 2002; Casper 2007).

The claim here is not that other economic groups—such as organized labor, regulators, the public or individual policymakers—do not exercise significant influence over the institutional trajectory of economic systems, or that these groups in some instances may not be pivotal actors whose support is necessary to sustain institutions over time. The rationale of a firm-centric theory of the modern market economy is that these groups rarely can sustain designs without the support of firms and that the latter have the power to undermine a large number of designs that are the function of social contracts if they chose to defect from multiple arrangements.[10] Moreover, the argument is not that firms set national policy, select national institutions, or are capable of intentionally designing perfect institutions that suit their needs. The rationale for focusing on firms is that through their behavior—in particular, how they adapt to changes in markets and their decisions to make material and social investments—firms shape the structure of the societal coalitions that exert the largest influence over the institutional designs that define economic models.[11] In other words, after governments have chosen to promote particular institutions, the behavior of firms that occupy pivotal positions in key domains influence whether governments are successful in implementing their preferred reform agendas.[12]

Because different parts of the business community play the role of contractual pivots in specific domains, governments must build coalitions *within* the business community if they are to successfully sustain or transform models of governance. If such coalitions include firms that are pivotal to sustaining designs in all major domains and the commitments of such firms to the designs championed by governments are credible, systems of governance are self-enforcing and patterns of consolidation possible. If the same firms conclude that extant designs are preferable to alternatives under an expanding set of external parameters (e.g., as changes occur in technology or the external market environment), their commitments become credible under a growing set of conditions and institutions are self-*re*inforcing.[13]

Under such circumstances, the conditions are met for governments to successfully implement strategies of institutional specialization.

When large segments of the business community are unwilling or unable to honor the social contracts that are the foundation of existing institutions, designs are self-undermining and a system of governance is characterized by systemic transformation. When institutions are self-undermining only in select domains while other domains remain self-enforcing, systems of governance are characterized by patterns of institutional recombination and hybrid forms of governance may be the result.

The particular type of business coalition that governments must secure to successfully implement structural reform depends on the particular model of governance they promote and their specific goals. When the goal has been to promote large integrated industrial conglomerates, as was long the case in post-war France where a centralized model was used, governments promoted a narrow business coalition. By contrast, when governments have sought to promote specialized manufactured goods that entail long innovation chains, a feature that many countries sought to emulate in the 1970s and 1980s, they have sought to create business coalitions that included large and small- and medium-sized enterprises, as well as the banking sector. In practice, this meant that governments sought to furnish designs across several domains of the economy in ways that met with the support of distinct constituencies within the business community.

Finally, when governments have sought to promote growth in high-end services such as in the financial sector or knowledge-intensive industries associated with the digital revolution, areas for which the liberal market economy is said to be well-suited (e.g., Soskice 1999; Casper 2007), they have also sought to build relatively broad support within the business community. In particular, they have sought to promote designs that have met with the approval of the financial sector, and they have sought to ensure support from large and smaller manufacturing firms.

Two Paths to Loyalty: Imperative and Motivational

At the center of structural reform are efforts by governments to shape corporate strategy in direct or indirect ways by means of particular economic institutions.[14] Governments looking to enhance the competitiveness of firms and alter a country's industrial composition seek to elicit patterns of investment by firms in new technologies and individuals' skills, specific patterns of industrial cooperation, and distinct relations between employers and organized labor. In broad terms, governments promote specific designs with the goal of influencing the product market strategies of firms with the ambition of generating economy-wide results.

Structural reform entails both direct and indirect ways in which the product market strategies of firms are influenced. However, governments cannot impose particular patterns of firm behavior because non-cooperation on the part of firms effectively means that the intended results are not achieved and the institutions promoted by governments lack the foundation for long-term stability (Hall and Thelen 2009). Governments, therefore, seek to elicit particular types of behavior of firms. Although governments may be unable to secure behavior on the part of firms that ensures intended or optimal outcomes, the sustainability of structural reform is contingent on ensuring that firms do not behave in ways that undermine the institutional core of reforms. As Russell Hardin notes in a discussion of the conditions under which stability is lasting, "[a] successful organization need not and likely cannot be expected to coordinate everyone optimally . . . [but] it *must coordinate modally* so that piecemeal violations of the coordination are not very disruptive (Hardin 1998, 431, emphasis added).

Governments regularly consult with the business community to ensure that its pivotal members behave in modally coordinated fashion. Government officials meet with representatives of the business community, address their annual meetings, and at times create formal bodies for regular consultation. The latter has been particularly common when the nature of competition has shifted radically for national industry and there has been a perceived need to update product markets and enhance the competitiveness of firms. In the early post-war period, as well as in the 1970s and 1990s, governments created a panoply of commissions, roundtables, and other vehicles to promote shared understandings between the public and private sectors on how to implement structural reform. Consultative organs and practices played important roles in aligning the expectations of disparate parts of the business community. However, the decisions of firms to adopt the type of product market strategies championed by governments turned in the long term less on persuasion than on firms' economic incentives to make particular kinds of social and material investments.

Governments seeking to build support for their economic reform agendas can use either imperative or motivational means to elicit loyalty among members of the business community.[15] The former strategy seeks to ensure loyal behavior through direct rewards and threats of sanctions, or by disabling the discretion of firms to behave in ways that would undermine the designs championed by governments. Governments employing imperative means attempt to shape corporate strategy through direct tools such as giving companies grants and subsidies, channeling favorable loans, and often by controlling the majority of seats on company boards. This approach has been popular in centralized market economies where governments embrace institutions of joint planning and held major ownership stakes in strategically placed firms. In centralized systems, governments also tend to rely on an extensive set of constraints on the market for corporate control, as well as manage the supply of credit in ways that make firms more likely to adopt the product market strategies championed by governments. Similar practices define the innovation system, where governments privilege particular kinds of research and development with the goal of promoting specific types of product market strategies. In post-war Europe, the paradigmatic case of the centralized market economy was France until the early 1980s (e.g., Shonfield 1965; Zysman 1977; Hall 1986; Schmidt 1996).

In addition to shaping corporate strategy in direct ways through supply-side reforms, governments employing an imperative approach have also tended to use macroeconomic policies in ways that benefit particular types of companies. For example, by controlling the value of national currencies, typically by ensuring that they are undervalued, governments may seek to boost the competitiveness of domestic firms in ways that reinforce structural reform. In similar ways, governments favoring centralized designs tend to adopt foreign economic policies that shield or promote particular industrial sectors rather than embrace multilateral agreements that cover a broader set of sectors, including those not directly targeted by governments in their national reforms (e.g., Adams 1989; Zysman 1978).

If governments expect that they will be unable to secure credible commitments from firms through various imperative means, they may introduce constraints that disable the discretion of firms to behave in ways that undermine institutions. This is typically done through legislative acts and regulatory statutes that limit the ability of firms to unilaterally overturn or escape existing obligations without significant sanction.

By contrast to strategies that rely on imperative means, those focused on motivational ones seek to elicit loyalty among firms by supplying institutions that match the preferences of firms. Such strategies attempt to ensure that firms voluntarily behave in ways that reproduce the designs championed by governments. They aim to shape firm strategy in indirect ways by putting in place institutional designs that give firms incentives to make specific types of investments, adopt particular product market strategies, and engage in distinct kinds of innovation. Strategies stressing motivational factors are particularly common features in decentralized systems of governance such as the liberal market economy associated with Britain after 1979 and the coordinated market economy in post-war Germany (Katzenstein 1987; Streeck 1992; Hall and Soskice 2001a; Culpepper 2003). Though their modalities vary, governments promoting these models seek to elicit patterns of behavior among firms that ensure stability in core institutions with the goal of producing long-term economic outcomes such as growth and employment. In contrast to imperative strategies, those stressing motivational means aim to gain support from the business community not by threatening to withhold direct support, but by supplying institutions that firms find more attractive than feasible alternatives. Efforts to disable the discretion of firms to act in ways that would undermine designs are more rare in decentralized systems than in centralized ones, though a significant feature of the coordinated market economy where statutory restraints are employed to encourage long-term contracting among economic groups.

The ways in which governments promoting liberal and coordinated market economies have sought to shape corporate strategy have varied. For example, in the former governments have favored systems of finance and corporate governance stressing large equity markets and fewer constraints on the market for corporate governance. By contrast, governments promoting the designs of a coordinated market economy have privileged designs that have given banks incentives to extend long-term loans. They preferred systems of corporate governance that have created strong blockholding arrangements in which firms have complementary interests (Deeg 1999; Hall and Soskice 2001b). Though both economic models are associated with decentralized systems of industrial relations, governments championing the liberal model have generally sought to promote high levels of flexibility in labor markets. Conversely, governments in coordinated market economies have promoted the expansion of a large set of institutions for non-market coordination as a means of fostering long-term relations between employers and employees. Both systems have distinct institutional advantages, as is evident in among other things their ability to contain wage inflation through different designs (e.g., Calmfors and Driffill 1988; Soskice 1991). Finally, differences have been apparent in the type of innovation system promoted by governments championing liberal and coordinated models, with those favoring the former devoting less attention to resolving basic public goods problems and the latter emphasizing private sector associations and public authorities in resolving market failures in this domain.

Motivational strategies to securing support within the business community also have macroeconomic corollaries. Though their success and particular emphases have tended to vary, governments in both liberal and coordinated market economies have employed monetary and fiscal policies with the goal of creating a propitious environment for large investments. Ensuring price stability has been a major priority and currency devaluations have tended to be explicitly ruled out as a means of boosting the competitiveness of firms because they have been seen to undermine firms' incentives to make large investments in productive capacity. Finally, governments employing motivational strategies have typically been associated with support for market liberalization and forms of multilateral regulation that prevent discriminatory practices.

Distributional Conflict

Institutional reform has distributional consequences within societies, including within business communities: some sectors will be relative winners from reform, others relative losers. Few areas of reform have had as significant distributional consequences as those targeting structural reform. In post-war Europe, attempts by governments to sustain and transform integral institutions of advanced capitalism were closely tied to efforts that favored some sectors and firms over others. The particular goals of structural reform, though somewhat different across countries, had some common themes across time. In the early post-war period, European governments placed particular emphasis on the creation of large-scale industrial companies with relatively undifferentiated product market strategies. By the 1970s, however, they had come to give more attention to the promotion of specialized firms in high value-added product markets. And, by the 1990s, a stronger emphasis emerged on knowledge-intensive production and on developing new markets in high-end services and advanced technologies.

Structural reform is a game of comparisons. Is one better off staying the course and privileging incremental reforms and moderate tinkering? Or is one better off radically altering designs embracing a radical departure in a new direction? Regardless of the answer, governments have always confronted trade-offs with distributional consequences for firms with stakes in the nature of economic designs. The manner in which governments manage these trade-offs, build support for reform in some constituencies, and compensate those who are relative losers is central to patterns of institutional development within market economies.

Because some economic models are better suited to promoting growth in some industrial sectors and other models better at stimulating growth in others, the model favored by governments constitutes necessarily a choice between imperfect alternatives. As market conditions change, however, firms with stakes in reform may conclude that a specific model is more imperfect than others. In other words, distributional conflicts do not appear only when governments attempt to change the structure of institutions. They may also exist, in fact intensify, if the institutional status quo persists. Because markets evolve, some firms will attach opportunity costs to preserving status quo institutions.[16] Such costs motivate firms to assess the balance of advantages and disadvantages associated with incremental and radical changes to existing arrangements. If governments depend on these firms to succeed economically and their opportunity costs are particularly large—that is, if the benefits forgone from maintaining the status quo and not adopting alternative designs are high—radical change is the rare means by which governments can secure the support from firms. Yet a radical reform path may present difficulties to governments for they may have negative repercussions for other firms and economic groups who are deeply invested in protecting status quo institutions.

Distributional conflict is particularly evident in cases where the institutional advantages on which some firms rely to develop their core competencies constitute institutional *dis*advantages to those firms whom governments are targeting for growth. In the early post-war period, for example, many of the designs promoted by British governments to create large industrial enterprises were opposed by the financial services industry and small- and medium-sized enterprises who sought to protect their stakes in historic designs. These cleavages were bridged only in the 1980s after a series of radical domestic reforms and a commitment by the British government to a new set of multilateral designs. In the 1990s reforms to Germany's financial system designed to spur growth in new high-tech markets through an expansion of equity markets was met with skepticism by large manufacturing firms, which feared that such reforms would undermine their access to patient long-term capital and erode institutional foundations of their international competitiveness. In that case, the historic coalition between commercial banks and advanced manufacturing firms was under threat and led German governments to devise ways to reduce the adjustment costs for the latter sector. In both cases, the ability of governments to successfully implement reforms to integral institutions of advanced capitalism hinged as much on their ability to reward sectors who saw potential benefits from reform as limiting the costs that other sectors expected from government agendas.

Adjustment Benefits

Governments' ability to secure support for their reform initiatives from the business community depends on how firms assess the advantages and disadvantages of being constrained by alternative designs. Such assessments produce appraisals of institutional differentials that are the result of several considerations, including how integral extant designs are to maintaining a firm's competitive advantage, how attractive feasible alternatives are, and whether exogenous factors such as technological shifts and international market and institutional conditions affect the merits and liabilities of historic and prospective designs.[17]

When firms determine that extant designs are preferable to feasible alternatives, an institutional differential is positive and firms' commitments to existing institutions are motivationally credible. The necessary conditions exist for governments to successfully consolidate institutions because firms will behave in modally coordinated ways that make extant designs self-enforcing. When positive differentials increase over time, firms' preferences for continuity become more intense and their commitments are credible under more parameters; institutions become self-*re*inforcing (Greif 2006). The conditions that produce such realities may be due to positive feedback effects and institutional complementarities, or simply because alternatives are very unattractive (North 1990; Pierson 2000).

Any action by governments that maintains or increases positive differentials through reform constitutes a situation where firms enjoy adjustment benefits. Such benefits may be the product of two sets of strategies. First, governments may implement incremental changes to specific institution that serve to marginally enhance the attractiveness of designs associated with the status quo. Depending on the nature of the institutional advantages of an economic system, such reforms may entail the reduction of constraints or the introduction of new ones.[18]

Second, reforms may entail adaptation benefits when governments initiate reform in different economic domains so that the overall effects of institutional interdependencies increases positive differentials. In these scenarios, reforms serve to create institutional complementarities that produce aggregate outcomes that enhance the positive differential associated with a particular institution (Porter 1990; Hall and Gingerich 2009; Hall and Soskice 2001b, 19–21). For example, a manufacturing firm that benefits from financial institutions that promote long-term financing may deem reforms in the corporate governance domain that increase concentrated shareholding arrangements to be enhancing the benefits of existing arrangements. Conversely, firms that favor a financial system with large equity markets may frame changes to corporate governance that reduce constraints on the market for corporate control to be a major benefit.

The effects of institutional interdependencies on firm strategy are evident in several areas, but their particulars vary across economic systems. The financial and corporate governance systems associated with the liberal model work to create an open market for corporate control. Such control has significantly aided firms that benefit from radical innovation strategies, including high-end financial services, biotechnology, and the many IT-related product markets (Soskice 1999; Casper 2001). Conversely, the combination of a financial system promoting long-term capital and a corporate governance system encouraging cross shareholdings have historically benefited firms engaged in incremental innovation strategies, including in the advanced and specialized manufacturing sectors (Streeck 1992; Hall and Soskice 2001a). Other examples of complementary relationships include those between labor markets and innovation system, where designs associated with the liberal market economy, such as greater flexibility in employment contracts, facilitate dynamic labor markets that benefit high-end innovation and service industries. By contrast, the industrial relations system associated with the coordinated market economy has a complementary relationship with parts of the innovation system because it facilitates the diffusion of new technologies (Streeck 1992).[19]

Because of the potential adjustment benefits from reforms that target interdependent institutions, governments often approach structural reform as a comprehensive project that targets designs in multiple domains of economic governance. Such strategies have two important consequences. They increase the potential that relationally specific feedback effects are generated through the coexistence of multiple and incentive compatible designs. Among such feedback effects are institutional complementarities, coordination, and network effects that help firms develop new and sustain existing competitive advantages (e.g., North 1990, 92–104; Milgrom and Roberts 1992, 106–108; Aoki 2000). Institutional complementarities, which exist when the presence of one institution enhances the value of a different one, have received particular attention as they have been linked to superior economic performance (Hall and Soskice 2001b, 17; Hall and Gingerich 2009).[20] Because of this potential, governments have strong incentives to promote comprehensive reform that increases internal coherence within economic systems. Internal coherence, understood as incentive compatible designs, reduces the relative costs of contracting for firms and other stakeholders. It also helps these specialize in particular market niches and to hone their core competencies as they face stiffer competition. Finally, comprehensive reforms, whether radical or incremental in nature, may serve to better align the incentives of disparate firms to adopt complementary product market strategies and thus further enhance the prospect that institutional differentials remain or become more positive over time.

Paradoxically, although greater levels of economic openness by virtue of exposing firms to higher levels of competition increases the potential value of institutional complementarities to firms, such developments make governments' task of sustaining these arrangements more difficult. Developments beyond the control of governments may lead to domain-specific preference transformation among pivotal firms who may be unwilling to reproduce particular designs with the consequence that the benefits associated with institutional complementarities decline for other societal actors. In post-war Europe, the potential for these types of developments increased as governments became bound by a larger number of international institutions that, foreseen and unforeseen, constrained the types of designs government could promote at home. For these reasons governments attached great importance to securing multilateral forms they thought would reinforce domestic reform programs and would prevent the erosion of those designs that were valued particularly highly by domestic constituencies on whom they relied to sustain their economic agendas.

Adaptation Costs and Losses

When markets change and new technologies emerge, firms reassess the relative value of extant designs. If firms pivotal to sustaining institutions integral to a system of governance experience preference transformations, the long-term sustainability of institutions—and even whole systems of governance—may be threatened. For example, if reforms in one domain end up being incompatible with existing designs in other domains, the institutional complementarities that other firms enjoy may decline and lead these to support further reforms. The defection of a pivotal sector from extant arrangements produces negative feedback effects that gradually undermine the commitments of others to reproducing designs. In such scenarios, formerly positive institutional differentials become negative and will, if discretion is not disabled, cause pivotal sectors to behave in ways that gradually generate self-undermining institutions. Studies have pointed to such processes in explaining major changes in the structure of post-war economic governance in Europe. For example, the defection in the 1990s of German commercial banks from the institutions that characterized the post-war coordinated market economy and of French banks from a system established in the late 1980s were crucial events that undermined major features of the corporate governance systems in those countries (Schmidt 1996; Culpepper 2005; Deeg 2005). Others have speculated that such developments may unravel whole systems of governance because the incentives of firms to support continuity in other designs declined significantly after radical changes in financial systems (Hall and Soskice 2001b, 57).

Firms frequently conclude that extant designs are not superior to alternatives. In such instances their assessments net a negative institutional differential and the status quo is consequently framed as entailing opportunity costs—that is, maintaining the status quo entails forgone benefits. These opportunity costs are technically speaking maladaptation costs because they may be eliminated through reform (Williamson 1996b, 5).[21] When maladaptation costs are sufficiently large to be considered consequential by firms for their long-term performance, they are the source of preference transformations. If governments are unwilling or unable to radically reform existing designs, they can only ensure that firms' commitments are credible through imperative means. They do so either by compensating firms through subsidies or other direct means, or by disabling firms' discretion to behave in ways that undermine designs.

Though associated in particular with centralized systems of governance, imperative means are also employed selectively in economies emphasizing decentralized forms of governance. For example, German governments used national and multilateral statutory strategies to disable the ability of large firms to undermine domestic rules governing mergers and the institution of codetermination. Similarly, following decentralization reforms in France during the 1980s, governments restricted the means by which firms could engage in hostile takeovers against the preferences of the financial sector and introduced statutory obligations in matters governing employment contracts that were widely condemned by the business community.

The potential for maladaptation costs is large and consequential in a competitive environment where political and economic groups search for efficient means to make use of their scarce resources. Thus governments committed to implementing structural reform are sensitive to the nature of such costs among domestic constituencies on whom they rely to successfully sustain reforms. But reforming institutions in ways that eliminate maladaptation costs for some sectors is not always politically feasible because changes in the status quo may have adverse consequences for other constituencies. For example, as scholars in the historical institutionalism tradition show, groups that have acquired investments in economic designs are often opposed to major reforms because they may lose access to those institutions they consider integral to their corporate strategies (Pierson 2000; Thelen 2004). This tradition points to what may be termed adaptation losses by contrast to maladaptation costs. Such losses involve instances in which shifts in the status quo entail the transformation of a formerly positive institutional differential into a negative one.[22] By contrast, maladaptation costs are instances when groups already frame the status quo as a liability (institutional differentials are negative) and where institutional reform constitutes an opportunity to secure benefits.[23]

The political challenge that confronts governments implementing institutional reform is how to reconcile demands for continuity among domestic groups confronted with adaptation losses from radical reform with those from groups that seek radical change as a means of eliminating maladaptation costs. In an open system of governance such as the modern advanced industrial economy, managing these types of distributional conflicts is not simply a matter of what designs exist at home—it is also a matter of how such designs are affected by the institutional environment beyond national borders.

The Open Economy and the Design Problem

In an open economy embedded within a fabric of multilateral institutions, the factors that influence firms' assessments of institutional differentials are both national and international. Governments that seek to engender loyalty among firms for domestic reforms must, therefore, attend to both sides of a governance dilemma known as the design problem (Goodin 1996; Roberts 2007). This dilemma concerns how national economic institutions are integrated internally within a state and how they are externally integrated into the international environment. "A well-designed institution," notes Robert Goodin (1996, 37) "would be one that is both internally consistent and externally in harmony with the rest of the social order in which it is set." Although governments are not always successful in ensuring that economic institutions remain "well-designed" over time, their ability to secure such outcomes, especially through action in the multilateral sphere, is often more a question of the extent of their "pluck" than of path-dependencies ("stuck") or fortuitous circumstances ("luck").[24]

Handling External Adaptation Losses

The reason that national economic models meeting Goodin's description can be said to be "well-designed" is that domestic groups face the prospect of neither adaptation losses nor maladaptation costs from maintaining the national status quo.[25] However, it is rarely the case that all domestic groups affected by multilateral designs agree that a national system is "well-designed." Invariably, multilateral designs will have domestic distributional consequences and induce some form of adjustment cost on one or more constituencies. In assessing the significance of such adjustment costs, externally induced adaptation losses and maladaptation costs should be distinguished.

When multilateral designs compel changes in domestic designs that constitute an asset to domestic groups, the former generates externally induced adaptation losses. These are situations where external designs threaten to reverse the sign of institutional differentials from a positive to a negative value. In the history of European multilateralism, such situations have been common, including when international agreements have forced governments to discontinue practices of economic discrimination that favored national firms through direct subsidies, targeted procurement strategies, and various forms of non-tariff barriers. The prospect of such losses has been apparent when legislative proposals in the EU have threatened to undermine long-standing national practices that supranational authorities deem discriminatory.

To ensure loyalty among firms when externally induced adaptation losses are large, governments employ strategies that range from launching legal battles in international courts, to attempting to mold multilateral designs in more favorable ways, to securing special dispensations from common rules. External adaptation losses may be the result of international legal decisions that force national authorities to rewrite national statutory codes in ways that eliminate the ability of domestic groups to maintain access to institutions they have considered assets. In such cases, governments often advocate in international courts on behalf of domestic constituencies that will be disadvantaged by multilateral rules. They are not always successful in their efforts, however. For example, the European Court of Justice (ECJ) determined that public sector savings banks in Germany constituted a breach of the EU's internal market and forced regional authorities to suspend preferential guarantees to public sector banks (for more detail see chapter 6). To those firms that relied on loans from such banks, that decision entailed significant external adaptation losses. Regional governments and small- and medium-sized enterprises argued that the ECJ's decision would undermine one of the cornerstones of post-war Germany's economic strategy, but the federal government was unable to prevent the external imposition of adaptation losses.

Another example is a case in which British governments launched a legal challenge to EU rules impacting what they considered crucial to maintaining the institutional advantages of a flexible labor market (see chapter 4 for details). They brought a case to the ECJ concerning the ability of British employers to exceed European rules on the number of hours individuals could work, but they lost the case. To mitigate the adaptation losses associated with this case, British governments secured special derogations through negotiations with other member-states. Although these may be considered to have been relatively small concessions, they allowed the British government to reassure the business community not only that adaptation losses were smaller than in the absence of their actions, but that the government was committed to defending the institutional integrity of domestic designs. The latter was important for it enabled governments to reduce the uncertainties that firms would otherwise associate with government (in)action and communicate their intentions with respect to institutional reforms.

EU regulations, which have direct effect and require governments to comply with multilateral rules, may also produce adaptation losses to domestic constituencies if they require governments to alter the national regulatory structure in ways that are detrimental to these constituencies. In negotiations over a common European legal identity for limited liability companies, governments rejected several proposals that would have forced them to rewrite national company codes with significant effects for the structure of corporate governance. For different reasons, governments in both Britain and Germany were concerned that common rules would impose adaptation losses on domestic constituencies. An agreement among EU members was reached after the adaptation losses for constituencies in both countries were significantly reduced, though with the consequence that many of the original benefits of the initiative were absent to groups championing an early resolution (Fioretos 2009). In that case, governments reduced external adaptation losses by placing the most contentious aspects of the original regulation in a directive.

Because directives give governments discretion in how they meet international obligations, they potentially reduce external adaptation losses relative to regulations. However, directives do not necessarily eliminate such losses. In many cases, directives are the product of qualified majority voting under EU rules and governments wishing to protect domestic designs may be unable to prevail in negotiations with other member-states.[26] Take, for example, a case in which French governments were strongly opposed to a directive that would affect the national system of corporate governance by eliminating the ability of French firms to employ national instruments that deterred hostile takeovers (see chapter 5). Though supported by the country's financial sector, the manufacturing sector was opposed because it would undermine a key mechanism by which companies ensured that investors developed long-term stakes in firms. By describing such mechanisms as a "loyalty bonus" that did not discriminate against foreign owners, the French government sought to protect domestic constituencies from externally imposed adaptation losses. In that case, a compromise among EU members eventually reduced the prospect of such losses and allowed the French government to claim that it preserved key features of national practice.

Governments in countries where low regulatory standards are a source on which firms establish their international competitive advantage are often concerned that efforts to harmonize national standards through directives will impose significant adaptation losses. For example, in Britain where the regulation of employment contracts are less extensive and where employee representation in company boards is not a legal mandate, governments have been adamant about ensuring that multilateral rules do not undermine national practices that are viewed as integral to the comparative institutional advantages of the liberal market economy. British governments have often been successful in thwarting such initiatives, usually with the support of Germany. However, they have not always been able to prevent multilateral agreements that threatened to impose domestic adaptation losses on firms. In instances where it has been particularly important for governments to reassure the business community that the comparative institutional advantages of the liberal market economy would not be affected, they have managed to secure special opt-outs from common EU rules, most notably during the negotiations over the Treaty on European Union. Although a particular opt-out was eventually surrendered, British governments used it to reassure the business sector of their intentions to protect firms from potential adaptation losses when the corporate sector had concerns over the future viability of a liberal market economy within the European Union.

Britain is seen as the paradigmatic case of a country seeking special dispensations in the form of opt-outs, but other governments have also sought special dispensations from EU rules as a means of reducing domestic adaptation losses. The case studies of Germany and France entail illustrations of how those governments sought special derogations from common multilateral rules as a means to minimize external adaptation losses and protect what governments considered integral elements of their national economic models.

Managing External Maladaptation Costs

It is often implied, and sometimes explicitly stated, that in resolving the design problem, governments seek to establish international designs that protect the domestic status quo. For example, Daniel Drezner argues that "a government's ideal point on [international] regulatory issues is its domestic status quo" (2007, 40). Governments' efforts to preserve the domestic status can be expected to be particularly strong when pivotal domestic groups face the prospect of significant adaptation losses. But protecting the domestic status quo is not an enduring concern for governments, who frequently support significant changes in domestic designs as a means of enhancing the prospect that structural reform is successful. In such instances, governments have strong incentives to support multilateral designs that enhance the prospect that domestic reforms eliminate the negative institutional differentials associated with maladapted designs.

Maladaptation costs may be externally induced. The use of directives, for example, though valuable in reducing potential adaptation losses, may create situations that produce maladaptation costs. Directives enhance regulatory competition between national jurisdictions and may cause domestic groups to conclude that maintaining historic forms of national governance entails opportunity costs that could be eliminated if the practice of other jurisdictions were adopted at home. In such cases, the institution of multilateralism plays a decisive role in transforming the preferences of domestic constituencies. However, it is not the prospect of external adaptation losses that is the motivating factor but the opportunity cost of not aligning national practice with multilateral standards that motivates preference transformations.

Through the multiple directives that constitute the single European market, competition in financial services increased significantly during the 1980s and 1990s. This caused banks that had traditionally employed product market strategies in which they relied on long-term relatively low-yield loans to domestic industry to advocate in favor of domestic reforms to national financial systems, which would make national practice conform more closely to multilateral norms. The relevant consideration in this context was the opportunity costs of not more closely aligning national designs with international norms. Both in Germany and France, this type of motivation transformed the preferences of pivotal sectors of the financial services industry and brought radical departures in national designs that eventually made them more similar in form to those found in liberal market economies than their own post-war models.

If externally induced maladaptation costs are larger than the value firms attach to extant national designs, firms' commitments to the latter lack credibility. These situations are a source of great concern to governments when they seek to preserve existing national designs. In discussions of national rules governing the workplace, firms in jurisdictions with less flexible rules often point to the reality that they compete with firms in jurisdictions where flexibility is greater. Some governments have sought to harmonize standards at the international level for the purposes of eliminating the prospect that external maladaptation costs will cause domestic designs to be undermined. Such efforts often fail because attempts by governments to harmonize standards upward as a means to eliminate maladaptation costs for its domestic constituencies represent the imposition of adaptation losses in countries where lower standards constitute the foundation for an economic model's comparative institutional advantages. To resolve such situations, governments looking to mitigate the prospect of high maladaptation costs have tended to promote the use of common minimum standards to reduce the negative institutional differential perceived by constituencies opposed to the status quo.

The use of common minimum standards helps governments mitigate domestic distributional conflicts. Because they permit countries to exceed standards, they allow governments to avoid the imposition of adaptation losses on domestic groups supportive of the status quo. At the same time, by establishing a common set of multilateral standards, they reduce the negative institutional differentials associated with the status quo by reducing maladaptation costs for those groups who preferred radical changes at home prior to a multilateral agreement. In this way, common minimum standards reduce the incentives of the latter to seek more radical changes in national designs. Common minimum standards do not eliminate the potential opportunity costs of operating in a setting with higher standards, but they may reduce such costs sufficiently to prevent preference reversals. They may thus ensure that the commitments of firms to extant designs remain motivationally credible despite the persistence of some maladaptation costs. In such situations, then, the ways in which the discretion of groups seeking to alter the original status quo is constrained are not by national means, but through the institution of multilateralism. For example, European agreements in the area of social policy, where common minimum standards are used extensively, can be said to have protected many domestic designs from experiencing more radical changes because both the incentives and the ability of groups seeking to alter the status quo were fundamentally different than had such standards not existed.[27]

The existence of external maladaptation costs are not always unwelcome by domestic groups. In cases where groups wish to transform national designs they deem less attractive than alternatives, high external maladaptation costs may be an effective vehicle to bring about domestic reforms. In these instances, governments and economic groups attempt to create "Trojan horse" effects whereby the incentives to eliminate maladaptation costs bring about domestic changes that would have been unacceptable in the absence of such costs. This has not been an uncommon tactic. For example, large German manufacturing companies have for most of the postwar period actively appealed to their government that less stringent international competition rules replace more restrictive ones at home. External maladaptation costs were the justification for why domestic reform was essential. German governments resisted as they considered such a trajectory harmful to the viability of small- and medium-sized enterprise sector. Because the latter sector has consistently been an integral part of the business coalition on which German governments have relied in implementing structural reform, resisting the demands of large firms was a more attractive option to governments than imposing high adaptation losses on smaller firms.

Adaptation Benefits and the External
Reinforcement of the Status Quo

Robert Goodin's definition of what constitutes a well-designed institution implies that the absence of adjustment costs is the critical issue governments will consider when they seek to resolve the design problem. This perspective overlooks that multilateral designs may contribute to situations in which open governance does not preserve but reinforces support for national designs. Membership in an international organization may itself be sufficient to reinforce firms' support for domestic reforms by producing externally induced adaptation benefits. Because multilateral institutions that reduce barriers to economic exchange and open new markets lengthen the time horizons of firms, reduce the potential risks of international exchange, and protect property rights, they often enhance the incentives of firms to make long-term investments in those resources that help them expand their profitability and market shares. Multilateral rules thus create opportunities for firms to exploit new scale and scope economies, which in turn generate positive feedback effects that potentially strengthen their commitments to national designs.

John Ruggie's (1982, 382) analysis of the post-war international economic order he termed the "compromise of embedded liberalism" was described as an arrangement with several "complementary" parts. These enhanced the willingness of the business sector to support domestic reconstruction projects and pay for the expansion of institutions associated with the welfare state. Barry Eichengreen (1993, 91) describes the European Payments Union, an early multilateral initiative designed to facilitate trade, in similar terms and calls it an "essential concomitant" to domestic reconstruction programs. The European Economic Community (EEC), which marks the origin of what became the EU, was significant for the same reasons. The EEC enlarged the opportunity for large manufacturing companies to increase their markets and in the process enhanced the value they attached to national reforms in both Germany and France. In contrast, Britain's delayed membership in the EEC significantly reduced firms' incentives to undertake large investments in productive capacity and reduced their support of major domestic reform programs that were initiated during the 1960s.

Multilateral designs also served to reinforce firms' commitments to national reforms in later stages of the European integration process. When governments resolved the design problem in ways that entailed no adaptation losses or maladaptation costs while expanding the opportunity of firms to exploit the institutional advantages of domestic designs, the institution of multilateralism strengthened firms' support for the domestic status quo. Such a process was evident in Britain during the 1980s when the financial sector attached greater value to domestic reforms following its government's commitment to the internal market program. Britain's financial services industry saw the latter initiative as integral to consolidating the advantages of a domestic deregulatory agenda and served to significantly increase the size of capital markets in London.

The implementation of Economic and Monetary Union (EMU) had a complementary relationship with those domestic designs that had historically facilitated moderate wage growth through the industrial relations system. Because such designs have been associated with a history of productivity enhancing agreements between employers and unions, the EMU regime helped German firms to significantly enhance their cost competitiveness in the 1990s vis-à-vis their main European competitors. EMU thus helped generate some specific adaptation benefits.[28] During the 1990s there was much controversy over Germany's industrial relations system, and the gradual implementation and consolidation of EMU did not eliminate such concerns entirely as much as it reduced the negative institutional differential that firms associated with parts of that system. As such the benefits from how the design problem was resolved were found in the manner in which it reduced the liabilities of domestic designs.

The cases highlighted here and explored at greater length in later chapters underscore that the credibility of firms' commitments to national designs was reinforced when national and multilateral institutions were incentive compatible. When such patterns occurred in multiple domains, multilateral designs served to preserve nationally distinct models of capitalism by making possible their continued consolidation. Indeed, in Germany during the 1970s and 1980s and in Britain during the 1990s and 2000s, the particular mix of multilateral institutions that were created significantly enhanced the value domestic groups attached to national designs and contributed to making possible sustainable patterns of institutional specialization. But the ability of governments to secure such outcomes was often limited to specific time periods and contingent on the nature of domestic reforms. Therefore, to identify when governments were successful or not in sustaining and transforming national designs requires a nuanced and context-specific understanding of how they resolved the design problem over time.

Systematic Process Analysis

The last section employed actor-centered institutional traditions to identify *general* conditions under which firms' commitments to government-led reforms are credible. Analytically, the *specific* conditions under which firms' commitments to government-led reforms are credible is a function of the assumptions that are made about the preferences and behavior of firms. As Ira Katznelson emphasizes, "large-scale comparative analysis is underspecified and incomplete when its microfoundations are left implicit, ad hoc, or undertheorized" (2003, 272). However, because theoretical traditions make different assumptions about the structure of preferences, the substantive study of institutional development should not be limited to one theoretical tradition. In such cases, studies run the risks of focusing on a narrow set of outcomes and leave unsaid whether alternative traditions that predict observationally equivalent outcomes are correct and potentially better placed to explain a larger number of cases.

Systematic process analysis aims to overcome the potential drawbacks of employing a single theoretical tradition in the study of institutional development (Hall 2003, 391–395; 2008). It is grounded in well-established social science practice such as the comparative method and process tracing, but as Peter Hall avers, "its crucial point is that the investigator should approach [a] case, not only with a principal theory, but with it and one or more theories that could plausibly be adduced to explain the outcome. The object is to test one theory against another" (2008, 309).[29]

Scholars have noted for decades that there are "pluralities of rationalities" (e.g., Simon 1957, 1997; Elster 1979). The rational choice institutionalist literature relies extensively on a particular model of rationality in which endpoint comparisons are the foundation on which preference orders emerge (March and Olson 1984; Simon 1997, 17–19). These so-called global rationality models inform large literatures and assume that social actors are primarily motivated by efforts to eliminate the opportunity costs of employing less advantageous solutions at a future date.[30] Global rationality models suggest that marginal differences in the advantages of employing an alternative in the future will presage preference transformations and, if experienced by pivotal social actors, will relatively rapidly lead to a stable new status quo. In the words of James March and Johan Olsen (1984, 737), these models assume that history is "efficient" in the sense that past investments and historical legacies do not matter in shaping the decisions or interests of political actors when they respond to new realities.

The reliance on global rationality models leads theories of institutional development to exaggerate the frequency, degree and speed with which radical reform occurs.[31] It also generates potentially narrow interpretations of instances where change is limited or incremental. From the vantage point of such models, suboptimal outcomes are the product of other institutions that prevent change (e.g., legislative barriers). Or they are evidence that pivotal actors are involved in multiple coordination games that lead them to give up the prospect of a stable new and more efficient equilibrium in one area if they get their preferred outcome in a different one (e.g., Tsebelis 1990). Yet it is possible that what this tradition sees as a sub-optimal outcome is a reflection of a different type of rationality and thus, from another perspective, not sub-optimal.

Historical institutionalism has long roots in political science and has emerged as a major tradition to the study of institutions by adopting a different approach to human agency (e.g., Thelen 1999; Pierson 2004; Katznelson and Weingast 2005a). It is heavily informed by implicit and at times explicit models of embedded rationality in which local (defined variously as national, regional, or firm-level) factors condition the behavior of social actors. Models of path dependence have been common in this tradition as a means to explaining persistent variations in similar types of polities. Recent studies have turned to a set of positive feedback effects to explain why social actors have reasons to voluntarily support continuity in extant designs (e.g., Pierson 2004; Thelen 2004). In this tradition, local culture, social norms, and the cumulative effects of the sequence by which designs have evolved explain why social actors have diverse stakes in their institutional environments. Preferences are the product of the type of investments actors make over time and transformations are rare and attributed to sudden and often unexpected shifts in the economic or political environment in which they find themselves.[32] But if global rationality models lead rational choice institutionalism to exaggerate the frequency with which radical reform occurs, then embedded rationality models can be said to be the reason that historical institutionalism tends to underestimate the extent to which economic institutions change in fundamental ways.

The type of assessments social actors make and to which global and embedded rationality models point can be readily observed in the historical archive. Firms regularly examine the costs and benefits of prospective alternatives, and they also regularly consider the costs and benefits of being bound by past designs. But the relative weight of such assessments varies over time. In periods of economic crisis and poor performance, firms tend to stress the type of comparisons that are highlighted in global rationality models. Past designs are more highly discounted in such cases and the primary goal of firms is to improve the conditions under which they will operate in the future. Studies of post-war Europe illustrate that the business community under such conditions has attached great costs to inaction and has been a vociferous agent of radical reform (e.g., Pontusson and Swenson 1996; Blyth 2002; Woll 2008). By contrast, in periods of relative stability and economic success, firms have been less keen to explore radical alternatives and tend to support measures that ensure continuity in designs (e.g., Swenson 2002). Such situations alter how firms frame the costs and benefits of change because their reference points are different. In the former example, the reference point (that against which the costs and benefits of maintaining the status quo is measured) was prospective in nature and firms framed the status quo as one entailing losses. In the latter example, the reference point was found in the past and maintaining the status quo was framed as one entailing gains. The relative attractiveness of alternatives and past investments matter, but the historical archive underscores that their consequences for how actors rank alternatives is situationally contingent, though far from accidental.

Behavioral Institutionalism

Behavioral economics offers means for incorporating situationally contingent dimensions such as framing effects in shaping preference orders and represents a valuable complement to comparative historical analysis. Although typically discussed in the context of theories associated with rational choice institutionalism, it is with historical institutionalism that it holds particular affinity. Both traditions begin from the premise that groups explicitly evaluate alternatives with respect to a reference point and that their preferences are not transformed if feasible alternatives offer only marginally greater benefits at a future point.[33] As such, both represent a departure from global rationality models and are more commensurate with one another than either is with rational choice institutionalism.

More specifically, what behavioral economics adds to historical institutionalism is a more nuanced theory of action of those who devise their economic and political strategies with reference to potential costs and benefits from specific institutional changes.

Historical institutionalism offers answers to why firms often hold different preferences over the designs of national economic institutions. Scholars working in this tradition document the powerful incentives that historical legacies may have on firm strategy and on the willingness of firms to support particular initiatives. Their work has been critical for a nuanced understanding of why corporate strategy and the evolution of national economic systems have varied over time (e.g., Pierson 1995; Thelen 2004). Contributors to this tradition also acknowledge that the preferences of firms and other social actors are not constant. Yet, short of sudden exogenous shocks or the accumulation of many incremental changes over long periods of time, it is unclear under what conditions preference transformations take place. Behavioral economics offers a dynamic model of how framing effects affect preference orders and of firms' incentives to support incremental or radical change as changes occur in the parameters that determine preferences. By doing so it offers logical and more conditional answers to the conditions under which institutions will be characterized by stability or radical changes than those offered by standard historical institutionalist models.

At the center of behavioral economics is the finding that whether social actors frame a situation as entailing losses or gains is consequential for it has an impact on the resources they are willing to expend to achieve their goals and for how they rank alternatives. Because social actors tend to exaggerate the value of their assets—a phenomenon called an endowment effect—they weigh potential losses more heavily than potential gains (Thaler 1980; Kahneman, Knetsch, and Thaler 1991). Endowment effects may be understood as the underweighting of opportunity costs, which is to say that someone is discounting the potential benefits from embracing an alternative (Thaler 1980, 44).

If firms' calculations are informed by endowment effects, governments that implement reforms with major distributional consequences have to expend greater resources to accommodate groups who confront adaptation losses than those who perceive potential maladaptation costs from the status quo or gains from reform. This approach also suggests that governments must offer greater compensation to potential losers from reform on whom they depend to successfully sustain or transform designs than is the case in a standard rationalist model and that transformative reforms, even when seemingly attractive, face greater obstacles unless they are framed as failures. Preference orders are not a function of evaluations of alternatives made in the absence of past experiences and realities, but contingent on the nature (positive or negative) and degree of change with respect to a particular reference point. Thus, a behavioral approach to the study of institutions expects the incidence of preference transformations to be greater than predicted by a standard historical institutional model. A corollary expectation is that radical reforms will become sustainable more quickly when firms' reference points shift and their assessments of past designs are revised.

The presence of endowment effects suggests that if institutions that are highly valued are threatened, say by a multilateral rule, governments must actively work to lower the prospect of adaptation losses if they are to secure domestic support. To ensure that domestic groups can credibly commit to domestic reforms, governments will have to secure compensations that are significantly greater than suggested by standard global rationality models. A related implication is that if a firm finds itself in the domain of losses and expects them to grow significantly, the speed with which their preferences will be transformed is greater than suggested by historical institutionalism. In the latter tradition, preference transformations are rarely rapid because of positive feedback effects. But the historical record suggests that firms frequently experience preference reversals as new information becomes available, including when others who rely on different designs are more successful (e.g., Weyland 2004). Behavioral models of rationality explain such situations with reference to shifts in the reference points that guide actors' evaluations and thus present a more dynamic approach to how actors assess institutional differentials over time than do its theoretical alternatives.

Behavioral economics also helps resolve a puzzle in the varieties of capitalism tradition. That tradition sees firms' preference in one domain as highly contingent on the structure of other domains, in particular if these have a complementary relationship. By contrast, behavioral economics finds that economic actors typically calculate their stakes separately in different domains (Thaler 1980, 2004). Known as mental accounting, this principle has important implications for our understanding of differential institutional change within economic systems as it a priori acknowledges that the same firm may frame one historic institution as a liability and another as an asset when external parameters evolve. As such, behavioral institutionalism departs from claims of strongly interdependent preferences that are associated with the varieties of capitalism framework and suggests that hybrid systems of governance may become just as stable despite being preceded by the disappearance of long-standing institutional complementarities.

Behavioral economics counters the tendency, especially among scholars critical of historical institutionalism, to describe that tradition as a deterministic one that expects paths once established to prevail after critical historical junctures. However comforting such depictions may be for those governments that are charged with reconstructing economic institutions after a crisis, it is not a reality that many governments have enjoyed. National economies are not QWERTY keyboards that once on a path move along a set trajectory because there are large costs to adopting alternatives (cf. David 1985). In fact, it is often the costs of staying the course that are on the minds of governments as they consider how they may sustain support for their reform agendas. Behavioral economics offers the tools for historical institutionalists to better contextualize these dimensions and how they impact the politics of institutional reform.

Research Strategy and Design

The following chapters adopt a two-fold research strategy to systematic process analysis that combines abstract theoretical models and detailed empirical research. They foreground how specific political governance dilemmas were resolved such as social coordination games and the design problem and they examine the historical archive for evidence of how these dilemmas were managed over time in diverse settings with the help of a multiplicity of historical and comparative case study methods.

The abstract theoretical part of systematic process analysis is most apparent in the next chapter. It specifies the conditions under which firms will credibly commit to the reforms championed by governments when they confront diverse constraints and are modeled according to the global, embedded, and behavioral rationality models. Several concepts—such as maladaptation costs, embeddedness, and multilateralism—pose significant challenges to the empirically oriented social scientist because there are no agreed on metrics for how to measure the concepts. The prospect of using a variable based approach to the social scientific study of institutions, at least in a historical context, is therefore limited. Yet, these concepts occupy center stage in several disciplines. The fact that economists cannot agree on how to measure maladaptation costs, that sociologists do not have a dominant operationalization of social embeddedness, or that political scientists vary in their understanding of what constitutes multilateralism has not stopped them from making the terms central to their study of institutions. Each concept has in fact been central to the evolution of major research programs in each discipline.

Alejandro Portes and Julia Sensenbrenner's discussion of how to operationalize the notion of social embeddedness captures the basic research challenge. They note that while embeddedness

> provides a very useful standpoint for criticizing neoclassical models . . . it suffers from theoretical vagueness. The observation that outcomes are uncertain because they depend on how economic action is embedded does not help us meet the positivistic goal of predictive improvement and theoretical accumulation. To fulfill these goals, we must better specify just how social structure constrains, supports, or derails individual goal-seeking behavior. (1993, 1321)[34]

The second part of the research strategy, designed to test the logical inferences of the three theoretical traditions, concerns engagement with the substantive archive on institutional reform in post-war Europe. Specifically, the empirical sections focus on how the manner in which governments in Britain, France, and Germany reconciled domestic reforms with multilateral commitments shaped their ability to gain support from pivotal sectors of the business community in their structural reform programs over time. The diverse outcomes that are apparent in these case studies ensure appropriate variation on the dependent variable and facilitate contextual and controlled comparisons across countries and time periods.

In the chapters that follow, the corporate sector is understood both in political terms ("business") and in economic and social ones ("firms"). The chapters rely primarily on three types of empirical data to identify how firms responded to the reform programs pushed by governments. They examine internal studies and public statements from business associations representing different sectors of national business communities. Along with other primary sources, such as personal statements by leaders of national business communities, such documents offer insights into the stated preferences of the business community with respect to national and multilateral designs. Chapters 4–6 also examine how firms responded to government reforms in terms of their investments in areas championed by governments and the extent to which they sought to publicly influence government reforms. Such information corresponds more closely to what scholars take to be the revealed preferences of firms.[35]

Finally, the comparative case studies also entail consideration of counterfactual questions. Active consideration of counterfactuals is critical to the goals of systematic process analysis for it is a means by which reasonable assessments and conclusions can be made about the implications of alternative assumptions about the motivations and behavior of those with stakes in and influence over the nature of institutional development. The idiographic and nomothetic counterfactuals that are explored in the following chapters are designed to identify whether the outcomes expected by behavioral institutionalism find grounds for support.[36] They include questions like what would have been the outcome of national reforms in the absence of the constraints posed by multilateral institutions, what the likely outcome would have been had multilateral designs taken a different form, and whether national patterns of reform would have been similar had governments opted for a different set of domestic designs.

Chapter 3

Three Models of Open Governance

Reform-oriented governments depend on support from the business sector to sustain and transform integral designs in the modern market economy. Thus, the conditions under which various business sectors are able to credibly commit to the designs championed by governments is a key analytical question for the study of institutional development in advanced market economies. Detailing firms' preference orders enables predictions about the type of business coalitions that form when the economic and institutional environments surrounding firms change and about the general conditions under which their commitments to government reforms are lasting. However, because scholars make diverse claims about the structure of firms' preferences and when these are transformed, studies reach different conclusions about the *specific* conditions under which firms' commitments are credible. This chapter specifies the logical inferences of and derives hypotheses from three perspectives of firms based in behavioral, global, and embedded rationality models. These hypotheses are examined empirically in later chapters.

The chapter employs discrete structural analysis to identify the conditions under which the three models expect the preferences of diverse firms to be strengthened, weakened, or transformed because of changes in internal and external parameters. Originating in the comparative economic organization literature (Simon 1976, 1978; Williamson 1991, 1996a), this method makes it possible to examine how variations in internal parameters such as the economic system in which a firm is embedded and the degree to which it depends on relationally specific social contracts interact with changes in external parameters like market integration and different forms of multilateralism to produce particular preference orders among firms over the design of national institutions. The chapter examines changes in external parameters sequentially in order to identify the independent and cumulative effects that different levels of market integration and distinct forms of multilateralism have for firms' preference orders. An appendix detailing the logical inferences of the behavioral, global, and embedded rationality models complements the narrative presentation.

Theorizing the Preferences and Behavior of Firms

A large literature on advanced market economies places the firm at the center of analysis. Firms are critical agents in transmitting market signals and potentially powerful political actors when coordinating their actions. The large majority of studies in political economy is centered on how the material interests of firms impact their policy preferences. The open economy politics literature, for example, links the material interests of firms that are exposed to international markets to firms' policy preferences (see Keohane and Milner 1996; Frieden and Martin 2001; Lake 2009). It finds robust links between export-orientation and support for free trade, globally oriented financial services firms and the deregulation of capital markets, and between import-competing firms and support for policies of economic discrimination. What this literature does not fully specify is the link between policy preferences and institutional preferences.[1] Because it relies on deducing preferences from economic theories based in factor endowment models, it offers no clear mechanism by which firms' material interests translate into specific views over the form of economic regulation. For example, no precise answer is given to why firms that are equally exposed to the same international markets and that support similarly high levels of free trade or financial service liberalization support alternative forms of national and multilateral regulation when they are embedded in diverse national settings. Consequently, under what conditions firms' commitments are credible to particular institutional forms cannot be specified.

Institutional theories of preferences look to overcome the lacuna in materialist ones. There are three alternative approaches to theorizing firms' institutional preferences anchored in global, embedded, and behavioral rationality models. Theories employing global rationality models suggest that firms' preferences are a function of careful weighing of prospective alternatives and that past investments in institutions are highly discounted. Such models offer potentially parsimonious theories of institutional development, but they have difficulties accounting for why firms embedded in diverse national contexts often prefer different types of institutions. Contributions to historical institutionalism and the varieties of capitalism traditions help address this lacuna in global rationality models. In these traditions, the ability of firms to harness material endowments is a function of the institutional context in which they operate and firms are modeled as actors with stakes in institutional designs (see esp. Hall and Soskice 2001a). The two traditions offer means of explaining why similar types of firms embedded in diverse national contexts often hold different preferences, but they lack specifics when it comes to the conditions under which preference transformations occur. This shortcoming can be addressed with the help of behavioral economics. As detailed in chapter 2, behavioral economics contributes intuitive and specific answers to how contextual factors, such as whether firms frame prospective changes as large or small and as gains or losses, affect their preference orders. These contributions are apparent when a behavioral model is contrasted with global and embedded rationality models.

Global Rationality Models

The rational choice institutionalist tradition relies extensively on global rationality models based on standard expected utility theory. Such models treat actors as utility maximizers that are primarily motivated by endpoint comparisons of the costs and benefits of prospective alternatives (Simon 1955; March and Olson 1984). Sunk and transition costs are immaterial in defining preference orders in such models and social actors are motivated by efforts to eliminate the opportunity costs of operating in an environment that is less efficient than feasible alternatives.[2] In these models, then, the principal concern for firms is the elimination of maladaptation costs. Firms' commitments to the designs championed by governments are motivationally credible as long as such costs are not present.

Global rationality models feature in several literatures that address the prospect of capital diversity in an open economy setting. What in the comparative political economy literature has been termed the political economy null hypothesis predicts that firms across diverse contexts prefer one optimal design and mobilize resources to bring about the gradual convergence of national models on the "global norm" (Weber 2001; see also discussions in Berger and Dore 1996; Drezner 2001).[3] In such accounts, firms' commitments to national designs that deviate from the global norm lack motivational credibility and are seen as the major mechanism leading governments to abandon extant designs in favor of models that eliminate the opportunity costs from not conforming to the global norm.[4] The end result is predicted to be the convergence of institutional designs across national economies.

Global rationality models are also central to scholars who address the potential consequences of how the external dimension of the design problem is managed, including within the literatures on systems and regulatory competition, as well as that addressing the "goodness-of-fit" between national and multilateral designs (e.g., Goodin 1996; Sinn 2003; Cowles, Caporaso, and Risse 2001).[5] These literatures speculate that national designs may converge because governments and domestic groups stand to benefit from eliminating externally induced maladaptation costs that exist when national and multilateral designs are not fully incentive compatible. The logic behind this contention—what may be called the multilateralism null hypothesis—is that in their efforts to maximize the national benefits of international cooperation, states seek to eliminate structural incongruities between the two levels of governance (see also Gourevitch 1996, 372).

For example, if multilateral business and social regulations are less extensive than national ones, governments and firms are expected to seek changes in national designs in ways that better align these with multilateral standards. Because neither governments nor firms or other domestic groups unilaterally can alter the structure of multilateral institutions, global rationality models of how the design problem is resolved expect that governments will adapt national designs to "fit" with multilateral ones. This process is expected to be most prominent where international cooperation is dense, highly formalized, and where international rules take precedence over national ones. For example, one large research project suggests and then concludes that membership in the European Union will cause "pre-existing differences among member states [to] slowly, and partly unnoticed, disappear" and will be replaced by "one common model" (Wessels 1996, 36; Wessels and Rometsch 1996, 328).

Global rationality models highlight a logic of adaptation that can be observed in the historical archive of deliberations within government circles and the business community relating to the question of what market economy model should be employed. Governments and firms regularly assess the costs and benefits of maintaining existing designs versus adopting alternatives. But these models highlight only one part of the factors that inform government action and patterns of adaptation among economic groups. By presenting the utility functions of firms as focused on one type of cost (the forgone benefits of not aligning national designs to the global norm or the multilateral order), other costs that potentially inform their calculations are excluded. History reveals that economic groups often are less concerned with whether government programs eliminate the opportunity costs from designs that are poorly aligned to the external environment than they are with the type of considerations highlighted in embedded rationality models, namely avoiding losses that would come from failing to protect national designs that are the foundation of their competitive advantage.

Their respective focus on maladaptation costs and adaption losses lead global and embedded rationality models to different expectations about when firms' commitments are credible and thus when institutions are sustainable over time. These are closely tied to how the two traditions account for preference transformations. In global rationality models, preference transformations occur even when small maladaptation costs can be eliminated, while adaptation losses must be absent in embedded rationality models. This is a consequential difference that has implications for when such models expect firms' commitments to different institutions to be motivationally credible. In the case of global rationality models, commitments are motivationally credible only when the designs that are most attractive under the status quo are supplied, while in embedded rationality models commitments may be credible even when designs that are less efficient persist.

Differences in the assumptions of these models also have implications for how traditions associated with the two models of rationality account for cases when their expectations are *not* borne out empirically. For example, accounts that rely on global rationality models frequently conclude that when a society does not change institutions in ways that are purported to be more efficient, it is due to the obstacles of other designs. From this perspective, firms desire radical changes, but their efforts are stymied because the distributional implications of the changes they seek lead other social actors to exercise their veto power in different settings to prevent radical reform.[6] Typically, attention is directed to the role of legislative designs that place high barriers to changes in economic institutions. In these accounts, governments that seek to engender loyal behavior among firms seeking radical changes can achieve such outcomes only through imperative means that constrain the exit option. In other words, the implication in global rationality models is that when patterns of radical change do not take place, governments have compelled rather than elicited credible commitments from firms.

Embedded Rationality Models

Historical institutionalism also points to the role of legislative and other institutions as constraints that may prevent rapid reforms. But in embedded rationality models the absence of radical reforms may be due to other factors as well, including the positive incentives that firms and others have to support incremental adjustment over fundamental transformations. The embedded rationality models that are at the center of the historical institutionalism and varieties of capitalism traditions suggest that the reason why economic designs do not change as frequently as predicted by global rationality models is because firms develop attachments to extant institutions (e.g., Bebchuk and Roe 1999; Thelen 1999; Pierson 2000). In these models, incremental adjustments and loyal behavior trump the prospective benefits of fundamental transformation and strategies of exit. From the perspective of embedded rationality models, firms' commitments to institutions may be motivationally credible even when attractive and feasible alternatives exist because the costs of forgoing institutional complementarities and other positive feedback effects may be greater than the potential benefits of transforming a specific institution.

Embedded rationality models inform many contributions to the literature on capitalist diversity. What may be termed the embeddedness hypothesis sees the setting in which firms are situated as highly consequential for how preferences are constructed and for how the merits of alternative designs are evaluated. Scholars examining the role played by where social actors are embedded sometimes reference sunk costs, but more typically focus on various positive feedback effects like increasing returns, network and coordination effects, and institutional complementarities (North 1990; Tzeng and Uzzi 2000; Hall and Soskice 2001a, 17–21; Thelen 2004; Crouch et al. 2005; Höpner 2005). Positive feedback effects, which are present when "the *relative* benefits of current activity compared with once-possible options increases over time," are thought to make economic groups less likely to give up their investments in extant designs because it entails adaptation losses (Pierson 2004, 20).

In embedded rationality models, the critical comparison that informs preference orders is not the differential between prospective alternatives, but rather the differential between past investments and the present. These models suggest that because national designs help firms acquire specific competitive advantages and greater competition makes sustaining such designs more important, firms will favor incremental over radical changes. Actors are modeled as having a strong status quo bias and their commitments to extant designs are motivationally credible as long as present designs generate positive benefits relative to past designs. In strict versions, local context lead social actors to reject options other than incremental adjustments to the status quo, "even if these alternative options would have been more efficient" (Mahoney 2000, 58).[7]

If global rationality models lead theories to overestimate the likelihood of preference transformations and radical change, embedded rationality models lead theories to underestimate such patterns.[8] For example, it is apparent that firms' preferences are transformed not only after major crises when the uncertainty about the future is great, but that they may incrementally change during periods of relative stability in ways that produce transformative results over time (Streeck and Thelen 2005b). Preference transformations occur also in domain-specific contexts despite the presence of institutional complementarities. In such cases, systemic factors are not as strong as typically thought in theoretical traditions that draw on embedded rationality models. This is not to say that institutional complementarities and other positive feedback effects are not important. Rather it is to underscore that embedded rationality models lack a theory of the conditions under which preference transformation occur absent sudden and radical changes in external environments.

Whether in the context of national responses to market integration or in the context of how the design problem is resolved, embedded rationality models expect a great deal more continuity in domestic designs over time and cross-national variations than appears to be the case in advanced market economies. Such models do not offer clear answers to what it will take for actors to voluntarily jettison their investments in extant designs and what alternative they will support. Recent studies reference the importance of opportunity costs in transforming preferences of key members of the business community, but it is not clear how large these must be for preferences to be reversed (Culpepper 2005; Deeg 2005). Without specification of such costs or some alternative mechanism by which preferences are transformed, historical institutionalism and other traditions employing embedded rationality models have difficulties identifying the conditions under which groups' commitments to extant designs are motivationally credible when external parameters change. They are thus also limited when formulating general explanations for when the behavior of social actors will make designs more sticky in some periods than in others, and why change is more common in some domains and countries than in others.

Behavioral Rationality Model

Behavioral economics makes subtle arguments about the calculations and behavior of social actors that help redress lacunae in global and embedded rationality models. One of its key finding is that actors' utility functions are informed by endowment effects. These exist when someone is willing to devote more resources to protecting an investment than to acquire the same asset (Thaler 1980; Kahneman, Knetsch and Thaler 1991).[9] Endowment effects have important implications for the conditions under which institutional commitments will be credible in environments characterized by high levels of uncertainty and great competition.

On the one hand, great levels of uncertainty will lead someone with investments in extant designs to be risk averse and seek to protect designs viewed as assets. In such cases, endowment effects will make the credibility of commitments to incremental change stronger than in global rationality model. This in turn has implications for social coordination games. It means, for example, that governments seeking the support of business must devote more resources to reassure firms than is the case in global rationality models, especially if the designs that firms value highly are threatened. On the other hand, high and rising levels of competition increases the potential costs of passing up opportunities to acquire more efficient designs. Behavioral theories therefore expect that firms that frame prospective alternatives as advantageous will experience more rapid preference transformations than is the case in embedded rationality models. If firms' calculations are shaped by endowment effects, a behavioral model suggests that governments must devote more resources to managing institutional differentials than is the case in an embedded rationality model.

Endowment effects may be thought of as a premium firms demand to give up an existing asset such as those institutions they consider a source of their competitive advantage. Because institutional investments are variable depending on where firms are embedded and may shift over time, they will attach differently sized premiums to specific designs. Preference functions are thus not given by comparisons of the differentials in costs and benefits between future alternatives alone (endpoint comparisons), but are the product of situational comparisons that are influenced by how alternatives compare to a specific reference point. However, premiums will not be infinite as suggested by a strict version of embedded rationality models. Only if the premium firms attach to the status quo is greater than the potential benefits from adopting new designs can firms be expected to willingly forgo attractive alternatives. Conversely, preference transformations take place when prospective arrangements alter institutional differentials so that the benefits associated with alternatives exceed the premium firms attach to extant designs. When the latter occurs, firms' commitments to existing arrangements are no longer motivationally credible.[10]

Unlike theories relying on global rationality models in which economic groups support radical change in national designs if there are opportunity costs from a poor fit with multilateral ones, behavioral institutionalism expects groups to support transformations only when the reduction in such costs is greater than the value they attach to extant designs. Rather than emphasizing differences in future values, this perspective stresses the size of change with respect to a specific reference point.[11] It also offers distinct expectations from a standard historical institutionalist model. Instead of expecting groups' preferences to be intact as long as continuity offers marginal benefits through positive feedback effects like increasing returns, a behavioral model expects preference transformations to occur when the benefits from supporting alternative designs are greater than the benefits associated with engaging in incremental adjustment.

A corollary expectation of the behavioral model is that when a negative differential contributes to preference transformation, actors should move quickly and willingly devote major resources to establish new designs (see Kahneman and Tversky 1984). All things equal, behavioral institutionalism therefore expects the speed with which new designs become sustainable to be greater than the standard historical institutionalist model. Finally, unlike embedded rationality models that see preferences as a function of complex considerations that involve systemic effects, behavioral economics stresses the primacy of domain-specific considerations (Thaler 2004). Consequently, this tradition is less skeptical that hybrid systems of governance will unravel than are standard historical institutionalist accounts informed by embedded rationality models.

Varieties of Governance and Market Integration

To assess the logical inferences of the three models of rationality requires that factors affecting institutional differentials can be adjusted in controlled fashion to make nuanced comparisons possible. Firms' incentives to stay loyal or exit according to the basic hypotheses of the global, embedded, and behavioral models may be captured by the relative resources they willingly devote to sustaining social contracts. In basic terms, institutions are formalizations of social contracts. When operating in a competitive environment, all social actors have incentives to conserve on the resources they devote to sustaining such contracts. The resources firms willingly expend to sustain social contracts may thus be treated as a function of three factors: the degree to which they are dependent on other social actors to achieve their own goals, the comparative costs of contracting in different institutional contexts, and how shifts in external parameters affect the relative costs of contracting.

Relational Investments

The more dependent firms are on others to achieve their own goals, the greater is the specificity of their social investments. The resources devoted to sustaining such investments, often termed governance costs, vary depending on how specific are social relations (e.g., Williamson 1991). In the extreme case of spot markets, social investments are minimal and endure only at the moment of transaction. In other cases, however, social actors will devote resources to first negotiate the structure of common constraints and to later ensure that these are upheld. Although the absolute resources devoted to sustaining specific social contract is greater than spot markets, firms that depend on others to achieve their goals willingly expend such resources.

The costs of sustaining similar types of asset-specific social investments vary with the type of system of governance in use. Though systems that favor market coordination are often assumed to be the most efficient form of governance in conserving on the costs of contracting, studies have long noted that the organization of social exchange solely through markets creates numerous potential problems, including various market failures. Ronald Coase (1937), for example, noted that though markets may seem comparatively efficient, firms themselves employ hierarchical forms of organization internally to conserve on the costs of sustaining social investments. Others find that centralized forms of governance also entail drawbacks, including inefficiencies when it comes to the collection of relevant information about markets (Hayek 1945). Yet other studies suggest that a third system of governance that relies on decentralized forms of coordination with the help of networks offers a superior way to conserve on the costs of sustaining socially specific investments (e.g., Amin and Hausner 1997).

Oliver Williamson (1985, 1991) explains how systems employing markets, centralized commands, and networks as the primary means to solving coordination problems impact the relative resources social actors must devote to sustaining similarly specific investments.[12] Figure 3.1, which reproduces one of Williamson's models with some additional notations, illustrates three important points. First, regardless of the system of governance used, the costs of contracting increase with higher levels of asset-specific investments.[13] Second, the rate of change in the costs of contracting varies in the three models: governance costs in a liberal model (L) rise faster with increases in asset specificity than do costs in either the coordinated (C) or centralized models (E). Third, the level of governance costs varies along sectoral lines. At low levels of asset specificity ($k1$) the liberal model is associated with lower governance costs than the alternatives, but at high levels of bilateral dependency ($k4$), governance costs are higher in liberal models than in coordinated ones, and similarly higher than for centralized models where costs are lowest. At the intermediate range ($k2$ and $k3$), coordinated market economies are consistently the least costly alternative, but the second least expensive form of governance varies.[14]

If the behavior of a typical firm is a function of the incentive structures embodied by existing institutions, then Williamson's model suggests that firms will cluster along sectoral lines in those settings that carry the lowest governance costs. Thus, a larger proportion of firms in liberal market economies will specialize in areas that are defined by low levels of asset-specific relationships. A larger share of firms with medium levels of asset-specific relational contracts should be found in coordinated market economies. Finally, firms that rely on highly asset-specific investments will be found in greater numbers in economies characterized by centralized models of coordination. These expectations correspond broadly with the empirical findings in the comparative capitalism literature, which documents how differences in the design and interaction of institutional domains shape the general strategy of firms in different sectoral and national contexts.[15]

Williamson's figure offers a foundation from which to examine rival claims about how market integration affects the credibility of firms' commitments to existing and alternative designs. Scholars agree that governance or what at times is called transaction costs cannot be measured empirically. They thus employ abstract

Governance
Costs *(Cx)*

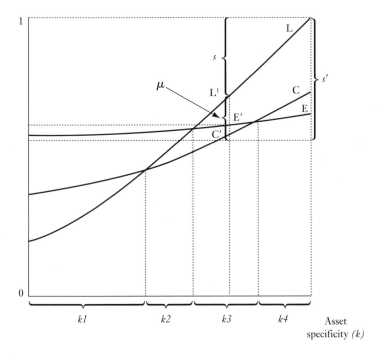

Figure 3.1: Comparative costs of governance
Source: Adapted from Williamson (1991).

models that allow them to compare how hypothetical variations in such costs affect how firms and other social actors will respond to changes in internal parameters like actors' dependence on asset-specific relational investments and the nature of the system in which they are embedded. Williamson remarks that "the measurement of transaction costs poses formidable difficulties. These difficulties are significantly relieved by looking at the issue of governance comparatively, so that the costs of one mode of governance are always examined in relation to alternative feasible modes. Differential transaction costs thus become the cutting edge" (1996b, 5).

When engaging in comparative institutional analysis, Williamson and many others working in the tradition of Weberian social science employ a method known as discrete structural analysis.[16] This is an actor-centered comparative institutional method that embeds social actors within diverse contexts in order to ascertain how hypothetical variations in internal and external parameters affect actors' incentives to rank some alternatives higher than others. This method, then, makes it possible to examine what role variations in the assumptions about firms' utility functions and patterns of adaptation play in shaping firms' preferences when they face common changes in the external environments but are characterized by diverse sectoral profiles (measured by asset specificity) and situated in different national contexts.[17]

Three Perspectives on Market Integration

Market integration is a defining characteristic of economic globalization and has generated an immense literature on its consequences for national economic systems. This literature has been dominated by two perspectives linked to theoretical traditions employing global and embedded rationality models. These models offer contrasting views of the conditions under which market integration reinforces, weakens, or transforms the propensity of firms to exit or remain loyal to the social contracts that sustain prevailing institutions. Figure 3.1 helps identify the conditions under which firms will prefer incremental change and remain loyal or opt to pursue radical change and prefer a strategy of exit according to these models.

In the figure market integration can be thought of as an exogenous event that presents firms bound by sectoral constraints and embedded in diverse systems of governance with the prospect of reducing the costs of social contracting by engaging in institutional arbitrage.[18] The choices associated with institutional arbitrage are captured in the figure by firms with a particular sectoral profile either switching lines or moving along a specific curve between two time periods. In Hirschman's terminology, the former represents a situation of exit (e.g., L to E') and the latter represents loyalty (e.g., L to L'). Firms' incentive to exit in pursuit of a model with higher governance costs is zero if they are bound by sectoral constraints ($k1$, $k2$, $k3$, or $k4$). If, however, there is a prospect for firms to reduce their governance costs while staying within the constraints of a particular sector—which would be a situation in which they slide down the curve from a higher to a lower level of governance costs within the parameters of an existing sector (e.g., L to L')—they would respond to market integration by remaining loyal.

Global and embedded rationality models offer different answers to how firms will respond to the opportunities of institutional arbitrage. Informed by global rationality models, the political economy null hypothesis assumes that firms are concerned with institutional differentials at a future date ($t + 1$) and thus expects firms to rank alternatives ($a, b, \ldots n$) according to strict comparisons of contracting costs in the future.[19] In these models, the utility function of firms is thus $U^k (a_{t+1} - b_{t+1})$, where k represents the sectoral profile, $t + 1$ a feasible future status quo, a the design currently in use, b an alternative model of governance, and where the sum of a and b represent an institutional differential. When the differential is positive, firms prefer continuity in extant designs, while they experience preference transformation if the sum is negative.

The global rationality model predicts that under conditions of economic openness, institutional preference orders will converge along sectoral lines across systems of governance on the alternative in which the costs of contracting are the lowest. The commitments of firms already embedded in the model of governance associated with the lowest costs are thus motivationally credible in such models. However, firms not embedded in the system of governance that carries the lowest costs undergo preference transformations and the credibility of their commitments to the status quo are undermined with greater levels of market integration. In the former scenario, market integration reinforces loyalty among firms and designs are self-enforcing and potentially self-reinforcing. In the latter case, institutions are self-undermining because firms experience preference transformations and are expected to pursue the exit option as a means to eliminating maladaptation costs.[20]

The utility function of firms in an embedded rationality model looks different and reflects calculations about the relationship between past realities and present circumstance. In this model, utility functions take the form $U^k((a_{t-1} - a_t) - (a_t - b_t))$. In strict versions of this model, even if the sum is negative (i.e., indicates that an alternative, b, offers lower costs of contracting), preferences may not be transformed due to perceived adaptation losses from transforming the nature of extant designs. The reason is that sunk costs or positive feedback effects associated with extant designs prevent preference transformations even when such a path would be more efficient in the terms of global rationality models. In other words, embedded rationality models expect firms to remain loyal and to eschew opportunities to exit. If market integration is understood as an opportunity to lower the relative costs of contracting by engaging in institutional arbitrage, the embeddedness hypothesis expects firms' commitments to extant designs to gain credibility. The intensity of these preferences will vary with the institutional context. As suggested by variations in the slope of alternative systems of governance in figure 3.1, preferences for continuity will be particularly intense among liberal firms, followed by firms in coordinated economies, and last by firms in centralized economies where the slope is much flatter. Moreover, preference intensities will be stronger among firms with highly asset-specific relational investments than among those with lower levels.

The hypothesis at the center of a behavioral rationality model differs in important ways from those informing the global and embedded rationality models. In contrast to a global rationality model and the political economy null hypothesis, the behavioral model does not expect preferences to change quickly as the relative attractiveness of alternatives marginally improves. Under certain conditions it even expects firms to prefer continuity despite apparent opportunities to significantly reduce the costs of contracting through exit. This is due to endowment effects, which lead firms to underweight opportunity costs. However, the behavioral model does not expect firms to always remain strongly committed to the status quo as does the embedded rationality model. Indeed, it suggests that exogenous changes short of major shocks are often sufficiently strong to produce preference transformations.

The behavioral model posits that firms' preference orders reflect a comparison of the difference in the cost from employing the same arrangement between two periods with the difference in the costs of employing discrete alternatives at a future time. Their utility function is thus $U^k((a_t - a_{t+1}) - (a_{t+1} - b_{t+1}))$. When the sum is positive, firms will be loyal and favor incremental changes. Conversely, when the balance of savings from engaging in incremental change and sustaining existing designs $(a_t - a_{t+1})$ are smaller than the differential between two alternatives in the future $(a_{t+1} - b_{t+1})$ firms experience preference transformations and their commitments to extant designs lack motivational credibility. In figure 3.1, savings from incremental change across time is marked s^i and the differential between s^i and savings from radical change (s^r) is marked μ. The behavioral model suggests that an actor's preferences will be transformed when $\mu > s^i$. In short, unlike the global rationality model in which the existing reference point is unimportant and only endpoint comparisons matter and the embedded rationality model where retrospective reference points are all-important, the reference point plays a more contingent role in the behavioral model.[21]

Central to the behavioral model is a revision of a key assumption in global rational models through the introduction of the endowment effect. Endowment effects exist if firms willingly forgo what appears to be the most attractive alternative under a standard expected utility model such as that which informs the political economy null hypothesis. Endowment effects are operationalized here in terms of a premium μ that is defined as the additional cost above the least costly alternative that a firm is willing to expend in order to retain an existing form of governance.[22]

When are Commitments Credible?

The appendix details the preference orders that emerge when the hypotheses associated with the global, embedded, and behavioral rationality models are derived for twelve types of firms that have diverse sectoral profiles and that are embedded in the three systems of governance (see appendix, tables B, C, and D). It shows that a strict application of the political economy null hypothesis leads to the expectation that firms will experience preference transformations and thus support radical change in six of the twelve cases that are represented in figure 3.1. At each of the four intervals of asset specificity (k) in the three alternative models of governance, two types of firms can reduce the costs of governance by switching to an institutional alternative with lower governance costs. The commitment by firms already embedded in the model of governance with the lowest governance costs are reinforced and remain motivationally credible. The expectation that six types of firms experience preference transformations contrasts with the predictions of the embedded rationality model in which preferences remain stable over time. Finally, if firms' preferences are shaped by endowment premiums in ways specified by the behavioral model, radical change will be preferred over incremental change in four of twelve cases. As the appendix details, this is because in all but four cases, the savings from incremental change are greater than the difference between alternatives in the future. (That is, in four cases, $\mu > s^i$ holds, and in eight of twelve cases, $\mu < s^i$ prevails.)

The four cases in the behavioral model where actors experience preference transformations are important for what models of governance are involved, how preference orders are affected, and for variations in the scope, timing, and sequence of institutional development across different models of governance. Three of the four cases where the behavioral model expects firms to prefer radical change concern the centralized market economy. In the case of firms with medium levels of asset-specific relational investments ($k2^E$ and $k3^E$), firms will prefer a coordinated market economy model, while in one case ($k1^E$) a liberal model is the preferred alternative. The fourth case of preference transformation is that of firms with low degrees of asset-specific relational investments in coordinated market economies ($k1^C$) where the benefits from switching to a liberal model exceed the endowment premium. Firms embedded in liberal settings confront no cases under high levels of market integration where the rate of the decline in governance costs will cause preference transformations.

The behavioral model predicts that with growing levels of market integration and opportunities to engage in institutional arbitrage, firms in liberal economies are least likely to experience preference transformations. Indeed, preferences in favor of incremental change intensify and create the preconditions for a self-reinforcing institutional equilibrium, making strategies of institutional specialization sustainable in liberal market economies. Meanwhile, institutions are most likely to be self-undermining in centralized market economies, because firms in those economies have the most to gain from a radical transformation. Moreover, because the rate at which governance costs decrease in liberal models is greater than in coordinated ones, the less dependent firms in centralized economies are on their existing social investments, the more likely they are to favor a liberal over a coordinated market economy model.

The three models of rationality in some cases predict observationally equivalent outcomes, but the underlying reason for the expected outcomes may vary. Although the four cases where the behavioral model predicts transformed preferences are part of the six cases predicted by the political economy null hypothesis, the model stresses a different logic of adaptation. Specifically, changes in firms' preferences are not assumed only to be a function of efforts to avoid maladaptation costs, but also to be a function of firms seeking to preserve institutions that constitute assets.

The behavioral model also makes more nuanced predictions than does a global rationality model. For example, in some cases, global rationality models are unable to offer clear predictions about which alternative firms will prefer because alternatives are associated with the same level of governance costs ($k4^L$; $k2^E$). By drawing explicit attention to the role of change vis-à-vis the reference point, the behavioral model predicts that in one of the two cases ($k4^L$) firms will not prefer a transformation because savings from continuity are greater than μ, while in the case of $k2^E$ it clearly identifies which of two alternatives will be ranked higher, namely that firms will prefer liberal over coordinated economy designs. Finally, the predictions generated by the political economy null hypothesis and the endowment hypothesis are directly at odds in one case. The null hypothesis predicts that some firms in liberal economies ($k3^L$) will experience a preference transformation and opt for coordinated economy designs because such models entail a lower absolute cost of governance, while the behavioral model predicts that these firms will continue to prefer liberal designs.

Empirical Expectations of Behavioral Model

The conditions identified by the behavioral model of when firms will support existing or alternative designs leads to distinct empirical expectations regarding the structure of business coalitions, which sector plays the role of a contractual pivot in a systemic setting, and what the likely trajectory of institutional development will be across diverse economies under high levels of market integration.

In liberal market economies, the behavioral model expects growing market integration to generate a broad coalition in favor of institutional continuity that spans all sectors of the business community. Indeed in an era of globalization, the symmetry and intensity of firm preferences grow, creating permissive conditions under which designs that are self-enforcing become self-reinforcing and thus enable a trajectory of institutional specialization. These expectations differ substantially from a situation in which economies are closed or levels of market integration are low. In the latter cases, the behavioral model expects that a cleavage exists within liberal market economies between firms that do not depend on high levels of asset-specific investments and that favor a liberal arrangement ($k1$) and firms that rely substantially on asset-specific relational contracts ($k2$ and $k3$) that are expected to support coordinated economy designs. Firms that are engaged in industries characterized by extensive and highly asset-specific relational investments ($k4$) are likewise expected to support a different arrangement, though a centralized one (see appendix, table D). In systemic terms, the pivotal sectors in this scenario are the firms with medium levels of assets-specific relational investments. However, because these do not share their preferences with either those with low or high levels of asset-specific investments, a liberal system is not expected to be particularly stable when the economy is relatively closed.

As market integration increases, firms will gradually experience preference transformations starting with those that have the lowest levels of asset-specific investments ($k1$). In other words, growing levels of market integration will create greater levels of cross-sectional preference symmetry in liberal market economies. Market integration thus serves not only to transform the preferences of firms in some sectors, but also enhances the credibility of firms' commitments to liberal designs, making it possible that a pattern of institutional consolidation transitions into one of institutional specialization in liberal market economies.

The picture is more mixed in the case of centralized market economies. Under low levels of market integration, there will be strong support across all sectors—

save the one with the lowest level of asset specificity ($k1$)—for a centralized model of governance and designs will be self-enforcing. However, with greater economic openness, divisions are expected to emerge between sectors. That is, firms with low levels of asset-specific relational investments will support a liberal model, those with medium levels will prefer a coordinated market economy arrangement, and those with high levels of relational investments will advocate institutional continuity along centralized designs. This cleavage is expected to persist, but the preferences of firms with low and low-medium levels of asset-specific investments gradually become more symmetrical as levels of market integration grow. When this occurs, the latter ($k2$ firms) becomes the pivotal sector that determines whether the business community is able to coordinate a transition to a liberal market economy model. However, because the preferences of firms with medium-high levels and those with high levels of asset-specific investments continue to differ, there will be great variation in the nature of institutional equilibria across domains of the economy. A trajectory of institutional hybridization is therefore the more likely outcome under high levels of market integration in centralized market economies.

Finally, in coordinated market economies, low levels of market integration are associated with high levels of preference symmetry across sectors in favor of continuity. The conditions also exist for a self-reinforcing equilibrium to emerge that supports a trajectory of institutional specialization. Under high levels of market integration, there is broad support in favor of institutional continuity in all sectors except for firms that rely on relational contracts with low asset specificity for whom market integration leads to preference transformations in favor of liberal designs. However, because the behavioral model expects the median firm in sectors characterized by medium levels of asset specificity to prefer continuity even under high levels of market integration, it predicts that a self-enforcing equilibrium prevails in coordinated market economies. Thus, even though market integration enhances the attractiveness of pursuing a liberal model, the behavioral model expects firms' commitments to a coordinated model to be credible in most sectors. The major difference between a situation where market integration is low and where it is high is that coordinated market economies may move from a set of self-reinforcing equilibria to a set of self-enforcing ones. This means that under high levels of market integration, processes of systemic institutional specialization are no longer sustainable.

Open Governance

If firms adjust to market integration in national isolation, then the hypothetical scenarios outlined thus far are sufficient to specify the expectations of the behavioral, global, and embedded rationality models. However, the modern industrial economy does not operate in isolation from international structures of governance and the constraints that shape firm strategy include a multitude of international institutions that stabilize expectations and regulate markets. Over several decades, industrial economies have become models of open governance in which national and multilateral institutions jointly shape the behavior of social groups, including firms' incentives to support or reject specific national designs.

The key mechanism by which multilateralism affects firms' commitments to domestic institutions is by impacting the institutional differentials that reflect firms' comparisons of the balance of costs and benefits of maintaining extant designs and radically transforming these. By impacting institutional differentials by increasing, for example, the attractiveness of maintaining the status quo or of pursuing alternatives, multilateral designs may transform, weaken, or reinforce the structure of domestic coalitions. Moreover, they may alter which sector plays the role of a pivot, and ultimately serve to generate patterns of institutional development that are different from those in which multilateral institutions are absent.[23]

The relative importance of multilateral designs in shaping firms' incentives to support national designs is a function of the extent to which designs at the two levels are incentive compatible and the intensity with which they interact. The degree of incentive compatibility is determined by the particular designs that exist at the national and multilateral levels. If multilateral institutions are typologized in similar ways to domestic ones—that is, whether they are more like those found in liberal, centralized, or coordinated market economies—there are nine potential forms of open governance.[24]

The nine cases of open governance, which are summarized in table 3.1, may be divided into three categories. One category entails cases (1, 5, 9) where the form of governance is the same at the national and international levels. These represent situations in which structures of governance at the two levels are incentive compatible. There are no adaptation losses or maladaptation costs and, by comparison to alternatives, prospects exist for adaptation benefits from open governance. In Goodin's (1996) words, these forms of open governance represent instances where solutions to the design problem are "well-designed" because internal institutions are in "harmony" with external ones.

A second category includes cases where institutions at the two levels of governance have a competitive relationship and incentive structures are incompatible.

TABLE 3.1
Nine potential forms of open governance

		Multilateral designs		
		Liberal	Centralized	Coordinated
National designs	Liberal	1. Liberal-Liberal	2. Liberal-Centralized	3. Liberal-Coordinated
	Centralized	4. Centralized-Liberal	5. Centralized-Centralized	6. Centralized-Coordinated
	Coordinated	7. Coordinated-Liberal	8. Coordinated-Centralized	9. Coordinated-Coordinated

These are cases where designs at one level are of decentralized nature (liberal or coordinated) and designs at the other level are centralized in nature (marked 2, 4, 6, 8 in table 3.1). In such cases, the comparative costs of contracting are higher than in the first category. The additional costs are due to externally induced maladaptation costs, and would be eliminated if national designs were transformed in ways that are incentive compatible with multilateral ones.

Finally, a third category entails the remaining mixed effects cases where national designs take the form of a liberal or coordinated economy and multilateral ones are the opposite (3 and 7 in table 3.1). Though the effects on the costs of contracting vary depending on the specific ways in which the design problem is resolved, mixed cases are associated neither with lower governance costs than incentive compatible arrangements nor with greater costs than incentive incompatible arrangements. For present purposes, mixed return cases are therefore treated as instances of incentive neutral combinations: that is, as instances where open governance is associated neither with adjustment costs nor with prospective adjustment benefits.

In addition to the level of incentive compatibility, the extent to which open governance alters the conditions under which firms will be loyal to national designs depends on the degree to which multilateral designs are more or less important than national designs in shaping the utility function of firms. Such variations may be thought of in terms of the intensity of interaction. Interaction intensity is low when multilateral designs exert less influence than national designs on firms' preferences, medium when they exert equally strong effects as national designs, and high when they are more important than national designs.

The Standard Hypotheses

Theories informed by global and embedded rationality models offer divergent predictions about the conditions under which firms' commitments to existing national designs are credible under open governance. The former is at the center of the multilateralism null hypothesis, which suggests that firms will prefer to adapt national designs in ways that make them congruent with multilateral ones.[25] Because firms are expected to rank alternative solutions to the design problem according to endpoint comparisons of the costs of contracting, such forms of adaptation are thought to be common. Firms' preference orders are expected to converge within sectors across economies (see appendix, table F). Thus, firms' commitments to national designs are credible when the extant arrangement is the one that ensures the lowest governance costs given the constraints of multilateral rules.

A comparison of the preference orders of firms assumed to behave according to the global rationality model and that are operating under conditions of closed and open governance, reveals some similarities (see appendix, tables B and F). However, the intensity of these preferences varies significantly, and thus the conditions under which firms' commitments to national designs are credible differ too. Under open governance, the opportunity costs of not securing the superior alternative are greater than under closed governance. This means that what may be a self-reinforcing equilibrium under conditions of closed governance may become a self-enforcing equilibrium under open governance. Moreover, situations that are self-enforcing in the former case may be self-undermining in the latter. The more intense the interaction between the two levels of governance is, the more costly it becomes for firms to sustain social investments in the national setting when domestic institutions are incompatible with multilateral ones. Consequently, according to the multilateralism null hypothesis, as open governance intensifies, the likelihood increases that the preferences of firms will converge across economic systems.

Models emphasizing a strict version of embedded rationality face some analytical limitations when applied to the context of open governance. Because these models assume that deep levels of national embeddedness lead firms to develop strong preferences for continuity at home, they offer no clear answer to how groups rank alternative forms of open governance beyond those arrangements that protect national designs. In these models, radical changes at the national level do not occur voluntarily, but only if multilateral agreements require countries to alter domestic designs. In short, embedded rationality models posit that as long as national institutions remain intact under open governance, firms' commitments to national designs will remain credible. That is, even in situations where groups confront high opportunity costs from not adapting national designs in ways that make them incentive compatible with multilateral ones, social contracts and thus national institutional trajectories may be characterized by great stability.

The Behavioral Model

The behavioral model identifies a distinct set of conditions under which firms' commitments to national designs gain or lose credibility. Adapting the operationalization of endowment premiums from the earlier discussion of economies as closed systems of governance to a situation of open governance, a behavioral model suggests that firms' commitments to extant designs are credible if the differential of incremental reforms between two time periods is more favorable than that between alternative endpoints in the future. As positive differentials grow, firms' commitments to extant national designs are reinforced. Conversely, if the sum of the difference between maintaining the same form of governance and transforming the existing national structure at a future date is smaller than the advantages from institutional continuity between two time periods, preference transformations occur and firms' commitments to existing designs lack motivational credibility.

Of the thirty-six cases of open governance representing firms operating in four distinct sectors in three different national economic systems and under three potentially different forms of multilateralism, predictions derived from the global and behavioral rationality models are observationally equivalent for the twelve cases of firms in liberal market economies (see appendix, tables F and G). In eleven of the remaining twenty-four cases, however, there are differences in the first-order preferences of firms that are guided by the precepts of the global and behavioral rationality models.[26] In these, the behavioral model finds that firms stand to lose more from radical change than from incremental change ($s^i_{xy} > \mu$). More specifically, the behavioral model expects—in contrast to the global rationality model—that firms in centralized economies will support a transformation in their existing form of governance with a growing preference for liberal arrangements with lower degrees of asset specificity and higher levels of open governance.[27] It also predicts that, with the exception of firms that rely on relational contracts with low levels of specificity, which will support a transformation in favor of a liberal arrangement, that all firms in coordinated market economies will support continuity in the existing form of national governance.

The behavioral model underscores that the same multilateral rules often have very different consequences for firms' commitments to national designs depending on where they are situated. These differences are not as stark as predictions based in strict embedded rationality models. For example, if national and multilateral institutions equally affect the behavior of firms and the multilateral form is of a liberal nature, then a firm embedded in a liberal economy that relies on highly specific assets will achieve its first preference (see appendix, table G). Consequently, its commitments to extant designs will be motivationally credible. Though a similar firm in coordinated market economies would face maladaptation costs under these forms of multilateralism, these costs may not be large enough to undermine its commitment to coordinated market designs. This is because it secures lower national costs of contracting than in the absence of open governance (appendix, table G).[28] Yet, for the same firm in a centralized market economy, a multilateral arrangement that is liberal in design imposes maladaptation costs greater than under a situation of closed governance. If the firm in a centralized economy is unable to block, alter, or gain opt-outs from the multilateral agreement, the credibility of its commitments to national designs are undermined.

The behavioral model expects that there will be much less convergence in firms' preferences under open governance than predicted by the global rationality model, but also more convergence than suggested by theories employing strict models of embedded rationality. Under low levels of relational asset specificity, there is substantial convergence in firms' preferences across economies. However, at slightly higher levels there is convergence only in the preferences of firms in liberal and centralized economies. Meanwhile, firms in coordinated economies generally prefer continuity. The picture is more mixed at somewhat higher levels of asset specificity with firms in liberal and coordinated economies preferring continuity at home, while firms in centralized economies vary significantly depending on the level of openness. Finally, among firms with highly specific relational investments, there is great diversity in firms' first-order preferences.

Empirical Expectations

The hypotheses derived from the behavioral model mirror in large part the situation under closed governance, but underscore that firms' preferences intensify in most cases of open governance. The appendix details that both preferences for the status quo (in *all* but one case of firms in liberal market economies and in *some* cases of firms in coordinated market economies) and for institutional transformation (in *most* cases of centralized economies and *some* cases of coordinated market economies) are significantly stronger under open governance. This suggests that depending on where an actor is embedded, open governance may both increase the urgency with which some firms will support the national status quo, as well as intensify differences among firms situated in alternative national contexts. In other words, in stark contrast to the multilateralism hypothesis, which expects greater preference symmetry across national and sectoral contexts, the behavioral model identifies several cases in which exposure to the same multilateral institutions will preserve and even intensify preference heterogeneity. As such, it identifies situations under which the expansion of multilateral rules may be significantly constrained due to pervasive asymmetries in the institutional preferences of core economic groups situated in diverse national contexts.

Placed in an empirical context, the behavioral model suggests that there is considerable variety in the conditions under which firms' commitments to national designs are credible under conditions of open governance. For firms in liberal market economies, commitments to national designs are reinforced under situations of open governance if multilateral institutions are liberal in design. Conversely, such firms confront higher adjustment costs if multilateral institutions take on other than liberal forms than do firms in either coordinated or centralized market economies. (This pattern is reinforced when relational contracts are characterized by low levels of asset specificity.) There is also greater symmetry in the preferences of firms across sectors under open governance, which means that patterns of institutional specialization are sustainable if multilateral rules are liberal in design. The expectations of the behavioral model also underscores why it is so important for governments in liberal market economies to secure multilateral designs that are liberal in design. It is because other forms impose significant maladaptation costs on firms and may lead the commitments of these firms to lack motivational credibility.

For firms in centralized economies, the situation is almost exactly reversed from that of firms in liberal market economies. Under open governance, firms in centralized market economies are more likely to experience preference transformations. Moreover, they are more likely to emulate parts of a liberal model than the designs of the coordinated market economy. As the intensity of open governance increases, the majority of firms is expected to be more willing than firms in other systems to jettison their support for centralized designs at home. The one exception is for firms that depend on high degrees of relationally specific contracts that will prefer a multilateral arrangement compatible with centralized national designs.

Thus, the behavioral model expects that the greater the level of globalization is and the more extensive multilateralism is, the less credible will be the commitments of firms to continuity in centralized designs. This is the case in all sectors except those characterized by high levels of relational asset specificity, which suggests that transformations will occur in several, though not all sectors. Consequently, rather than wholesale systemic transformation, national trajectories are expected to follow a pattern of institutional recombination if multilateral rules take liberal forms.

Finally, in coordinated market economies, open governance undermines the credibility of some firms' commitments to existing national designs. Firms that rely on relatively low levels of relational asset specificity and that can easily substitute their extant contracts with new partners abroad, such as investment banks and high-tech industries in radical innovation sectors, are more likely to prefer the designs of a liberal market economy under conditions of open liberal governance. In other sectors, however, there is a general preference for continuity.[29] Thus, firms' commitment to institutional continuity at home remains credible under most forms of open governance, making self-enforcing national institutions possible. The major difference between a situation of closed governance and one of open liberal governance is that the systemic nature of institutional development goes from a situation entailing the preconditions for institutional specialization to one of institutional consolidation. However, should firms in sectors characterized by medium levels of relational asset specificity experience preference transformations, the national trajectory is more likely to become one of recombination as the preferences of firms in those sectors would be transformed.

Conclusion

The political realities that generate diverse patterns of institutional development in advanced market economies are more complex than the stylized discussion in this chapter suggests. Firms alone do not determine the outcome of all consequential political battles surrounding capitalist institutions. Decisions by governments, the actions of unions and other interest groups, the results of elections and economic crises, political institutions that give greater voice to some views than others, unintended outcomes from earlier reform and the unanticipated ones stemming from multilateral agreements often have important consequences for the trajectory of reforms. Nevertheless, there are good reasons for why the political economy disciplines devote so much attention to firms. They are key players in mediating market signals, occupy critical positions in the economic activities that generate growth and employment, and are pivotal actors in the social contracts that sustain institutions over time. The conditions under which members of the business community will support or oppose reforms is therefore necessary though not always sufficient for the purposes of identifying when market economies are characterized by particular patterns of institutional development.

This chapter detailed how three models of firms' preferences shape the expectations of alternative theoretical traditions with respect to empirical patterns of institutional development. Beyond the specific implications of these models, the chapter has three broader ones that concern the behavioral model and its contributions to the study of institutions and market economies.

First, a behavioral model of firms suggests that although globalization generally enhances the attractiveness of liberal models of governance for firms across national and sectoral contexts, firms will in some cases expend resources to resist institutional convergence on a liberal model. Reforms in that direction impose higher levels of governance costs for firms with significant investments in extant designs. In particular, this is the case for firms with highly specific relational investments in coordinated market economies for whom the benefits from switching to a liberal arrangement are outweighed by the benefits of engaging in a process of incremental reform. Because the costs and benefits of altering existing national designs depend on where a firm is embedded and the type of sector in which it is engaged, it is possible that firms can credibly commit to reproducing extant designs in both liberal and coordinated market economies under high levels of market integration. This is a conclusion reached in other studies too (e.g., Hall and Soskice 2001a; Pontusson 2005), but this chapter underscores the importance of distinguishing between two patterns of systemic continuity. Market integration enables extant equilibria to become self-reinforcing in liberal market economies, thus making possible sustainable patterns of institutional specialization. However, most equilibria are only self-enforcing in coordinated market economies. Thus, though stability will characterize the latter system, it will be more easily undermined than those found in liberal market economies.

The behavioral model also leads to different expectations in the case of centralized systems of governance where it finds that a cleavage exists between sectors that experience a preference transformation in favor of liberal designs and sectors that prefer incremental shifts in the status quo. It thus expects that centralized market economies will not quickly experience a full systemic transformation in the direction of a liberal model. Rather, the model suggests that centralized economies are likely to experience trajectories of institutional recombination as economic globalization increases. It expects this pattern to be reinforced if multilateral designs are liberal in nature.

A second implication concerns firms' incentives to support alternative systems of governance if they are not exposed to market integration. The behavioral model expects the trajectories of the three economies under globalization to differ significantly from when these economies are relatively closed and market integration low. Under the latter scenario, there is significant heterogeneity in the preferences among firms in liberal economies and such systems will not be self-enforcing. Rather, a strong cleavage emerges between sectors with lower and higher degrees of asset-specific relational investments. However, this cleavage narrows under higher levels of market integration and some forms of open governance. Meanwhile, in coordinated economies, low levels of market integration create greater preference homogeneity among sectors and more intense support for incremental reform. The behavioral model thus expects that institutions will be self-reinforcing if the level of market integration is not very high. A similar pattern of stability is expected in the case of centralized market economies.

Finally, the behavioral model expects that when the intensity of interaction between national and multilateral designs is weak or when these are incentive compatible, open governance will reinforce the credibility of firms' commitment to national designs. Open governance can thus make both patterns of institutional consolidation and specialization more prominent. In contrast, when in a competitive relationship to national designs, multilateral institutions impose adjustment costs that serve to undermine firms' commitments to nationally distinct designs and thus make it more likely that the institutional trajectory of an economy will be different. Multilateralism, in short, may alter the intensity of firms' willingness to support different national designs, and may alter which sector is the pivotal one in shaping the general trajectory of an economic system.

Chapter 4

Britain

From Replacing to Reinforcing a Liberal Market Economy

For most of the post-1945 period, Britain was an economic laggard routinely criticized for having failed to establish an institutional foundation that could sustain a competitive and innovative modern industrial economy. Politicians, the business sector, and scholars widely attributed Britain's inability to maintain its historically prominent position among industrialized countries to the structure of its national system of economic governance, especially to the absence of economic institutions underwriting long-term social contracts. Particular criticism was directed at national institutions that made up the financial, corporate governance, industrial relations, and innovation systems.

To modernize the industrial base of the economy, British governments undertook repeated, often comprehensive reform programs. The direction, scope, and outcome of these reforms varied significantly across three distinct post-war periods. Efforts to introduce designs more akin to those found in centralized and coordinated economies in the 1960s and 1970s failed to be sustainable despite an initially broad political consensus and extensive support among key sectors of the business community. In contrast, against a background of little partisan consensus and open hostility among many economic groups, a comprehensive reform program that aimed to establish a liberal market economy was gradually consolidated in the course of the 1980s. Finally, in the 1990s and 2000s, Conservative and Labour governments successfully reinforced the core of the liberal market economy and a pattern of institutional specialization became evident.

This chapter examines the factors that contributed to differences in the institutional trajectory in the three periods, specifically why some designs proved sustainable and others not. Particular attention is given to the nature of support within the business community and the extent to which firms in different sectors were able to credibly commit to structural reform agendas championed by governments. The underlying rationale behind a government's structural reform agenda is to influence corporate strategies through policies and institutional innovations in ways that make firms more competitive in existing and new product markets. The chapter finds that the ability of governments to shape corporate strategy in ways that made institutional reforms to the British market economy sustainable was a function of how governments reconciled domestic reforms with their foreign economic policies.

This chapter departs from a majority of studies in the voluminous literature on Britain's failed and successful reforms after World War II. The primary emphasis within that literature has been on domestic factors. The inability of governments to sustain early post-war reforms is often attributed to the organizational capacity of economic groups, the structure of state-society relations, or an entrepreneurial elite averse to innovation (e.g., Wiener 1981; Beer 1982; Hart 1992; Wood 2000). Meanwhile, the consolidation of the liberal market program in the 1990s is typically seen as the product of new economic ideas or the reduction in the ability of labor unions to shape government agendas following reforms in the 1980s (e.g., Hay 2001; Howell 2005, 131–173).

Although domestic factors played major roles in shaping the British trajectory after 1950, attention to such factors cannot fully account for institutional developments over time. The weak organizational capacity within the business sector is often identified as a reason that firms were unable to commit credibly to government reforms and has been used to explain the failure of structural reforms in the 1960s and 1970s. Yet firms were able to credibly commit to government reforms during and after the 1980s when their organizational capacity was less significant. Research seeking explanations in the structure of state-society relations overlook that there has been no fundamental transformation of that structure since World War II. Similarly, accounts arguing that an elite consensus in the 1980s served to consolidate reforms in that decade overlook that institutional innovations proved unsustainable in the early post-war decades when there was a stronger political consensus on the nature of institutional reform (albeit on a different type of market economy). Other studies suggest that early post-war reforms were doomed to failure because of the historical legacies of British capitalism presented an inhospitable foundation for centralized and coordinated economy designs (e.g., Elbaum and Lazonick 1987). The implication is that institutional transformations cannot occur in economic systems due to entrenched path dependencies. A related inference is that the restoration of the British liberal market economy in the 1980s was an inevitability given nineteenth-century historical legacies of such forms of governance.

Neither the failures of early reforms nor their sustainability in later periods were inevitable. In each period, outcomes were contingent on factors that were temporal and variable in nature, such as the extent to which firms were exposed to or insulated from international markets, the legacies of preceding reforms, and the nature of British governments' foreign economic policies. Attempts to restore and reinforce the liberal model after 1979 were less a function of a historic commitment to liberal forms of governance than the legacies of discredited post-war alternatives. Yet the lack of alternatives was by itself not a sufficient condition to ensure the consolidation of the liberal model.

To account for the consolidation of liberal reforms in the 1980s, as well as the failure of earlier reforms and the eventual reinforcement of the liberal agenda during the 1990s and 2000s, the analytical scope must be extended beyond domestic institutional factors. In particular, explicit consideration must be given to how Britain's membership in multilateral organizations affected the ability of governments to implement domestic reforms. This chapter shows that the nature of governments' multilateral commitments profoundly shaped corporate strategy and affected the terms under which firms' commitments to national reforms were credible. It finds that domestic reforms were significantly undermined in the first period because Britain's foreign economic policy—specifically the protracted uncertainty surrounding its membership in the European Economic Community (EEC)—undercut the incentives of the manufacturing sector to shift corporate strategy and also reinforced a cleavage between that sector and the financial industry. In the 1980s, by contrast, the British government aligned domestic and foreign economic policies in ways that brought about a convergence in the institutional preferences of the two sectors and that gave manufacturing firms across several sectors strong incentives to support the liberal market project at home. In the 1990s and 2000s, British governments made explicit commitments to multilateral liberalization programs in Europe and successfully ensured low external adaptation losses by blocking the introduction of some rules and gaining special opt-outs from others. Such actions enhanced the motivational credibility of firms' commitments to national economic designs and reinforced core institutions in the liberal market economy.

Table 4.1 summarizes the direction, scope, dominant features, and aggregate trajectory of reforms in the British market economy. The outcome of these reforms was not preordained because of the nineteenth-century legacies of laissez faire capitalism or rising levels of economic globalization. Instead they were deeply contingent on how governments managed the design problem during three distinct periods of structural reform.

Failed Transformation

In the course of the first half of the twentieth century, the liberal economic model that had characterized Britain during the Victorian era was rejected and gradually gave way to stronger reliance on state intervention and forms of collective governance. Two world wars pushed the country farther away from its laissez faire past and by the mid-1940s Britain had became what historian Eric Hobsbawn described as "the most state-planned and state-managed economy ever introduced outside a frankly socialist country" (1968, 245). The first post-war Labour government dismantled many war-time programs, but a major role was retained for the state in economic management. Full employment and industrial reconstruction were the primary policy objectives, and the centralization of economic management re-

TABLE 4.1
Institutional developments in the British market economy

	1950–1973	1979–1991	1992–2008
Direction	Centralized model (centralized coordination: planning, expansion of public ownership and regulation)	Liberal model (market coordination: deregulation, liberalization, privatization)	Liberal model (market coordination: liberalization, deregulation)
Scope, mode, dominant features	Comprehensive	Comprehensive	Limited
	Finance Banking system largely intact; government control over credit increased; limited risk capital	*Finance* Radical: banking; deregulation of capital controls; expansion of risk capital	*Finance* Incremental: expansion of investment-oriented banks and equity markets
	Corporate governance Management autonomy in key firms limited; government large shareholder; constrained market for corporate control	*Corporate governance* Radical: expansion of management autonomy; diffuse shareholding; reduction in constraints on market for corporate control	*Corporate governance* Incremental: reduced constraints on market for corporate control
	Industrial relations Attempts to enhance coordination among social partners and extend collective bargaining; employment contracts not flexible	*Industrial relations* Radical: social partner autonomy expanded; minimal collective bargaining; enhanced employment flexibility	*Industrial relations* Incremental: enhanced flexibility in employment contracts.
	Innovation Extensive subsidies to firms; competitive relations between large and small firms; limited support for public research	*Innovation* Radical: end to discriminatory subsidies; competitive relations between large and small firms; little support for public research	*Innovation* Incremental: more cooperative relations between large and small firms; increase in public support for research
Aggregate outcome	Failed transformation	Consolidation	Specialization

mained strong through practices of government-directed demand management and the nationalization of key industries (Middlemas 1986a; Middleton 1996).

Representing a quarter of world trade in the early 1950s, governments and the business community projected that British industry would enjoy a set of favorable conditions for economic growth, and they sought to gradually relax the constraints that had characterized the war-time economy. With access to inexpensive factor inputs and protected market in the Sterling Area, and with growing demand for industrial goods in Europe, North America, and elsewhere, manufacturing firms expected to be major beneficiaries of the post-war boom and advocated greater economic openness and reduced state intervention. By the end of the decade, however, exuberant expectations were replaced by a gradual surrender to the realities of relative economic decline. Economic performance no longer matched pre-war figures, and Britain trailed the French and German economies in all major categories of economic performance, including the critical category of productivity growth.[1] In the wake of lagging economic growth, continued balance of payments problems, and a declining share of global manufacturing exports, the decade ended with a new national debate about the institutional nature of Britain's market economy.

Modernization Through Centralization

Prompted by its own experience with centralized economic management during the war and by the positive demonstration examples of other industrialized countries in the early post-war period, a broad political consensus emerged in the 1960s on introducing designs that centralized economic management. To spur economic modernization in the industrial sector, a Conservative government embraced an ambitious agenda of economic planning in the early part of the decade. Described by the prime minister as "fruitful in every sense of the word" (Macmillan 1973, 37), centralized economic planning was thought to be a superior mean by which to coordinate disparate parts of the corporate sector. Though the reliance on planning would gradually recede, the emphasis on centralized coordination remained intact, as evident in the unprecedented number of new government ministries, tripartite councils, and institutions for non-market coordination that were introduced throughout the 1960s and that characterized the next decade as well (Middlemas 1986b).

Though they at times favored reforms in different domains, Conservative and Labour governments agreed that in the absence of institutions promoting centralized coordination, firms would fail to undertake the necessary shift in corporate strategy to more capital intensive production. A failure to undertake such a shift, it was broadly agreed, would constitute significant opportunity costs at a time when international demand for industrial products was significant. The goal of centralizing economic coordination was to spur a transformation in the corporate landscape from one dominated by comparatively small-scale, often crafts-oriented, and under-capitalized manufacturing companies to one characterized by large, scale-intensive, and specialized mass manufacturing firms that could compete success-fully in advanced industrial markets. Through comprehensive reforms to nearly all areas of the national economy, British governments sought to encourage firms to make long-term investments in productive capacity by enhancing their incentives to coordinate with one another and with unions.

Enhanced coordination was designed to push firms toward sharing information with one another and avoiding the pattern of autonomous adaptation that had gen-erated sup-optimal investments in asset-specific technologies and comparatively low levels of productivity growth in the 1950s. In the industrial relations domain, centralized coordination was expected to help firms secure moderate wage settle-ments with unions and encourage employers to make greater investments in peo-ple's skills. Governments also directed funds to specific firms and industries with the goal of encouraging innovation in product markets thought to have particularly large prospects for growth.

However, British governments did not significantly reform the financial system. A major government report that enjoyed broad backing concluded that although the lending practices of some banks were a matter of concern to the long-term vi-ability of large and smaller manufacturing firms, the basic structure of the financial system was sound and there was sufficient capital available to modernize produc-tion without significant reforms (HMSO 1959). Buttressed by a large financial in-dustry that sought to maintain the basic structure of the extant system in which it had significant investments, radical reforms to the banking system were absent, though credit restrictions would be used intermittently during the 1960s.

The sustainability and success of the centralization agenda depended on govern-ments getting Britain's manufacturing firms to voluntarily commit to undertaking the sought-after shift in corporate strategy.[2] Reforms targeted large manufacturing firms as the pivotal sector, while smaller firms operated in what has been described as "an atmosphere of political hostility, or at best indifference" (Carnevali 2005, 103). In the early 1960s, Britain's large manufacturing firms welcomed the gov-ernment's centralization agenda.[3] Speaking to the liabilities of the historic laissez faire model, president of the Federation of British Industries (FBI) Hugh Beaver concluded that "there is nothing now to be said for the old Victorian freedom of action, even if it were still practicable." In the same context, Beaver (1959) de-fended an economic reform agenda built around centralized coordination, saying that "the Government, every and any government, must play a considerable part in our industrial affairs. There must be, to a large degree, over-all planning; it is not sufficient for the various parts of industry to be efficient, industry must be *able* to be an efficient and effective machine as a whole."

Reforms aimed to provide manufacturing firms with access to a new set of in-stitutional advantages that would assist them in securing skilled labor, moderate wage growth, and encourage innovation and technology diffusion. The creation of institutions that could foster competitive advantages in these areas was thought to be essential to ensuring that the business community would undertake a joint shift in corporate strategy. But the sustainability of the institutions that provided these advantages depended on firms actually undertaking the shift in corporate strategy that governments were promoting. If firms did not alter their product market strategies, their commitments to new institutions would be undermined over time. Consequently, governments were intent on creating a mutually reinforcing relationship between institutional reform and corporate strategy whereby, in the initial stages, changes in the former would produce the latter, and further on the latter would sustain the former. Though large manufacturing companies initially supported and embraced calls for institutional reform, a combination of domestic and international factors gradually undermined their willingness to shift corporate strategy and thus undercut the credibility of their commitments to key designs in the government's reform agenda.

Domestic Obstacles

Government reforms in the industrial sector during the 1960s focused on the creation of large capital-intensive manufacturing firms. To achieve such a transformation, firms needed access to long-term capital and be assured that their investments would be rewarded. Gaining sufficient access to capital proved difficult, however. British banks were extensively engaged in commercial lending and were not oriented toward long-term loans to the manufacturing sector. Owing to the imperial era, banks were focused on international markets and had few incentives to shift their resources to the domestic sphere given sluggish growth in Britain (Reddaway 1968). Meanwhile, manufacturing firms who cited the "lack of capital" as a major reason for why they experienced poor productivity growth (Associated Industrial Consultants 1962) were confronted with a choice to either accept more government intervention in the supply of capital or target markets where success could be sustained without major new infusions of capital. For fears that the former option would further expand government control in industry, manufacturing firms opted for the latter strategy (Wood 2000). The consequence of their choice was that they privileged fixed capital strategies over making major new investments in technology and human capital. This significantly undercut their incentives to pursue more specialized and scale-intensive product markets.

A second obstacle to the transformation in corporate strategy was due to the choice of macroeconomic policy tools. Firms willingly make major investments in people and plant when the value of such investments is sustained over time and when competition is such that the failure to invest entails significant opportunity costs. During the 1960s and 1970s, however, British governments had difficulties sustaining an economic environment that was conducive to long-term investments. Known as the "stop-go" period, governments would stimulate the economy by expanding aggregate demand, in the process creating major inflationary pressures and balance-of-payments problems. The tools that were used to restore balance, such as currency devaluations, tariff barriers, import surcharges, high interest rates, and credit restrictions in turn often reduced firms' incentives to make large long-term investments. Devaluations, including one in 1967 of 14 percent, dampened the corporate sector's willingness to make significant capital investments because firms could maintain market shares by exporting more goods and services at lower prices as a substitute for enhancing productivity through capital investments.[4] High tariff barriers on industrial goods and import surcharges had analogous effects by protecting firms from international competition.[5]

Similarly, by increasing interest rates to stem inflation, the government reinforced a long history among firms to rely on retained earnings and limit borrowing from domestic banks. This practice was further encouraged by targeted credit restrictions designed to steer capital to large manufacturing firms. Because the sums were insufficient to fill financing gaps, multiple social market failures that had long existed were reinforced, especially pertaining to long-term investments in skills and productive machinery (Broadberry and Crafts 1996). Credit restrictions also served to dissuade banks from reorienting their long-term lending practices toward domestic reconstruction. In addition, as a government report eventually concluded, credit restrictions had deleterious consequences for smaller manufacturing firms that relied heavily on loans but were side-lined by government initiatives that were directed at larger firms (HMSO 1971a). Thus, despite a plethora of new institutions designed to mitigate coordination failures and create the conditions for a shift toward higher-end production, government policies lessened those prospects and instead reinforced cleavages between the financial and manufacturing sectors and between larger and smaller firms within the latter.

The Costs of Multilateral Uncertainty

The domestic reform agenda of British governments had similarities to those found elsewhere in Europe. However, because other European economies grew more quickly in the same period they were able to absorb macroeconomic fluctuations more easily and mitigate the type of investment disincentives that befell the corporate sector in Britain. A key reason that European economies grew at a higher level and were able to create the conditions under which national firms' could credibly commit to corporate restructuring was the expansion in international markets following a significant shift in foreign economic policy through the embrace of economic multilateralism.

In the same speech FBI president Beaver (1959) acknowledged the liabilities of laissez faire capitalism and spoke of the merits of centralized governance; he also stressed that domestic measures alone would not be sufficient to transform British industry. Industrial renewal would require a resolution to the uncertainty surrounding the country's multilateral trade commitments, which in Beaver's words had contributed to a "period of twilight . . . confusion and . . . despondency." However, rather than providing firms with greater clarity over the nature of the country's multilateral commitments in the 1960s, British governments exacerbated the uncertainty surrounding firms' access to foreign markets.

British governments were strongly supportive of multilateral initiatives in the 1940s and 1950s, in particular those associated with the Bretton Woods conference and the Organization for European Economic Cooperation. However, unlike the large industrialized countries in Europe, British governments and large parts of the business community saw the major multilateral initiatives on that continent in the 1950s either as a potential threat to domestic economic and industrialization agenda (McKinlay, Mercer, and Rollings 2000), or as having uncertain and potentially negative effects (Milward 2002, 187–216). Instead, following the failure of the International Trade Organization and with the future of the General Agreement on Tariffs and Trade (GATT) unknown, British governments were focused on establishing a global free trade area among industrialized countries. When these efforts failed as an alternative to the EEC, Britain formed the European Free Trade Association (EFTA) with six smaller European economies in 1960. Though EFTA was welcomed by British business, the latter did not see that organization as a long-term solution (Sherwen 1970; Bromund 1999, 357–401).

Securing membership in the EEC would soon become an all-consuming priority for the British government and the business sector alike. The year EFTA was formed, the government underscored that gaining access for British firms to their fastest growing markets in the EEC on terms equal to those of their main competitors was a key requirement for creating a dynamic, specialized, and scale-intensive industrial sector. Though at times questioned on political grounds, the government acknowledged that "[a] decision to join the [EEC] would be a political act with economic consequences, rather than an economic act with political consequences" (Macmillan 1960). One widely debated government study noted that the success of EEC was found in the "dynamic of the new large common market and the scale on which . . . industries can think and plan. To share in that dynamic requires us to be 'in'" (Lee 1960). Continuing in more frank language, the same study addressed the long-term effects of multilateral alternatives on corporate strategy:

> [EFTA] is not a despicable grouping in economic terms . . . [However,] it is doubtful whether a heterogeneous and scattered group . . . can develop a real cohesion or even continuity . . . [EFTA] is bound to be a weaker economic group than [EEC]. This is likely to have a profound psychological effect on United Kingdom industry. . . . The conclusion is inescapable—that it cannot be compatible with either our political or our economic interests to let the situation drift on indefinitely on the basis of a divided Europe, with the United Kingdom linked to the weaker group. (Lee 1960)

In 1961, the Macmillan government decided to pursue membership in the EEC. Its application had enthusiastic support within the business community, especially among large advanced manufacturing companies that expected the combination of economic centralization at home and accession to the EEC would transform their sector into a dynamic one by making possible economies of scale, greater specialization, and substantial increases in domestic investments (FBI 1961).[6] Throughout the 1960s, the major business association stressed that membership was essential for industrial modernization, "particularly for those [firms] requiring heavy capital expenditure on plant and on research and development" (CBI 1966). The manufacturing sector continuously noted that it willingly accepted the anticipated short-term costs from adjusting to higher levels of competition in Europe, because these were seen as small by comparison to the long-term costs of remaining outside the EEC and minor relative to the expected long-term benefits from EEC membership (CBI 1967a, 1967b).[7] British governments framed the issue of membership in similar language, and justified it in terms of the "dynamic advantages" it would have on the modernization of British industry over time (e.g., HMSO 1970, 1971b). Meanwhile, remaining outside was thought to place Britain in "a position of progressive competitive inferiority" (Official Committee on Europe 1966, 5).[8]

Efforts to avoid the costs to the domestic economy and industry from non-membership initially proved unsuccessful. Both in 1961 and in 1967, the French government vetoed British applications. Only after securing membership in 1973 and reaffirming that membership in a national referendum in 1975 did the uncertainty surrounding Britain's membership significantly recede. Meanwhile, the lack of clarity had had profound consequences for corporate strategy with major effects for the willingness of firms to support domestic reforms. The centralization agenda was the means by which British governments would meet their ambitious targets of annual growth, around 4 percent. However, achieving such rates required a yearly increase in British exports of some 5 percent (Tomilson 1990, 262), which could be realistically secured only in Europe given the sharp decline in exports to the Sterling Area and growing demand for manufactured goods in Western Europe. By not gaining access to European markets on terms equal to those of their competitors, firms in all major industries instead deferred investments in personnel and equipment and chose to pursue traditional product market strategies (Owen 1999). Thus, rather than undertaking the necessary investments to compete in higher value-added product markets in Europe, firms adapted in ways that reinforced old corporate strategies.[9] This made it more difficult for British governments to achieve the targeted rates of economic growth at home. It also undermined the incentives for firms to embrace domestic reforms and thus undercut the credibility of their commitments to the institutional innovations at the center of the government's economic reform agenda.

The prolonged uncertainty over Britain's membership in the EEC reinforced what had been a long-standing cleavage between the manufacturing and financial sectors (Newton and Porter 1988). British governments reasoned that EEC membership would encourage British banks to invest more actively in the modernization of British businesses and their expansion into European markets. Without membership, however, the incentives for British banks to forego their competitive advantage in global markets were practically non-existent. This served to increase the manufacturing sector's reliance on retained earnings and further reinforced less capital-intensive production techniques. Similarly, with Britain outside the EEC, the incentives for its banks and foreign investors to place greater shares of their investments in Britain were significantly reduced because economic growth was expected to languish and because the barriers to exporting earned capital were thought to be greater than if Britain were a member of the EEC (HMSO 1973).

Self-Undermining Reforms

The economic institutions at the center of a government's structural reform agenda are self-undermining when shifts in the internal or external environments of the business sector serve to reduce the number of firms that can credibly commit to the type of corporate strategies on which a reform agenda depends. Self-undermining institutions were a dominant feature of the British market economy throughout the 1960s as a declining number of firms were making the type of investments championed by governments. Though there was initial backing for many government programs and the manufacturing sector had positive views of centralized coordination from the war years and framed such designs as superior to feasible alternatives, support waned relatively quickly.

The willingness of the manufacturing sector to undertake expensive capital-intensive investments in plant and people was limited by a combination of domestic policies and innovations that lacked internal coherence as well as by foreign economic policies that encouraged the continuation of historic product market strategies. At the domestic level, the failure to implement reforms to the financial system in ways that provided sufficient capital for industrial modernization and a macroeconomic policy that undercut firms' incentives to make new productivity-enhancing investments lessened the value of other reforms, including those in the industrial relations domain.

The manner in which governments managed the design problem in this period further undercut the prospects that firms in the manufacturing and financial industries would adopt complementary product market strategies and transform the country's industrial landscape in ways sought by the former. In particular, the high levels of uncertainty surrounding firms' access to their fastest growing markets (namely, the EEC) stalled shifts in corporate strategy and lessened the depth of support governments enjoyed within the manufacturing sector for their domestic reform agenda. This uncertainty also reinforced the financial industry's commitment to global markets and lessened their incentives to increase domestic lending, thus further deepening the historic cleavage between those two sectors. In addition, the attention given to large manufacturing firms at the expense of smaller ones generated a major cleavage within that sector, delaying modernization and preventing governments from making up for the lack of deep support among large firms with broader support within the business community.

The lack of support within the large advanced manufacturing sector targeted as the pivotal one for its reform strategy deepened cleavages within the business community and undermined the transformative governance agenda of the 1960s. The failure of structural reforms in this period ushered a period of incremental reforms that lasted for nearly a decade until a new period of comprehensive reform was launched. This time, however, the leitmotif was not replacing the liberal model, but rather its construction.[10]

Gradual Transformation

The 1980s was a transformative decade in post-war economic governance. Like the 1960s, the principal goal was to restore British industry to a position of global competitiveness through a comprehensive agenda of institutional reform. Beyond that commonality, the two periods differed significantly. Unlike the 1960s when the emphasis was on rejecting historically liberal institutions of governance and the goal was to transform pre-war legacies, the reforms of the 1980s sought to construct a liberal market economy model and aimed to transform post-war institutions. As such, Britain's strategy of structural reform was moving in the opposite direction of those implemented by Europe's large industrialized economies where the trend was toward greater use of institutional designs associated with the coordinated market economy model. The most lasting difference was that unlike in the 1960s—when governments were unable to sustain broad support from the business community and therefore failed to consolidate institutional reforms—a broad coalition of business interests gradually came to support the innovations of the 1980s.

Modernization Through Decentralization

A Conservative government under Margaret Thatcher (1979–1990) devised a comprehensive set of reforms targeting all major areas affecting corporate strategy. In many respects, this reform agenda inverted the role that macro- and microeconomic policies had played in the previous period. Rather than relying on macroeconomic policy to promote growth and employment and on microeconomic initiatives to contain inflation, the Thatcher government had developed a plan to use the former to secure price stability and the latter as the means by which to encourage industrial modernization (Howe, Joseph, Prior, and Howell 1977). A shift from demand-management to targeting price stability through monetarist policy tools, especially by curbing the growth of the money supply, was the defining feature of the new macroeconomic regime. Also key were major changes in fiscal policy, including a commitment to budgetary restraint and tax reforms, especially reduced government support for industry and lower corporate taxation rates. Together, these reforms were designed to put an end to the stop-go pattern that had characterized earlier decades and to resolve the persistent investment disincentives that had confronted firms for decades.

Reforms to the financial, corporate governance, industrial relations, and innovation systems were comprehensive, radical, and internally coherent. In all major areas, the main emphasis was on crafting institutions that would protect market incentives and promote decentralized coordination among economic groups and individuals. The labor market was liberalized and major changes in the industrial relations system brought about a decentralized firm-level system of wage bargaining (Howell 2005, 145–151). The government also deregulated product markets, gradually privatized nationalized industries, and placed a strong emphasis on securing a business environment with minimal environmental and social regulations (Riddell 1989; Vogel 1996, 65–136).[11] In addition, capital markets were deregulated and greater levels of competition were introduced in financial services (Story and Walter 1997, 224–247). Among other initiatives, a major financial reform package in 1986 ("Big Bang") was introduced that ended an old price fixing cartel and brought about a significant expansion of equity markets. These reforms stressed a highly decentralized system of governance in the financial sector and were complemented by developments in the area of corporate governance that enhanced management autonomy and reduced constraints on the market for corporate control. Finally, in a major departure from earlier practice, the government terminated the use of institutions for centralized coordination and consultation with organized economic groups.

With the liberal market economy often heralded as a model for economic modernization in the 1990s, it is easy to presume that the Thatcher reforms were bound to be sustainable over the long term. But the consolidation of that reform agenda was anything but inevitable. Undertaking the type of institutional transformation championed by the Thatcher government entailed significant political and economic challenges. For an electorate long used to full employment as a public priority, the high levels of unemployment that followed labor market reforms and major cuts in government support to firms generated intense public opposition.[12] Business leaders also expressed major reservations. The shift in monetary policy brought high interest rates and a major liquidity crisis in the early stages. This led representatives of the major business association to publicly condemn the government's policy, including the director general of the Confederation of British Industry who called for a "bare-knuckle fight" with the government (Keegan 1984, 155). The government's unilateral end to close consultations with the business sector and higher levels of competition following market liberalization also met with resistance from manufacturing firms in several sectors and, to a lesser extent, in the financial industry (Boswell and Peters 1997, 142–149).

Because of the broad nature of opposition to the early stages of the Thatcher government's reform agenda, speculation was rife that the government would undertake a similar u-turn to secure its reelection as a Conservative government had done in the early 1970s. Scholars also expressed skepticism about the long-term prospects of the Thatcher reforms.[13] At the time, it was the German and Japanese versions of the coordinated market economy model that were seen as the future for industrial renewal and few observers expected the liberal market economy to be politically sustainable or economically successful (e.g., Hart 1992). Thus, for example, Peter A. Hall concluded mid-way through the Thatcher reforms that "preliminary indications suggest that the changes Thatcher has inspired are still far from permanent" (1986, 130).

Effects of Old and New Institutions

What happened to make the transformative reforms of the 1980s sustainable? The success of Thatcher's reforms depended on convincing firms in several sectors to adopt corporate strategies that benefited from high levels of contractual flexibility. This meant persuading firms of the merits of abandoning decades-old efforts to reform the institutional landscape of the British economy and move away from designs that were conducive to highly specific relational investments and long-term contracts. In practice, it entailed encouraging firms to attach less importance to competing with German and French firms in high value-added specialized supplier and advanced manufacturing markets in favor of corporate strategies targeting low-cost mass manufacturing and services on the one hand, and high value-added specialized services, on the other hand. Despite early reservations to its reforms and the successes of countries pursuing other models of governance, the Thatcher government was gradually able to build broad support within the manufacturing sector and the financial services industry for its transformative agenda.

Behavioral institutionalism helps explain why the government was able to secure broad support within the business community. As the previous chapter detailed, under growing levels of international market integration most firms in liberal market economies prefer continuity in extant designs because these are associated with lower governance costs than alternatives.[14] These preferences grow more intense if the designs of different domains produce tangible adaptation benefits. Though originally not apparent to firms, such benefits had become evident by the mid-1980s through a set of complementary reforms. A stable macroeconomic environment together with financial reforms providing greater access to capital encouraged a significant increase in investments by firms in new technologies (CBI 1988a, 6). Similarly, inflation containment in combination with a system of decentralized wage bargaining placed downward pressures on wages and provided institutional advantages to firms pursuing cost-sensitive product market strategies. These developments benefited manufacturing companies of all sizes, including small- and medium-sized enterprises, which the Thatcher government explicitly targeted as a means to broadening support for its economic reforms.

A different set of adaptation benefits emerged due to changes in the financial system and the labor market. The combination of a dynamic equity market and a flexible labor market significantly aided firms in the information-technology and science-oriented industries targeting radical innovation practices. Both these industries benefited from the type of high-powered incentive structures that the liberal market economy stresses, and Britain became an increasingly attractive place for software and pharmaceutical industries (Soskice 1999). The same mix of institutions also helped Britain to provide a hospitable environment for high-end financial services, which expanded rapidly in the course of the 1980s (Story and Walter 1997). Finally, the emphasis on a flexible labor market, reduced union power, and generally low taxation and regulatory burdens attracted firms targeting cost-competitive mass manufacturing and significantly expanded the service sector.[15] The outcome was that the Thatcher government gradually broadened support among many traditional and new manufacturing firms, as well as from the high and lower end of the service industries.

The emergence of the broad business coalition was facilitated by the fact that firms had few investments in post-war designs and thus confronted no significant adaptation losses from reform. Alternatives to the liberal model had been discredited, and notwithstanding some differences within the business community, there was broad support for the liberal reform agenda (Boswell and Peters 1997, 161–178). Yet, as the 1960s had illustrated, the rejection of past designs and the embrace of new ones are not sufficient conditions to ensuing that firms' commitments to national institutions are credible. Governments in open economies must also give firms assurances that access to international markets is secured on terms that give firms' incentives to adopt product market strategies that exploit the institutional advantages of national designs. Unlike in the earlier period when British governments failed to provide such assurances, the Thatcher government was able to do so successfully in the 1980s through a major shift in the country's post-war multilateral strategy.

The Multilateral Dimension

Margaret Thatcher is frequently invoked for her critical attitude toward Europe, and she has become an icon among Euroskeptics. However, to suggest that the Thatcher government was indiscriminately opposed to European integration is not only incorrect, but it obscures the ways in which her government successfully consolidated a transformative domestic agenda. By committing Britain to a set of ambitious European reform programs, the Thatcher government sought to assure national and foreign firms that they would have simultaneous access to a unique set of institutional advantages in Britain while also gaining entry to European markets on non-discriminatory terms. This combination, reasoned the government, would strengthen the motivational incentives for firms to support domestic reforms.

The centerpiece of Thatcher's foreign economic policy was the promotion of the internal market program that would abolish barriers to trade in goods and services and to the mobility of capital and labor in the EEC by 1992. Although her government was far from being the only champion of the internal market, Thatcher attached particular importance to it and later described the program as "very much a British initiative" (Thatcher 2002, 372). A larger European market would increase the size of the home market for British companies and thus encourage specialization and scale-economies (CBI 1980; Moravcsik 1998, 322–324). As it promoted the internal market program, the Thatcher government was deeply concerned that international market liberalization occurred on terms that complemented domestic reforms and that the potential for external maladaptation costs be minimized. It sought, in short, to resolve the design problem in ways that safeguarded the comparative institutional advantages of the liberal model.

One set of safeguards that greatly concerned the government were protections against non-tariff barriers (NTBs). Britain's unilateral liberalization of domestic goods and capital markets in the early 1980s made the Thatcher agenda particularly sensitive to other EEC countries employing NTBs as these could potentially undermine the relative value firms attached to basing their operations in Britain. If process and product-related NTBs in Britain's major export markets were extensive, the comparative advantage firms would gain from investing in Britain would be limited significantly. Moreover, with firms in other member-states confronting large adjustment costs due to trade liberalization, the pressure on governments to employ NTBs and other forms of protection was expected to increase. The recourse by governments to national vetoes was also expected to rise and thus to potentially stall the multilateral liberalization program on which the Thatcher government counted to make its domestic reforms a success.

The Thatcher government feared that the extensive use of NTBs and national vetoes would place firms into a similar position they were in before the country joined the EEC. The legal and institutional barriers to investing in Europe had become the primary obstacle to British firms for expansion in Europe (Millington and Bayliss 1991). To create a scenario whereby expansion in Europe would be feasible, the government sought agreement on a set of multilateral rules that would promote market integration that covered NTBs, as well as ensured that individual governments would be unable to undermine the liberalization agenda by vetoing specific agreements. The former issue by comparison to the latter was relatively uncontroversial. In invoking the principle of mutual recognition and giving powers to the European Court of Justice to enforce an internal market without barriers, member-states reached agreement on how to reduce the prospect of the extensive use of NTBs. This helped the Thatcher government reassure the domestic business community that economic discrimination in Europe would neither threaten firms' incentives to base their operations in Britain nor their expansion in Europe.

However, the long-term viability of the multilateral liberalization agenda could be reasonably secured only if majority voting replaced the right of governments to employ national vetoes in the Council of Ministers by invoking a "vital" national interest. Despite the fact that a British agreement on such a significant shift would entail a surrender of some national sovereignty—a matter of particular concern among many Conservative parliamentarians—the Thatcher government strongly supported such a step as a means to ensure the implementation and long-term viability of the internal market program.[16] Following extended negotiations, Britain and other member-states signed the Single European Act (SEA) in 1986 that introduced qualified majority voting in areas relating to the internal market. The initiative, which was welcomed by the British business community, effectively served as a second safeguard that reinforced the motivational credibility of firms' commitments to domestic reforms for it reduced the prospect of externally induced adaptation losses.

The two sets of safeguards resolved the uncertainties that had revolved around foreign markets and increased firms' incentives to make long-term investments that would enhance productivity. For the financial services industry, the internal market program was a particularly welcome development following the deregulatory agenda at home. Without barriers to capital mobility in Europe and a set of multilateral financial services directives that established the principle of home-country supervision of banks and investment houses, national and multilateral reforms were incentive compatible and offered adaptation benefits to the financial industry. It was now able to exploit the institutional advantages of the liberal market economy, such as a light regulatory touch and liberal takeover rules, to attract significant overseas capital and to manage nearly half of all stock-market equity in the EEC by the end of the Thatcher premiership (Story and Walter 1997, 259–280). To the government this was a crucial development for several reasons. As the manufacturing sector was becoming a net-importer, the expansion of exports in financial services became key to spurring economic growth and maintaining external balances. More important in the long-term, this development created capital for future industrial modernization, which had been in short supply in the past. In this respect, the internal market program ushered a process in which financial services firms and the manufacturing sector gradually moved toward complementary product market strategies and where the incentives of the former to invest in the latter increased with the prospect of larger markets abroad.

Finally, the Thatcher government needed to ensure a third set of safeguards to consolidate its domestic reform program. It was greatly concerned that multilateral initiatives in a wide-ranging set of areas affecting firm strategy would reduce the comparative institutional advantages of domestic designs. Its efforts to minimize externally induced adaptation losses were apparent in several areas, notably with respect to initiatives that would affect domestic reforms in the areas of corporate governance and industrial relations. In the early 1980s, the Thatcher government vociferously campaigned against the so-called Vredeling Directive, which sought to enhance employee representation in multinational corporations and thus ran counter to the model of corporate governance championed at home.

In particular, the government reasoned that mandating multinationals to embrace forms of representation more akin to those found in coordinated economies would undercut the incentives for foreign firms to make investments in Britain. Later in the decade during the negotiations over the internal market, similar concerns informed the Thatcher government's opposition to the European Company Statute (ECS). The ECS was a long-standing initiative that had been renewed and that included provisions for board representation by employees in public limited companies that chose to incorporate under European rules. The Thatcher government reasoned that in the proposed form, the ECS threatened the institutional foundations of its domestic system of corporate governance and potentially also the larger reform project (Fioretos 2009).

The Thatcher government successfully blocked both initiatives and in the process reassured domestic and foreign firms that it was intent on preventing external adaptation losses and would protect key national designs from being undermined by multilateral initiatives. Its opposition to the Vredeling Directive was greeted not only by national firms (CBI 1980, 17; 1984), but also by multinational companies who would gradually turn Britain into the preferred location for corporate headquarters in Europe (Cowles 1994, ch. 4). The government's rejection of the ECS, which was the only specific initiative Thatcher (1988) singled out in her most famous speech on Europe, was welcomed by the business community as a way of protecting management autonomy and preventing a potential return to features associated with the failed reforms of the 1960s (CBI 1988b).

Great concerns also existed over the prospect of multilateral rules undermining the institutional integrity of national reforms in the industrial relations system and the labor market more generally. Championed by European Commission officials and member-states with strong commitments to coordinated economy designs, the European Council decided in 1988 to make the "social dimension" of the internal market program of equal importance to its economic dimension. This raised major concerns in Britain and the Thatcher government consistently approached the extension of European social policy with an eye to how multilateral designs would affect the institutional integrity of its domestic agenda. The government rejected the Community Charter on the Fundamental Social Rights of Workers, an initiative that aimed to establish common minimum standards in matters relating to employment, thus preventing the incorporation of such ambitions into the treaty structure.

The government also strongly opposed specific initiatives aimed at harmonizing workplace conditions. Because Britain had the fewest restrictions on part-time work in Europe, a European directive regulating working time was framed by the government and the business community as entailing large adaptation losses because it threatened the comparative institutional advantages of the liberal model. The logic of the Thatcher government's opposition to multilateral rules was clear: European rules that were incompatible with the institutional core of the liberal market economy would be opposed, even if the opposition came at a significant diplomatic cost to the government within the EEC. As in the case of the Vredeling Directive and the ECS, the government's opposition to the Working Time Directive enjoyed wide support within the business community (CBI 1984; 1985, 29–30). Indeed, rather than framing the government's recalcitrance to support deeper integration as evidence of hostility to the EEC, the business community saw it in the opposite terms, namely as an assurance that the government would protect the comparative institutional advantages of the liberal market economy.

Sustainable Reforms

Early on during Thatcher's premiership, British business stressed that it was crucial that there be an integrated solution to the design problem. As described by a leading CEO and former chairman of the National Enterprise Board in a discussion of structural reform, "unresolved issues" in supply-side domains "all relate to problems created by our institutional arrangements. But the UK context includes EEC today" (Knight 1982, 5). The business community argued throughout the 1980s that domestic reforms alone would not be sufficient to restore the competitiveness of British industry. Despite descriptions of Britain, and the Thatcher government in particular as a "reluctant" or "awkward" partner in the EU (e.g., George 1998), the Conservative government in the 1980s was deeply committed to a major expansion of multilateral institutions as a means of consolidating domestic reforms. Notwithstanding a philosophical outlook that often suggested otherwise, the Thatcher government was highly cognizant of the interdependence between its national reform project and its foreign economic policy. Specifically, it reasoned that the implementation of reforms in key areas of the liberal market economy such as the financial, corporate governance, and industrial relations domains were contingent on securing stable access to international markets. But such access had to be established on terms that avoided the prospect of externally induced adaptation losses, in particular in those economic domains that constituted the core of domestic reforms.

The manner in which the Thatcher government resolved the design problem in the 1980s had major consequences for its domestic reform agenda. Unlike in the 1960s when the preferences of the financial and manufacturing industries were not aligned, an integrated solution to the design problem in the 1980s brought a convergence in the institutional preferences of the majority of firms in the two sectors. This facilitated the emergence of complementary product market strategies by large firms in both sectors that revolved around exploiting the comparative institutional advantages of the liberal market economy. A similar process occurred within the manufacturing sector as smaller manufacturing firms modernized their plants and became more integrated into the production chains of larger ones. With such broad support, the government created the conditions for the emergence of a set of self-enforcing institutional equilibria in the financial, corporate governance, and industrial relations domains. As such, it made possible the consolidation of a liberal market economy during a period when most other European governments pursued reforms in a very different vein.

The Politics of Institutional Specialization

British governments were singularly committed to advancing the liberal market economy model during a third period of institutional innovation. Despite important changes in the composition of the British government and the international environment, there remained a steady focus in the 1990s and 2000s on promoting and protecting the core institutional advantages of the liberal market economy. Neither expectations that the Conservative government under John Major (1991–1997) would roll back its predecessor's programs (e.g., Dorey 1991; Holliday 1993), nor predictions that a Labour government under Tony Blair (1997–2007) would undertake a major reversal of the same programs materialized. Instead, both the Major and Blair governments went to great lengths to enhance and defend the institutional core of the reform agenda that originated in the 1980s. And by broadening and deepening the support for the liberal market economy among firms in multiple sectors, the two governments created the conditions for a sustainable trajectory of institutional specialization.

Specialization is a pattern of institutional development in which the coherence of an existing model of governance is enhanced and reforms in disparate domains increase levels of incentive compatibility between specific institutions. For firms with investments in extant designs, this is often an attractive trajectory because it increases the aggregate returns they reap from the institutional advantages of an existing model. As a pattern of institutional development, it has several parts that are observable in the actions of governments. First, governments frequently commit themselves publicly to promoting existing structures of governance and, as a means to assuring pivotal economic groups that their stakes in extant designs will not be devalued, commonly denounce alternative models of governance. In addition, statutory provisions are often introduced as a means of reducing the chances that rival alternatives emerge. Second, to deepen and broaden support for extant designs, governments focus on enhancing and creating new complementarities between the core institutions of a particular market economy. This is done by increasing the incentive compatibility between institutions and by minimizing the negative effects that existing or prospective designs may have on the institutional advantages of the current model of governance. Finally, efforts to overcome or minimize the comparative institutional disadvantages of a given system of governance tend to be gradual and are a second-order priority that is pursued as long as the core advantages of a given model are not eroded.[17]

For a pattern of institutional specialization to be sustainable over time, firms must be motivationally inclined to adopt corporate strategies that rely primarily on exploiting the institutional advantages of the model in question. They must deem these superior to alternatives under an expanding set of conditions such as greater levels of competition, the emergence of new technologies, or new multilateral rules. In Britain after the early 1990s, sustaining a pattern of institutional specialization meant that governments needed to provide firms with incentives to employ and extend the use of product market strategies that relied on flexible social contracts and low levels of asset-specific relational investments. These are institutional advantages for firms in the lower end of the mass manufacturing and service sectors, in the upper-end of the latter (e.g., financial services), as well as in industries characterized by radical innovation practices (Hall and Soskice 2001b). Following the Thatcher government, which had targeted its structural reform agenda toward firms in these sectors, the Major and Blair governments successfully deepened support for the core of the liberal market economy within the financial sector and among large and smaller manufacturing firms.

Promoting the Core

The structural reform agenda of the Major government was nearly identical to that of the Thatcher government. In a series of white papers on how the competitiveness of British firms could be enhanced, the government stressed the same themes as its predecessor (HMSO 1994, 1995, 1996). Achieving low rates of inflation and sustaining a stable macroeconomic environment was seen as a prerequisite to closing the investment and productivity gaps that characterized British firms in relation to those in other major industrialized countries. Its strategy also mirrored those of the Thatcher government in other areas, in particular in its emphasis on labor market liberalization and financial deregulation. However, following criticisms within the business community about the detached nature of government offices during the Thatcher years, the Major government expanded the role played by the government in promoting British industry. Though it maintained a strong emphasis on protecting market incentives and rejected a strategy of "picking winners," it favored the expansion of formal consultations with business about how to enhance competitiveness (HMSO 1994).

The Blair government's economic agenda followed closely that of its predecessor. Immediately upon taking office, the new government announced that it would adopt the same macroeconomic priorities and tools as had the Conservative governments in the 1980s and 1990s. To allay fears within the domestic and international business communities that the new Labour government would exercise greater discretion in macroeconomic policy, the important Monetary Policy Committee of the Bank of England was granted independence in setting interest rates. In addition, new rules for fiscal stability were introduced, and a Financial Services Authority was established to promote stability and responsible behavior in the financial sector (HM Treasury 2002). The use of devaluations was explicitly ruled out as these would compromise long-term growth, and instead the government stressed the importance of budgetary discipline and price stability. In the words of the new Chancellor of the Exchequer Gordon Brown, the Labour government aimed to "create a modern framework that could command confidence and credibility" (*Financial Times*, 17 May 1997). Although the reform to the Bank of England was indeed a "modern" move given similar trends elsewhere, the overall policy objective did not so much signal a departure from earlier practice as much as it underscored continuity.

A high degree of continuity also characterized the Blair government's reform agenda in the financial, corporate governance, industrial relations, and innovation systems. It explicitly rejected previous Labour Party programs such as the National Plan of 1965 and the Alternative Economic Strategy of the 1980s and declared that there was "no going back to nationalisation or to corporatist management of the economy" (*Guardian*, 8 April 1997: 1). Blair (1997) spoke instead of a "third way between laissez-faire of the last 20 years, and the model of statist and corporatist policies that used to be fashionable." Though nominally described as a departure from its predecessors, the institutional core of the agenda did not much differ from that of the Major or Thatcher governments. The Labour Party's election manifesto could not have been clearer on this point than when it pledged to "leave intact the main changes of the 1980s in industrial relations and enterprise" and when it committed itself to promoting "the enterprise of the market and the rigour of competition" (Labour Party 1997).

Framing the institutional status quo as the superior strategy to ensure competitive firms, the Labour government had in the words of Chancellor Brown "no intention of indulging in change for change's sake" (*Financial Times*, 5 June 1997).[18] Rather than rolling back Thatcher's labor market reforms, the new government praised Britain as the "envy of continental Europe" for its flexible labor markets and touted the benefits of having a less regulated labor market than the United States (*Financial Times*, 5 May 1997; see also Blair 1997). Similarly, the Prime Minister openly supported the privatization agenda by previous governments, and his stated goal of creating "a culture of enterprise" echoed his Conservative predecessors who had spoken of restoring an "enterprise culture" (*Financial Times*, 2 March 1997).

The Blair government also extended institutional reforms begun by its predecessors. It implemented changes to competition rules that were originally drafted by a Conservative government. It also amended the Financial Services Act to enhance the attractiveness of the British financial system to domestic and foreign investors. The financial system was frequently criticized for being the source of short-term thinking among firms (e.g., Hutton 1995). But the Blair government explicitly invoked and rejected reforms that would have brought about a German-style alliance between manufacturing firms and banks for the purposes of building a foundation for long-term capital intensive investments (Blair 1996, 94–95). Instead, consistent with a pattern of institutional specialization, it introduced reforms that enhanced flexibility and entrenched a light regulatory system in the financial services industry. Simultaneously, it supported the reduction of constraints on the market for corporate control and encouraged an active takeover market. By the late 1990s, Britain was home to Europe's largest equity markets, had become the most active arena for domestic mergers and acquisitions, and also recorded more than twice the number of hostile takeovers domestically than the combined total for all of continental Europe (Martynova 2006, 60–66).

There were some departures from the Conservative agenda. During the course of its first term, the Blair government gave greater attention to knowledge-intensive industries such as the information technology, pharmaceutical, and biotechnology sectors. Each of these industries depended on access to substantial sums of risk capital and individuals with advanced education and training. Britain's liberal market economy provided a comparative institutional advantage in the provision of venture capital through a dynamic stock market and a large financial services sector willing to accept substantial risks for high potential rewards. However, the same system had historically been seen as a liability in the domain of human capital formation (Finegold and Soskice 1988). The latter was a major preoccupation for the new government, but reforms emphasized the creation of incentives for individuals to acquire new skills and not the creation of new non-market institutions for coordination among employers.

Similar patterns of reform were evident with respect to the innovation system where the government extended more public support for research and development and spearheaded programs to attract firms to research clusters, but where the type of coordinated and government-led programs familiar from Germany and France or from the early post-war period were missing (Casper 2007). Although reforms in these areas were important, the government's agenda did not represent a fundamental change in the direction of economic governance as much as it constituted an attempt to mitigate some of the institutional disadvantages of the liberal market economy without compromising the internal coherence of that model.

The commitment by the Major and Blair governments to the core of the institutional blueprint introduced during the 1980s secured broad support within the business community. The gradual emergence of positive feedback effects from the reforms of the 1980s made firms in the pivotal sectors more strongly committed to the liberal market economy.[19] They now had significant investments in the liberal market economy and framed continuity as the superior strategy. In addition, higher levels of international competition, as explained in earlier chapters, made designs that encouraged market coordination more attractive to firms embedded in liberal market economies. This is the case in particular for firms in those sectors that governments in the 1990s and 2000s saw as pivotal in their industrial strategies, namely the financial services and radical innovation industries. But as in earlier periods, the ability of the government to sustain a broad business coalition required that the design problem be resolved without significant compromise to the institutional advantages of national designs.

The Institutional Core and Multilateralism

If the Thatcher government had made the alignment of its national and multilateral strategies a necessity to restore the liberal market economy, its successors turned such an alignment into a virtue. Both the Major and Blair governments repeatedly expressed their commitments to ensuring that Britain would be at "the heart of Europe," and they attached particular importance to underscoring their commitment to the internal market and to securing a European architecture that emphasized deregulation and flexibility.[20] Membership was to be the catalyst for the expansion and renewal of domestic industries and the means by which a major increase in foreign direct investment would occur. Major's reform strategy spoke of turning Britain into the "Enterprise Centre of Europe" (HMSO 1996), and the Blair government talked about turning Britain into "Europe's corporate headquarters" and making it "the best place to do business in Europe" (Blair 2000).

With the internal market program implemented, the long-term sustainability of the domestic reform agenda was largely contingent on preventing the introduction of multilateral rules that could undermine its integrity. In the 1990s and 2000s, this would at times prove to be a major challenge to British governments. Following the implementation of the internal market program, demands proliferated among other member-states for the expansion of European-level regulations in areas affecting the financial, corporate governance, industrial relations, and innovation systems. Though the trend in several countries was toward more liberal designs at home, there were demands by major constituencies within other large member-states that European rules be adopted that would forestall greater convergence on the British model. With qualified majority voting firmly established and an economic downturn in Europe, such demands appeared more likely to become a reality and represented in the eyes of British governments and its business community potential adaptation losses that threatened the institutional advantages of domestic designs.

The biggest challenge to the Major government and the foundations of its domestic economic program came in the context of the negotiations surrounding the Maastricht Treaty in the early 1990s.[21] Core issues during the negotiations included the construction of a new supranational industrial policy focused on innovation and research and development activities, the expansion of social policy, and agreement on the details surrounding economic and monetary union (EMU). Developments in each of these three areas represented potential threats to the institutional coherence of the Major government's domestic program. A proposal for a Commission-directed industrial policy was opposed, for it was seen to distort the market incentives stressed in the liberal market economy. Because the Major government was committed to budgetary austerity in the domain of industrial subsidies, it opposed a European-level industrial policy since such a policy could generate "subsidy auctions" in which governments engaged in competitive bidding to attract industry. Given its goal of attracting such investments by offering the "right" institutional environment, the Major government was concerned that other governments would undercut firms' incentives to invest in Britain by offering direct financial assistance (HMSO 1994, 84–86).[22]

With greater levels of international competition fostered by the internal market program, concerns grew among other member-states that some countries (notably

Britain) would engage in "social dumping" whereby they would attempt to attract business by maintaining low social standards. The fear among these member-states was that such practices would encourage a race-to-the-bottom dynamic and bring a radical reduction in social provisions throughout the EU. During the Maastricht negotiations, proposals were put forward to bring within the treaty structure measures that would curb the ability of countries to engage in social dumping. A "social chapter" to the treaty was proposed that would cover social benefits, freedom of association, fair compensation, and enhanced dialogues between employers and unions. The Major government saw these provisions as a direct threat to it providing a low-cost and deregulated business environment. Those provisions, clarified one government official, were "absolutely anathema to freeing up labor markets . . . [and] it made absolutely no sense to import European-level labor market regulations to Britain" (Foreign and Commonwealth Office 1996).

Finally, the Maastricht negotiations aimed to finalize an agreement on EMU to commence in 1999. Member-states were to relinquish monetary authority to a European central bank and agree to meet and observe several strict economic performance criteria. Though John Major had been a strong proponent of Britain participating in earlier European monetary arrangements, his government was adamantly opposed to EMU.[23] In part this position reflected an effort to placate members in his own party who were strongly opposed, but it also reflected an institutional rationale that was closely associated with his government's concern with how to sustain the liberal market economy. That economy provides a competitive advantage to firms relying on relatively low-cost production and thus made industrial producers concerned with the long-term effects of being locked into a fixed exchange-rate regime. Lacking wage-setting institutions that can control labor costs, autonomy over the exchange rate presented a particularly important tool to restoring cost-competitiveness should prices escalate at home (Soskice 1990).

Despite the many reservations the Major government had over the Maastricht Treaty, it was not in a position to veto an agreement. The latter strategy would have reopened the issue of Britain's commitment to European multilateralism and undermined the ability of the government to secure support for its structural reforms within the business sector. At the same time, accepting the proposals put forth by other member-states presented similar risks as they entailed adaptation losses to British firms and could potentially erode the very national institutional advantages on which the Major government's structural reform strategy rested.

In an effort to mitigate high externally induced adaptation losses, the Major government adopted a hardnosed negotiation position. In the case of industrial policy, it gained support from Germany to block any significant expansion of the European Commission's discretionary authority and instead agreed to an expansion of non-discriminatory programs devoted to research and development. In the social policy and monetary domains, however, there was little support for Britain's unwillingness to agree to new rules. Yet, after extended negotiations, the Major government was able to secure a singular opt-out for Britain from the treaty's social chapter and one from the final phase of EMU. The two opt-outs avoided potential adaptation losses and enabled the Major government to resolve the design problem in ways that assured the national business community both that the institutional core of the liberal market economy was protected and that Britain was fully committed to European integration.

Though questions have been raised about the extent to which the opt-outs actually saved British firms from higher production costs, their effect on the willingness of firms to invest in Britain are not in doubt. The principal purpose of the government strategy was to provide assurances to firms that it would protect the core of the liberal market economy while securing access to European markets on non-discriminatory terms. In the words of one official, opt-outs would provide the "best of two worlds: free access to 370 million consumers and low social costs [at home]" (HM Treasury 1996). The government reasoned that if firms saw its assurance of protecting the institutional architecture of the liberal economy as credible, firms were more likely to adopt corporate strategies that exploited the institutional advantages of the liberal model and thus enhance the sustainability of the government's reforms. While a business survey found that 72 percent of British firms supported the opt-out from the social chapter (Greenwood and Stancich 1998, 157), the prime minister noted in Parliament that the agreement "will not impose damaging costs on British industry and workers. I feel, as so many employers in this country and abroad feel, that it will give a competitive advantage to this country, not a competitive disadvantage" (House of Commons 1991–1992, 280–281).[24]

At first glance, the Blair government's criticism of its predecessor's European social policy agenda suggested that it was willing to depart from the latter's strategy of attracting firms to Britain by opting-out of European agreements. The electoral manifesto of the Labour Party (1997) included a promise to sign the EU's social chapter, which the Blair government did the same year it took office. However, a closer look at the Blair government's approach to this and related issues reveals more continuity in its EU policy than significant departures. The importance the Labour government attached to assuring the business sector that it would protect the core of the liberal model was apparent in several cases. Although it signed the social chapter, the Blair government went to great lengths to assure large- and medium-sized firms in Britain and foreign investors that it would prevent any new multilateral rules from imposing adaptation losses and more generally undermine the institutional advantages of the domestic labor market system. Claiming that the Maastricht Treaty's social protocol "will not impose the so-called German or European model of social and employment costs," Prime Minister Blair added that European initiatives that would do so in the future would be opposed "if necessary by veto" (*Financial Times*, 11 March 1997).

The Blair government continued to defend British derogations from the Working Time Directive. The directive, which set a maximum target of forty-eight working hours per week and that established rights to holidays and breaks during the work day, had been strongly opposed by Thatcher and led the Major government to challenge its legality in the European Court of Justice.²⁵ Britain lost the case, but the Blair government secured derogations, which enabled employers in Britain to opt-out from some of the constraints imposed by the directive. When some member-states and the European Parliament sought in 2005 to end Britain's special status in the area, the Blair government again promised the largest business association that it would "not agree to anything that surrenders our opt-out on working time" (Blair 2006b).²⁶

The Blair government also chose not to end the British opt-out from EMU. Quickly upon taking office, the new government outlined five criteria that had to be met before Britain would join others in EMU. In addition to noting that Britain would need to converge its basic macroeconomic indicators on other members of EMU, the criteria centered around the long-term effects of the common currency on investments in Britain, its ability to adjust to changing markets, and the specific effects on the financial services industry and employment. The manufacturing and the financial services sectors in the past had been supporters of closer monetary cooperation. The Labour government sought to assure these industries that it was committed to protecting essential features of the economic policy that had been initiated in the 1980s under Thatcher. It provided these assurances with respect to macroeconomic stability by retaining the opt-out in combination with domestic institutional innovations that gave the business community greater confidence that there would be no fundamental departure from the strategy of its Conservative predecessor.

The commitment of the Blair government to protect the core of the liberal market economy through a particular engagement with the EU was evident in other areas too, including in the domains of financial services and corporate governance. It complemented domestic reforms to financial services centered on reducing regulatory fragmentation with a multilateral strategy that promoted targeted financial services harmonization within the EU. Although its regulatory agenda enhanced public oversight, the government championed a principles-based approach over a rules-based one at both levels. Long a supporter of an integrated European financial market, the government pushed for a Financial Services Action Plan that would reduce the prospect of economic discrimination within the EU while preserving national discretion in regulating such firms (HM Treasury, Financial Action Services Authority, and the Bank of England 2003). For example, unlike in the case of social policy where it supported extensive national discretion and common minimum regulations at the multilateral level, the government backed an arrangement that combined the preservation of national discretion with a maximum regulation principle. The government reasoned that the latter arrangement would help British firms gain access to larger markets while preventing other governments from introducing discriminatory practices or collude within the EU to increase standards substantially beyond those in Britain. In this way, the Labour government successfully shifted some regulatory authority to the public sphere while enhancing the potential benefits from European integration for British firms without the prospect of any significant adaptation losses to these from new multilateral institutions.

The Labour government extended its predecessor's reforms to the corporate governance system, though it placed a stronger emphasis on statutory means of enforcement (Keasey, Short, and Wright 2005). Among other legislative initiatives, the Blair government undertook the first revision of the Companies Act in twenty years in 2006, which consolidated the trajectory of earlier reforms and included reductions in the constraints on the market for corporate control. The Act also served to implement the EU's Takeover Directive, one of the most controversial initiatives in the organization's history that pitted Britain against countries with less liberal corporate governance codes (Höpner and Callaghan 2005).

One of the cornerstones of the liberal market economy is an active market for corporate control in which hostile takeovers are a key feature. Negotiations over an EU directive designed to level the playing field proved controversial elsewhere in Europe because early proposals were more closely aligned to British practice than in other countries where defensive mechanisms allowed major owners to frustrate hostile takeovers. Supportive of original proposals, the Blair government was concerned with protecting the integrity of domestic designs and with enabling British firms to launch bids for European companies without facing higher hurdles abroad than they did at home. It actively campaigned for an EU directive that promoted the principles of equal treatment and one-share-one-vote and that entailed a breakthrough provision that would allow bidders to overcome the privileged voting rights that large owners held in some countries.[27] However, with strong opposition to the proposals favored by Britain from other member-states, a compromise was needed to reach an agreement.

The exclusion of provisions that would have enabled British firms to launch takeover bids abroad on the same terms they could at home led the British regulatory body in charge of mergers and takeovers to describe the EU compromise as one of "very little benefit" (Takeover Panel 2004, 13). Thus, there were no significant adaptation benefits from the new Takeover Directive. More important, from the vantage point of the Blair government there were no adaptation losses, which would have been politically costly. Instead, the compromise introduced multilateral statutory protections of national discretion in the area and thus reinforced the existing corporate governance system in Britain.

Sustainable Specialization

The Major and Blair governments resolved the design problem in similar ways and had similar goals. Both governments preserved the investments that major manufacturing and services sector firms had in the liberal designs that were introduced in the 1980s. Both promoted multilateral designs that maintained access to an integrated European market while avoiding large externally induced adaptation losses. Behavioral institutionalism helps explain why governments in liberal market economies would be so concerned with ensuring that domestic and multilateral designs be incentive compatible. The sectors that British governments targeted in their industrial strategies—high-end financial services, radical innovation firms, and low-costs mass manufacturing and services companies—had benefited significantly from earlier reforms and therefore had a major investment in sustaining the liberal market economy's institutional architecture. Furthermore, the increase in governance costs to such firms from operating under multilateral rules that are incentive incompatible with domestic designs were comparatively large and made the Major and Blair governments particularly sensitive to potentially high adaptation losses that were induced externally.

The manner in which the Major and the Blair governments integrated their domestic and foreign economic policies in a period that saw the emergence of new technologies, a significant rise in economic globalization, and a proliferation of new multilateral institutions ultimately reinforced the credibility of firms' commitments to the core of the liberal market economy. The incremental reforms overseen by the two governments to the country's financial, corporate governance, industrial relations, and innovation domains had in the course of the two decades become self-enforcing under a larger number of parameters (i.e., had become self-reinforcing), thus producing the conditions under which a trajectory of institutional specialization was sustainable.

Conclusion

Neither the failure to implement a reform agenda stressing centralized governance in the 1960s, nor the success of governments in consolidating and later reinforcing a liberal market economy model after 1979 were historical inevitabilities that can be traced to the legacies of economic liberalism in Britain. In each case, the ability of governments to build sufficient support within the business sector to implement their structural reform agendas was a product of their policy and institutional choices, and not simply a legacy of nineteenth-century laissez faire capitalism. As Karl Polanyi (1944) remarked about the nineteenth century and Steve Vogel (1996) has noted with reference to the 1980s, sustaining a liberal market economy has historically been a product of an active government or a visible hand, not of an inactive government or of Adam Smith's "invisible hand." But the visible hands of governments in the postwar period have not been limited to the domestic sphere—their foreign economic policies, in particular their multilateral commitments and strategies, played integral roles in shaping the trajectory of Britain's market economy after 1950.

The international economic environment changed significantly for British firms after World War II. Protected colonial markets ended, European markets gained in importance, and a period of economic globalization fostered intense levels of competition in major product markets. To manage the process of international market integration, industrialized states adopted a large number of multilateral institutions that significantly altered the context in which British firms operated. Shaping the specific terms on which British firms would be exposed to international markets and the manner in which they would be impacted by multilateral rules became critical elements in the structural reform agendas of post-war governments. This chapter underscores the central role that governments assumed in shaping the specific manner in which international developments affected corporate strategy and ultimately whether institutional designs at the center of their structural reforms were undermined or reinforced.

The chapter's attention to how governments resolved the design problem helps it revisit some common explanations of Britain's institutional trajectory after 1960. For example, rather than arguing that the reforms of the 1960s were doomed to fail because of the historical legacies of liberalism in Britain, it links the lack of institutional sustainability to the policy choices of governments and how these undermined firms' incentives to make long-term investments in productivity enhancing technologies. By highlighting temporally contingent factors such as government decisions that enhanced the uncertainty surrounding British firms' access to foreign markets, the chapter details the microfoundations for why firms in pivotal industrial sectors failed to credibly commit to the type of corporate strategies championed by governments in this period despite their initial support for reforms. Early membership in the EEC may not have rescued the government's reform strategy, but failure to gain membership made it nearly an inevitability and something governments worked actively, though unsuccessfully, to prevent.

This chapter also revisits a common understanding of post-war reforms concerning the ability of the Thatcher government to consolidate its agenda. That process is frequently explained with reference to the emergence of new ideas and a significant decline in the power of labor unions, but this chapter underscores the institutional foundations for why firms came to support the liberal market economy. It links the emergence of support among firms to the absence of their investments in the designs from the post-war period and the growing incentives they had to support liberal designs during a period of greater international market liberalization. Though neither of these dimensions were the making of the Thatcher government, that government adopted a multilateral strategy that reinforced the manufacturing and financial sectors' incentives to adopt product market strategies that revolved around exploiting the institutional advantages of the liberal model. For the first time in the post-war period the deep cleavage that had existed between the two sectors was bridged and generated a strong and broad business coalition on which the government could sustain its structural reform agenda. In other words, rather than characterizing the Thatcher government as a reluctant supporter of European multilateralism in general, the chapter underscores that it successfully consolidated the liberal market economy through its support for specific forms of European multilateralism.

Gaining access to international markets was by itself not sufficient to ensure continued support for the liberal market economy among British firms, much less a strategy of institutional specialization during the 1990s and 2000s. British governments actively sought to prevent multilateral designs from imposing external adaptation losses that could undermine the core designs of the liberal market economy. These efforts were the opposite of government inaction and were viewed by the business community as essential to safeguarding the institutional foundation on which they had developed their core competencies and competitive advantages. "By shielding us from parts of Europe, those not like us," one business representative stressed, "the government has protected our competitive edge at home and abroad" (CBI 2006). It was by reconciling domestic and multilateral designs in ways that avoided large externally induced adaptation losses that the Major and Blair governments were able to deepen support within a broad business coalition. That coalition, which came to include the financial services industry as well as large and smaller manufacturing companies, made it possible for these governments to implement reforms that sustained patterns of institutional specialization.

By the time of the 2008 economic crisis, the liberal market economy enjoyed broad support within the corporate sector and across both major parties. Despite the severity of that crisis and calls for stricter rules in the financial domain, neither the British government nor its industry called for reforms that would alter the core of the liberal model. Indeed, by comparison to earlier crises in post-war history that occasioned proposals for comprehensive and radical shifts in economic governance, the British government's responses to the crisis stood out for its advocacy of incremental national reforms and the extensive attention given to securing multilateral rules that would strengthen the protection of the former (e.g., Brown 2009). The conditions for continuity in the liberal market economy following the 2008 crisis, much like after 1979, was thus one that the British government saw as highly conditional on innovations in multilateral designs and how successfully it could prevent such designs, especially within the EU, from undermining the core features of its particular variety of capitalism.

Chapter 5

France

*The Centralized Market Economy
and Its Alternatives*

Unlike most European economies that quickly sought to reduce their reliance on centralized forms of economic governance after World War II, French governments significantly expanded the scope of such designs. Through a comprehensive reform program of key economic institutions and the introduction of a dense fabric of formal and informal institutions that were designed to foster joint planning and adaptation within and between the public and private sectors, French governments exercised great control over corporate strategy. Scholars and policymakers widely credited these reforms for transforming the "pointillist character" (Ehrmann 1957, 320) of the country's economic landscape from one defined by a large number of small firms to one in which large manufacturing firms were the dominant engines of economic growth and employment (e.g., Shonfield 1965; S. Cohen 1977; Fourastié 1979).

Though French governments would continue to play a major role in shaping the country's economic trajectory, the centralized system of governance that is so closely associated with post-war France proved relatively short-lived. Even before they were declared the source for the country's "thirty glorious years" of economic expansion (Fourastié 1979), key building blocks were eroding as pivotal sections of the industrial sector became unable to credibly commit to the type of corporate strategies championed by French governments. During the late 1950s, changes in the international economy and foreign policy decisions originally designed to reinforce the domestic reform agenda gradually served to undermine the ability of governments to ensure sufficient support within the national business community for industrial strategies based on a centralized model of governance. Attempts to further centralize economic governance in later decades proved unsustainable and led governments in the mid-1980s to introduce decentralized forms of governance that bore similarities to the coordinated model of capitalism. However, by the late 1990s, the emphasis on such designs had been abandoned and greater weight was placed on ones associated with the liberal market economy. Through a process of institutional recombination, the French market economy gradually emerged as a hybrid system of governance. By the 2000s, the French economic model combined institutional forms in the financial and corporate governance domains that had significant similarities to those found in liberal market economies with designs in the industrial relations and innovation systems where legacies of centralized governance coexisted with decentralized designs introduced in the 1980s.

In advanced market economies, governments attempt to achieve general goals such as economic and employment growth by shaping the incentives of firms to adopt particular product market strategies. The nature of corporate strategy and adjustment is key to processes of structural transformation and to whether governments will successfully maintain or attain levels of economic growth that ensure political stability. There are, however, important differences in the particular means employed by governments that favor centralized and decentralized modes of governance and in the type of coalitions they build within the business community. Governments employing the former exercise great authority through statutory and fiscal means and have typically used subsidies and extensive ownership stakes to directly influence corporate strategy in a narrow set of sectors. They have also tended to shape corporate strategy through numerous constraints on the market for corporate ownership and to orchestrate mergers as a means of establishing large lead firms that smaller ones have been compelled to follow. In contrast, governments relying on decentralized models have generally sought to establish support within the business community through institutions that have been designed to align the incentives of a broader set of sectors to pursue complementary corporate strategies, including the financial and manufacturing sectors.

In practice, differences between centralized and decentralized models have meant that governments moving from the former to the latter arrangement have had to find functional replacements to the role played by public authorities in resolving coordination problems, including in the provision of capital and in support for industrial innovation. In France, where the transition toward greater reliance on decentralized forms of governance began in the 1980s, the type of business coalition that could consolidate such a shift was slow to emerge due to the legacies of earlier reforms. Only in the early 2000s, decades later than its large industrial neighbors, had such a coalition formed and the conditions emerged under which a hybrid system of governance characterized by extensive decentralization was sustainable.

This chapter examines the nature of institutional development in key economic domains during the early post-war period, the 1970s and 1980s, as well as in the decade and a half preceding the 2008 global financial crisis. There was a great deal more institutional experimentation in post-war France than in other countries. As summarized in Table 5.1, patterns of institutional development were variable over time, as well as distinct from those of Europe's other two large economies. Unlike Britain where attempts to introduce centralized forms of governance failed in the early post-war period, French governments successfully consolidated such forms in multiple domains. Also unlike Britain, where a liberal agenda was consolidated, and Germany, where a pattern of institutional specialization was sustainable in the second period, French governments were neither successful in implementing a partial liberal reform agenda nor in sustaining a comprehensive program of institutional specialization that sought to expand centralized governance. Finally, though there were greater similarities between the three economies after the early 1990s, differences existed in the timing and scope of French reforms.

The national trajectory of French capitalism was heavily impacted by the manner in which governments resolved the design problem. French governments persistently tried to shape multilateral institutions in ways that would facilitate the consolidation of their domestic reform programs. Their efforts met with important successes and they were able to secure forms of multilateralism at key junctures in the post-war era. But governments failed in several instances to secure their preferred form of multilateralism. Moreover, some multilateral agreements to which France was party, such as the European Economic Community (EEC) and the internal market program, had long-term effects that governments had difficulties reconciling with their domestic ambitions. These undermined long-standing institutional practices and pushed governments to undertake more significant changes in economic governance than were the cases in Britain or Germany. By the 2000s, however, French governments had successfully resolved the design problem in several key areas of the economy in ways that created broad support within the business community and made possible the consolidation of a hybrid system of governance.

This chapter explains why and when different forms of economic governance across a range of domains were stable and others characterized by more change. Presented in a set of analytical narratives of the extent to which governments were able to secure patterns of corporate behavior that could sustain the core designs of their industrial strategies, the chapter brings attention to the role of historical legacies, shifts in international markets, and the multilateral environment in shaping firm strategy. Only after French governments aligned national reform with the multilateral designs that were taking root in the late 1980s and early 1990s were they able to broaden the basis of support within the business community and produce the conditions under which a hybrid system of governance paradoxically was more stable than early post-war reforms that were internally more coherent.

The Gradual Consolidation of a Centralized Market Economy

France is often seen as the paradigmatic case of a centralized market economy. However, in historical perspective broad labels like *dirigisme* and *statism* that are used to describe France mask significant discontinuities in the designs governments have promoted and that have defined the country's market economy over time. Drawing a direct line from Jean-Baptiste Colbert's rationale for centralized economic management and mercantilism in the seventeenth century to France's post-war market economy obscures major departures from a centralized model in

TABLE 5.1
Institutional developments in the French market economy

	1950–1973	1974–1991	1992–2008
Direction	Centralized model (coordination through administrative hierarchies)	Multiple agendas (partial decentralization during 1970s; more centralization 1981–83; great decentralization and experimentation with coordinated designs after 1983)	Mixture of liberal designs and legacies of centralized and coordinated designs (greater market coordination)
Scope, mode, dominant features	Comprehensive	Variable	Comprehensive
	Finance Large public ownership of banks; government control of credit; government supply of risk capital (limited)	*Finance* Expansion of public control of credit through 1983, extensive deregulation afterwards; nationalization of banks (1981–1983), followed by privatization; limited risk capital until late 1980s	*Finance* Radical: expansion of investment-oriented banks; privatization of banks completed; increases in equity markets and risk capital
	Corporate governance Public ownership and control of boards high; significant constrains on market for corporate control	*Corporate governance* Expansion of government control through 1983, high state ownership; privatization, private blockholding late 1980s; constraints on market for corporate control high, lifted somewhat late 1980s; limited expansion of employee representation	*Corporate governance* Radical: major reductions in blockholding and constraints on market for corporate control

Scope, mode, dominant features	*Industrial relations* Limited autonomy for social partners; government influence on practice of collective bargaining; stable employment contracts	*Industrial relations* Social partnership autonomy stable through mid-1980s, more decentralization later; government regulation of employment contracts high; some expansion in collective bargaining	*Industrial relations* Incremental: expansion of decentralized bargaining; mixture of new constraints and enhanced flexibility in employment contracts
	Innovation Extensive subsidies to firms; conflictual relations between large and small firms; extensive support for public research	*Innovation* Expansion of direct support through late 1980s; conflictual relations between large and small firms until late 1980s; public research greater	*Innovation* Incremental: reduction in direct firm support; cooperative relations between large and small firms stronger; expansion in public support for research
Aggregate outcome	Consolidation	Failed transformation (1970s); Failed specialization of centralized model (1981–83); Partial consolidation of decentralized reforms (late 1980s)	Recombination (stable hybrid after mid-1990s)

some periods, as well as exaggerates the inevitability of the latter's consolidation after World War II. During the late nineteenth century, economic management in France had largely followed a liberal vein. Governments played key roles, but the mode of economic governance was far from centralized in nature (Palmade 1972; Kuisel 1981). The chief architects of economic management in the last decades of the nineteenth century and before World War I opposed using the state as provider of public goods. Minimal market regulation was a hallmark, and price controls of goods and wages were rejected. Stock-market capitalization was high by international standards; notably, it was twice that of the United States at the outbreak of World War I (Rajan and Zingales 2001, 61). Monopolies were also opposed with the exception of the financial sector where economic concentration was partially endorsed (Kuisel 1981, 8).

The liberal period of economic governance ended with the inter-war economic crisis and World War II when governments in France, as elsewhere, significantly expanded centralized forms of economic governance. Yet, when the provisional government of Charles de Gaulle (1944–1946) opted for a project of economic reconstruction that emphasized a centralized model of governance, it was not a foregone conclusion that key designs of that model would remain in place some twenty years later. French governments faced significant political and organizational obstacles in implementing a structural reform agenda based on centralized forms of governance. There was initially much contestation over what form of governance should be employed. Major divisions existed between supporters of decentralized and centralized models within the early governments and the civil service. Early post-war governments were also under pressure to minimize the role of the business sector in economic management given that the latter had been implicated in the collaborationist Vichy government (Kuisel 1981; Shennan 1989).

Moreover, securing cooperation from the business sector for a model of economic modernization in which the autonomy of firms was significantly constrained constituted a major challenge. In contrast to the type of centralized model that characterized socialist economies after the war, the model employed by French governments was of an indicative nature—and "rested in concertation, not on subordination" (Michalet 1974, 113). Significant parts of industry were nationalized and governments exerted a great deal of direct control over many companies. However, the long-term success of government reforms relied ultimately on the ability and willingness of firms to adopt the product market strategies championed by governments and to undertake major investments in plant and people during a period of great domestic and international uncertainty. In addition to the skepticism of many firms toward a model of governance in which their autonomy would be significantly constrained (Ehrmann 1958, 284–294), governments had to overcome the challenges of a highly fragmented business community that lacked well-established institutions for joint coordination. The latter meant that it was easier for governments to overcome opposition from some sectors of the business community. However, it also entailed a significant obstacle to ensuring that the business community as a whole would remain committed to an integrated and ambitious project of structural reform.

Early post-war governments initiated a comprehensive set of domestic reforms designed to shape the corporate strategy of French firms, in particular their investments in plants, technology, and skills. They also gradually shifted the country's foreign economic policy from one that was relatively closed and that favored centrally regulated and sector-specific forms of international market integration to one that was more open and accepted broader forms of economic multilateralism. This partial transition to an open system of governance and the manner in which governments reconciled designs of economic governance at the national and multilateral levels proved highly significant in shaping corporate strategy and ultimately in determining the fate of the domestic governance agenda across time and sectors of the economy.

Domestic Foundations of Centralized Governance

Between 1945 and the mid-1970s, French governments introduced an ambitious set of plans designed to spur a major transformation of the economic landscape through the expansion of industry and to construct a sustainable foundation for economic modernization of the manufacturing sector. They prioritized the creation of large industrial enterprises and were guided by a general formula, which stated that about 20 percent of firms would be responsible for 80 percent of industrial production (Shonfield 1965, 138). The particular emphasis in the economic plans evolved from an emphasis on six basic industries to a stronger emphasis on boosting the productivity and size of advanced manufacturing firms. To implement their reform agendas, governments introduced two complementary sets of institutions designed to shape corporate strategy across the business sector.

One part of the reform agenda involved efforts to create an internally coherent economic system through innovations in all major domains of economic regulation that were designed to push firms toward adopting scale-intensive production techniques across a range of industries (Baum 1958; Sheahan 1963). Centralized control over the financial and corporate governance systems was key to this agenda. Through government-intermediated credit and public ownership of significant parts of the banking system and large manufacturing firms, governments controlled about 50 percent of corporate investment (Kindleberger 1963, 154; see also Zysman 1983). Economic concentration was encouraged through mergers orchestrated by government officials, who also exercised significant direct control over the activities of large companies through the appointment of managers (Fanto 1998). Finally, centralized governance of large parts of the corporate landscape was facilitated by technical and elite educational institutions that fostered close relations between government agencies and the nationalized and private industrial sector by creating a cadre of officials who shared a common understanding of the tools and goals of economic management (Maclean, Harvey, and Press 2006).

The logic of a centralized system of governance also permeated reforms to the industrial relations domain. Governments significantly expanded social benefits and increased wages to make structural reform politically sustainable, but they were concerned that such initiatives would undermine the modernization of industry and the international competitiveness of firms (Ehrmann 1957, 434–445; Howell 1992, 37–60). Both employers and unions were relatively weakly organized by international standards, and there was no significant expansion of institutions for non-market coordination. Instead, governments influenced company strategy by determining benefits and wage structures. Though the latter were nominally set through collective bargaining at the industry level, governments shaped wages by setting minimum compensation and by using the so-called extension procedure.[1] Several amendments were made to the industrial relations system after 1950, especially in the wake of 1968, but its basic structure remained intact until the early 1980s.

The 1950s also saw a significant expansion and centralization of public authority in the innovation domain. Scientific priorities and innovation patterns remained closely tied to the goals articulated by government officials (Fernez-Walch and Romon 2006). A strong emphasis was placed on funding big public research facilities oriented toward the basic sciences. Large public subsidies were also directed to select companies and governments encouraged mergers among smaller firms and their incorporation into larger ones (Sheahan 1963). The corollary of this strategy was that little attention was devoted to strengthening the ties between large and smaller firms as a means of creating integrated production and innovation chains.

Given the fragmented industrial landscape and low levels of business coordination that had historically characterized France, post-war governments reasoned that supply-side reform would not be sufficient to align the interests of firms across diverse sectors. Designed to be complementary and partially guide the priorities of governments, a large administrative apparatus in the form of modernization and planning commissions was introduced to facilitate the joint planning and forecasting between public officials and the corporate sector. Described by their primary architect as "the king-pins of the whole planning system" (Monnet 1978, 237), these commissions were originally attached to the office of the prime minister to assure their relative autonomy from ministries. In reality, they worked closely with select ministries to promote their agendas, in particular the Ministry of Finance (Zysman 1983, 100–112). Anchored in the notion of an "economy of concertation" (économie concertée), industrial groups, employers, unions, as well as farmers and other interests were compelled to work jointly with public officials (S. Cohen 1977; Hall 1986).[2] The principal aim of planning was to reduce the investment uncertainty for firms and to ensure that the corporate sector had adequate supplies of capital, skilled labor, and technology. To its early architects, economic planning was not about expanding the scope of the government's direct control of firms, but constituted a mechanism for joint deliberation that would bring about "convergent action" among firms (Monnet 1978, 258).

Notwithstanding intense political battles over the structure of French capitalism and much skepticism toward the expansion of government authority during the latter part of the 1940s, the centralized governance agenda was largely deemed successful by the basic industry. Economic reforms and joint planning had contributed to a major expansion and fundamental changes in the basic industry and brought significant improvements in the standard of living to French citizens. Although concerns persisted about the international competitiveness of its industry, economic and productivity growth was robust by the country's historic standards (Caron 1979, 242–308). However, other policy choices reduced the comparative institutional advantages of the centralized model beyond basic industry and lessened the incentives of firms in the advanced manufacturing sector to continue making major capital investments. Large and persistent balance of payments problems played a key role in this context as they curtailed the resources governments could extend to industry. That problem was exacerbated by governments that frequently chose to extend aid to poorly performing firms, which increased public debt and reduced the resources available for expanding firms in the advanced manufacturing sector. While temporarily boosting exports and limiting import-competition, currency devaluations also reinforced a cautionary approach by firms to major investments in plant and technology.

Ultimately, neither the relative successes nor the failures of French governments in transforming industry during the 1950s can be attributed to their domestic choices alone. The success of the basic industry and the limited success of the advanced manufacturing industry in the 1950s, as well as the latter's success in the 1960s, were all closely linked to the manner in which French governments reconciled domestic reforms with their foreign economic policies.

The Multilateral Dimension

Because post-war governments lacked sufficient resources to finance industrial expansion and the country lacked natural resources that were integral to the reconstruction of basic industry, they sought quickly to establish a set of multilateral institutions that were complementary with domestic reforms. Particular emphasis was placed on securing forms of international cooperation that would provide long-term assurances to French industry about their access to natural resources and outlets for industrial goods. As John Zysman (1978, 256) notes, the country's foreign economic policy was during the early post-war period in many ways "an extension of domestic strategies." But it was neither uniform across time, nor of a sort that ensured the long-term sustainability of a centralized system of economic governance.

To make possible its long-term goals of industrial modernization based on the terms laid out in the First Plan (1946–1952), the French government rejected the type of multilateral programs of trade liberalization favored elsewhere in Europe. Instead, it promoted a sectoral approach that was limited to those products most

directly affecting its basic industries. Based on extensive assessments of the potentially negative consequences for domestic reconstruction efforts from the broad
scope of international market integration preferred by the United States, Britain,
and eventually Germany, France favored narrowly targeted multilateral designs
with a limited sectoral scope. In the early stages, particular attention was given
to securing natural resources like coal and coke to rebuild basic industries. The
major repositories for coal and coke were located in Germany, and France in the
late 1940s was importing seven times more coal from the United States than from
its European neighbor at a significant surcharge (Lynch 1984, 237). This was not
a sustainable foundation for establishing competitive manufacturing firms. It was
necessary to ensure access to the natural resources and close the competitiveness
gap that had long existed between French and German steel producers. To achieve
these goals, French prime and later foreign minister Robert Schuman and the principal architect of the First Plan Jean Monnet spearheaded an initiative that would
regulate continental Europe's coal and steel resources at the international level.
Their initiative became the foundation for the European Coal and Steel Community (ECSC) in 1951.

The ECSC represented French efforts to foster political reconciliation with
Germany and simultaneously secure an international environment that would be
supportive of its early domestic reconstruction plans. An integrated European market of coal and steel governed by multilateral institutions was deemed imperative
by Monnet and his supporters to consolidating structural reform at home (Lynch
1984). Their key motivation was to secure a set of multilateral institutions that
would assure domestic industry that modernization was not only desirable, but feasible. French and German steel and iron producers had a pre-war history of extensive cooperation, including a joint cartel, and the former was strongly supportive of
domestic and international initiatives that protected high levels of concentration. In
their consultations with domestic industry through the modernization commissions,
the importance attached by French firms to securing long-term access to German
resources was made clear to public officials. "[F]or us," declared one steel executive,
"[t]here's no choice . . . it's either [the ECSC] or extinction" (Monnet 1978, 318).

Through the ECSC, French governments fundamentally altered the contractual
context in which basic industry operated. That context was no longer defined by
domestic constraints or bilateral treaties, but by an internationally regulated market
that offered predictable access to the key natural resources needed to successfully
modernize basic industry. Through a set of multilateral designs, including a supranational authority and joint planning, both the size of the supply and commodity
prices could be easily ascertained and thus incorporated into the domestic planning
apparatus. The change ushered by the ECSC transformed France's basic industry, restored and in some cases significantly expanded levels of production beyond
pre-war levels and those that had prevailed at the signing of the ECSC agreement
(Baum 1958, 39). Furthermore, the composition of the industrial landscape shifted
and became characterized by a smaller number of larger enterprises that could more

effectively compete in international markets (Caron 1979, 278–308). In the eyes of French policymakers, the foundation had been laid for the further modernization of the advanced industrial sector.

Successfully establishing competitive firms in advanced manufacturing markets proved to be a greater challenge than expected. As it became clear that the Marshall Plan would only temporarily help French governments fill domestic investment gaps, governments contemplated a series of multilateral alternatives that could sustain a trajectory of economic recovery without relying on foreign assistance.[3] The creation of economic unions was explored with other European economies, including a customs union with Italy (1947) as well as an international payments and customs union with Belgium, the Netherlands, Luxembourg, and Italy (1949–1950). The latter included an international investment bank that was designed to address the financing gaps. However, that plan was opposed by France because it was considered incompatible with its domestic modernization agenda. In particular, the government had reservations over potential adaptation losses for they feared that the plan would lessen their control over the domestic nationalization program of banks. With the momentum of the First Plan in place and a declining balance of trade, the French government opted instead for a protectionist trade policy in the early 1950s. In contrast to other governments, which supported international trade liberalization as a means of spurring structural transformations of their industry, the French government stressed in the Second Plan (1954–1957) the importance of reducing imports from industrialized states. Rather than attempting to compete with other European companies, the government sought to modernize the advanced manufacturing by stimulating domestic demand and encouraging exports to the Franc Zone, which had represented 42 percent of foreign sales in 1952 (Adams 1989, 178).[4]

French officials reasoned that greater trade liberalization, strongly advocated by the United States, Britain, and Germany, would only be sustainable for French industry after firms had been fully modernized. The emphasis they placed on implementing a less open strategy had the opposite effect, however. It limited the ability of firms to raise funds from international trade and, rather than encouraging a shift toward greater investments, reinforced a strategy of expansion that relied on retained earnings and government subsidies. In the early 1950s, these forms of financing made up 80 percent of total financing for French industry (Lynch 1997, 100). Because public resources were limited and retained earnings relatively low due to government-determined wage structures and inflationary macroeconomic policies, the attempt to speed up the modernization of the manufacturing sector by rejecting multilateral market liberalization reinforced the opposite pattern in corporate strategy from that sought by governments. The ability of strongly performing French companies to raise funds through exports was reduced and lessened their incentives to make large capital investments for the purposes of scale-intensive production. In other words, though ostensibly designed to enhance firms' incentives to make long-term investments, the government's policy of shielding domestic markets and rejecting European calls for encompassing free trade agreements instead stymied the modernization of the advanced manufacturing industry in the mid-1950s by impeding the very shift in corporate strategy sought by governments.

By the late 1950s it had become apparent that France's foreign economic policy was undermining the government's structural reform agenda at home. Rather than seeing trade liberalization as a threat to domestic reforms, the government and the majority of large manufacturing firms now framed the former as a strategy entailing high opportunity costs (C. Balassa 1978, 344–399; Lynch 1997, 169–187). The status quo was seen as more costly than securing access to foreign markets and led France to support the creation of the EEC in 1958.[5] Described by the French president as "nothing less than a revolution" in the practice of post-war economic management (de Gaulle 1970, 143), the EEC committed France to a common external tariff and to observing the free mobility of goods, services, capital, and people within the community. French support for international market liberalization was far from indiscriminate, however. The country's advanced manufacturing firms remained less competitive than their German counterparts, and French governments were concerned that the EEC would undermine their ability to selectively help and target specific industries as well as their ability to successfully sustain joint economic planning. To protect the core of the domestic modernization program and mitigate the negative consequences for industry from greater levels of competition, French governments sought to limit externally induced adaptation losses through a series of initiatives.

Lacking a history where competition law served the purpose of protecting the market mechanism and where it played a key role of managing inflation, French governments were particularly concerned that the EEC would limit their ability to orchestrate mergers between firms and control factor prices (Gerber 1998, 183–187). They therefore opposed the strict competition rules sought by Germany. Though restrictive competition rules were included in the 1958 Treaty of Rome, national autonomy remained the norm and allowed French governments to exercise significant discretion in the type of subsidies they gave domestic firms and also in their effort to modernize the structure of the advanced manufacturing sector through large mergers. As such, what existed on paper did not challenge the practice of economic governance in France. Rather the growth of the European market gave the French government and industry the impetus to further increase economic concentration and boost the size of leading industrial enterprises.

With a less productive industry and higher social costs than its competitors, the French government became a strong champion of multilateral rules that would harmonize the social costs of production as a means of reducing maladaptation costs. The emphasis fell on the social security contributions of employers (*charges sociales*) and on the conditions of work, including wages (*conditions de travail*). Because French provisions in these areas were subject to national legislation (unlike in Germany where employers and unions enjoyed great autonomy), employers and the government saw international harmonization as the best way to ensure that French standards were sustainable without its producers facing competitive disadvantages (C. Balassa 1978, 437–442). Though French industry insisted that social harmonization be achieved prior to greater trade liberalization and the government was strongly committed to ensuring such outcomes, the latter was unable to prevail over the opposition of Germany and other prospective member-states. Instead, the Treaty of Rome included language that committed the EEC to achieving greater similarities in social and working conditions, but offered no actual provisions for bringing about such outcomes.

In addition to seeking agreement on international forms of market regulation that were compatible with domestic designs, French governments sought to enhance their ability to forecast market conditions through numerous proposals for multilateral planning in the early 1960s (MacLennan 1964). These initiatives bore little practical fruit. Other European governments were not keen on committing themselves to joint planning, and the feasibility of such a project was slim given the large and diverse market that the EEC represented. Higher levels of competition, heterogeneous economies, and divergent macroeconomic practice introduced great uncertainties and eventually contributed to undermining the effectiveness of domestic institutions of economic planning (B. Balassa 1965). Although formally still in place, France's planning commissions would gradually cease to be a major vehicle by which governments shaped corporate strategy and instead became research-oriented organizations with advisory capacity to government officials.

Temporary Consolidation

After having been a reluctant supporter of international market liberalization and not particularly successful in shaping the specific rules of the EEC, the decision by French governments to be part of a common market reshaped the contractual environment for the advanced manufacturing sector in ways that domestic reforms had failed to achieve on their own. Higher levels of market competition increased the opportunity costs for firms that maintained existing product market strategies and that limited investments in new skills and technology. By offering access to foreign markets that were growing rapidly in the 1960s, firms were able to cover their losses in the Franc Zone, gain access to more capital through larger earnings, and undertake costly investments with greater confidence. Between the EEC agreements in 1958 and 1968, for example, the destination of French exports was fundamentally reoriented: goods to EEC members nearly doubled to 43 percent of total exports, while those to the French Overseas Union were reduced by almost two-thirds and those to French North Africa declined by 80 percent (Adams 1989, 178).

Like the coal and steel industry that had benefited from a new contractual environment following the formation of the ECSC in 1951, the advanced manufacturing industry was a significant beneficiary in the 1960s of the government's support of multilateralism. The uncertainties that had characterized the country' multilateral engagements during the late 1940s and much of the 1950s were reduced by the creation of the EEC and gave large manufacturing firms strong incentives to adopt corporate strategies that prioritized long-term investments in scale and innovation intensive production. When these recorded significant growth in the 1960s, it was not simply a validation of domestic reforms. It was to a large extent a validation of a radical, if delayed, shift in how French governments had integrated domestic reforms within a new multilateral trade system.[6]

France's foreign economic policy in this period may have been what Zysman described as an "extension" of what they were doing at home, but it would be incorrect to infer that this policy reflected a coherent national or a consistent grand strategy after the war. The ability of French governments to consolidate an agenda of centralized governance was contingent on events beyond their control and evolved over time as they contended with how to gain access to international resources and markets in ways that reinforced rather than undermined domestic priorities. Domestic programs were designed to provide firms with long-term assurances in order to enhance their willingness to make the type of investments French governments saw as essential to transforming industry. Here the long-term exposure to international competition that membership in the EEC brought was key for it increased the opportunity costs to firms from maintaining the status quo and created strong incentives to undertake long-term investments in productive capacity.

From the perspective of early post-war policymakers, the integral role played by shifts in how the design problem was resolved was paradoxical. The original expectation was that a closed system of economic management defined by centralized forms of governance in which the government selectively opened sectors to international competition was a better strategy by which to achieve the goals of structural transformation. In reality, it was only after French governments adopted a foreign economic policy that exposed industry more broadly to international markets that firms in the pivotal advanced manufacturing sector were able to credibly commit to the corporate strategies championed by governments.

Also paradoxical was the fact that France's commitments to international market liberalization through the EEC gradually undermined the foundation for centralized governance at home. Though industrial efficiency and economic growth would be the highest in the four years after the agreement on the EEC, greater levels of competition also pushed firms to seek more autonomy from government officials. By the mid-1960s, the French business community had become divided over the merits of centralized forms of governance with officials of the largest business association declaring that "The authority [of corporate decisions] cannot be divided" (CNPF 1965). During the decade that followed, efforts by French governments to further centralize economic governance had self-undermining qualities because of an international economic and institutional environment that reduced the incentives of large firms to follow the lead of their government.

Unsustainable Reforms

French governments successfully transformed the country's economic landscape in the 1950s and 1960s and significantly narrowed the competitiveness gap with Germany. But the perception that it was domestic reforms and the promotion of large firms that were the source of success delayed governments from adapting their structural reform strategies to new market conditions and the focus fell instead on incremental changes to the planning system (Hayward 1984; Boyer 1997). By the mid-1970s, however, persistent difficulties in containing inflation and the growing realization that French industry was not well-positioned to compete in more specialized product markets precipitated an intense period of institutional innovation that centered on how to modernize industry. Characterized by lengthy political debates about the merits of centralized and alternative systems of decentralized governance, the 1970s and 1980s can be divided into three distinct episodes of economic reform in which governments sought to redesign basic building blocks of the French market economy.

In the latter half of the 1970s, the first concerted post-war effort was made to reduce the role of governments in economic management and to expand the functions played by markets in shaping corporate strategy. These reforms marked a major departure from earlier decades and frequently drew comparisons with the liberal reform agenda in Britain (e.g., Hall 1986, 189; Levy 1999, 60–62). But there were major differences in the nature and outcome of reforms between the two countries. As French governments introduced a greater role for market forces in shaping corporate strategy, they maintained a focus on encouraging economic concentration within the manufacturing sector and expanded centralized forms of governance within the financial and corporate governance systems. Also unlike reforms in Britain that eventually were consolidated, those in France failed to be sustainable and were abandoned by 1981.

During a second period of reform in the early 1980s, a Socialist government rejected the partial liberalization agenda of its predecessor and instead promoted a comprehensive expansion of centralized forms of governance. Exhibiting the characteristics of a strategy of institutional specialization built on the foundation of early post-war designs, these reforms proved to be self-undermining and were quickly abandoned. Marking a radical shift with earlier reforms, a third period of institutional innovation began in 1983 after which both Socialist and Conservative governments steadily shifted from an emphasis on centralized to decentralized forms of governance. There was extensive support within the business community and a broad political consensus that the decentralization agenda be accompanied by an expansion of the type of institutions of non-market coordination found in coordinated market economies rather than the designs championed in Britain during the same time. Yet key innovations would prove sustainable only in the short-term.

The Failure of Partial Transformation

The structural reform strategy of Conservative governments in the 1970s focused on the creation of national champions, that is large firms that were to be technology and innovation leaders in designated product markets. From having supported both existing large companies and those struggling to stay competitive in the early part of the decade, governments eventually targeted select industries of the future and promised to reduce aid to declining sectors after the middle of the decade. During the presidency of Valéry Giscard d'Estaing (1974–1981) the principal goal was to bring about a shift in the structure and composition of the manufacturing sector by pushing large firms to redeploy their resources toward new product markets in more advanced and higher value-added niche markets (*politique des créneaux*). Large advanced manufacturing firms were expected to withstand competition in international markets better and to serve as locomotives for economic modernization that would gradually also improve the competitiveness of smaller and more specialized manufacturing firms (Groupe de Réflexion 1974).

In implementing their reforms, Conservative governments side-lined institutions of economic planning, which had become less effective following the creation of the EEC (see B. Balassa 1965; Hayward 1984). They also reformed the nature of industrial support, implemented a program of market liberalization, and gradually moved macroeconomic priorities toward price stability. The shift in economic management from earlier periods was particularly sharp during the premiership of Raymond Barre (1976–1981). The Barre government sought to boost corporate profits to fill financing gaps, stressed budgetary discipline and a stable exchange rate (Cohen, Galbraith, and Zysman 1982; Spivey 1982). At the center of its program was an ambitious reform agenda that expanded the role of markets in shaping corporate strategy and that selectively reduced levels of government intervention. Price controls were abolished, equity markets expanded, and promises were made to limit cartels through stronger enforcement of anti-trust legislation. However, lacking a well-capitalized banking sector that could credibly fill capital demand for industrial investments, centralized modes of governance were retained in the financial and corporate governance domains as a means of shaping corporate strategy in ways thought to encourage industrial modernization.

After intermittently employing credit restrictions in the 1950s and 1960s, an encompassing system of such restrictions (*encadrement du crédit*) had been introduced in 1972. Credit restrictions were designed to help governments directly influence how much money banks could lend to firms and households and aimed both to achieve structural reform and to contain inflation (Zysman 1983). By allowing governments to decouple the lending rates of industrial and non-industrial borrowers and determine which firms and how much subsidized capital they would get, credit restrictions allowed governments to exercise direct influence over corporate strategy as well as influence the composition of industry more broadly. With a limited number of parties involved and constrained by rules set by the government, the system of credit restrictions entailed relatively low contracting costs and promised high levels of cooperative adaptation within the private sector (Cohen, Galbraith, and Zysman 1982, 72).

Notwithstanding the advantages of a centralized model of credit allocation for some firms (especially export-oriented ones that were privileged), the system of credit restrictions also had negative feedback effects that prevented the sought after shift in product market strategies within the advanced manufacturing sector. By primarily directing funds to existing large firms, the financial system reinforced corporate strategies that sought to exploit existing comparative advantages in mass markets at the expense of greater diversification. Credit restrictions also stymied the expansion of the financial sector by containing competition among banks and limiting their ability to raise more capital. This in turn made manufacturing firms more dependent on increasing their own profits and on gaining access to capital supplied by government programs. Increasing profits was a significant challenge in a period characterized by depressed international demand. Meanwhile, reliance on direct government support and protection proved itself problematic because the willingness of governments to direct resources to industries of the future gradually waned.

Although a commitment to budget austerity placed limits on the support the Barre government was willing to extend to industry, growing levels of unemployment made it less prone to redirect support from failing industries to those targeted for excellence. As firm closings grew significantly in the latter half of the 1970s, the Barre government directed support to less competitive firms to stem rising unemployment.[7] In this context, the early version of the national champion strategy had unintended negative consequences and served in part to undermine new structural reform initiatives. The former's focus on establishing single competitive firms, including in basic and less competitive industries, meant that when a large plant was closed the government faced high political costs given that such plants often affected large regions of the country in adverse fashion (Berger 1981). By extending support to firms that were losing competitiveness, the Barre government thus both undermined the very signals that were designed to promote market-discipline and reduced the resources available to future-oriented industries that lacked adequate access to capital (e.g., telecommunications, computers, aeronautics).

In addition, by rationing credit to the small- and medium-sized enterprise sector, credit restrictions reduced the prospect that firms would adopt complementary product market strategies and smaller firms remained detached from the structural reforms championed by the government. Efforts to improve the competitiveness of small- and medium-sized firms by actively encouraging their incorporation into larger conglomerates also had negative feedback effects because the liabilities that characterized the weaker part of industry were often diffused throughout the new entities. For example, wages tended to rise to the level found in firms with the highest remuneration and managerial hierarchies were left intact rather than restructured (Berger 1981, 229). Consequently, rather than leading to the rationalization of industry or enhancing the competitiveness of both large and smaller firms, the reform strategy of the Barre program reinforced the structure that had characterized French industry for decades.

The foreign economic policy choices of the Conservative governments reduced the incentives of firms to make major investments in plants and people. Firms' decisions to make such investments and adopt new product market strategies are heavily influenced by the nature of demand for their products and by the macroeconomic environment. Both these dimensions were characterized by significant uncertainty throughout the 1970s. International economic crises depressed external demand and Conservative governments were reluctant to support greater levels of trade liberalization for fears that such initiatives would further erode the competitiveness of French firms. At the same time, persistent balance of payments problems placed major constraints on the ability of the government to boost domestic demand. The uncertainty surrounding demand for advanced manufacturing goods significantly tamed the incentives of the country's large firms to shift corporate strategy in ways that entailed major new investments. Because this meant that those firms that were to be the leaders of reform could not credibly commit to significant modernization, the institutional elements of structural reform were self-undermining.

Macroeconomic strategy in the 1970s further contributed to undermining the credibility of firms' commitments to the structural reform agenda that governments promoted. The international fixed exchange rate regime that had been a major anchor in the post-war period ended in 1971. Efforts were made to stabilize the franc and reduce inflation through domestic and international programs. At the domestic level, credit restrictions along with price freezes and incomes policy were the key tools, but recourse to these proved ineffective over the long term. The economy was persistently "overshooting" and the currency's value moved beyond that which would help it restore balance in trade (Loriaux 1991). Periodic devaluations were employed as a means of reducing the value of the franc and to restore balance to foreign trade and external payments. Though this practice had positive effects on exports in the short-term, it had negative long-term consequences for the economic reforms of Conservative governments. In addition to increasing the cost of imports and causing a rise in inflation, devaluations reduced the incentives of large firms to make long-term investments as their market shares were protected without the need to make significant new capital investments to upgrade their production lines.

To bring greater stability in the exchange rate, France had been engaged in extensive negotiations with other European economies over deeper levels of monetary cooperation since the late 1960s. It had supported a set of floating exchange rate arrangements that tied the franc to a basket of European currencies. However, with substantially greater levels of inflation than its primary trading partner Germany, governments struggled to remain within the parameters that had been agreed and were twice forced out of a floating exchange rate arrangement (Frieden 2001). Only toward the end of the decade, when macroeconomic performance worsened considerably, did the Barre government endorse proposals for a new multilateral monetary regime that limited national discretion when it accepted German preconditions for a new system of monetary cooperation, the European Monetary System (EMS). Described by President Giscard d'Estaing as a "zone of stability," EMS would "stabil[ize] prices for half France's foreign trade . . . [and] be a factor of confidence and encouragement to invest" (quoted in Lorioux 1991, 253). However, by the time the EMS was established in 1979, unemployment and plant closures had reached post-war records. The manufacturing firms that had been targeted for modernization had recorded only modest progress toward establishing viable product market strategies in new high value-added segments of industrial production. Moreover, progress had come with other significant costs, including a large public deficit and limited structural reform in the country's small- and medium-sized enterprise sector (Berger 1981).

The Barre government confronted a new international economic environment characterized by significant instability. However, the failure of the domestic structural reform agenda cannot be attributed to international economic crises alone. Throughout the 1970s, governments had persisted in their emphasis on economic concentration and failed to resolve internal contradictions in their reform plans, weakening the incentives of large as well as smaller manufacturing companies to redirect their product market strategies. Resources devoted to helping large manufacturing firms to modernize and boost their competitiveness were insufficient and firms operated in an institutional environment characterized by pervasive uncertainty about the long-term benefits of major capital investments. Amplified by a foreign economic policy that protected French firms from international competition and thus did not impose any significant costs on firms that resisted modernization, domestic reforms created a situation in which the commitments of the pivotal advanced manufacturing sector to the structural reform strategy of Conservative governments lacked credibility.

Failed Specialization

The Barre program proved deeply unpopular and in 1981 led to the first major electoral victory for the Socialist Party since the 1950s. Under the banner of "rupture" to underscore its commitment to rolling back the reforms of its Conservative predecessors, the new government of President François Mitterrand introduced an ambitious and comprehensive reform program that included changes in the financial, corporate governance, innovation, and industrial relations domains. Public authority in economic management was significantly expanded and greater levels of economic concentration were promoted while market-based signals and allocation mechanisms were tamed. Keeping with this enhanced version of the post-war model of centralized governance, the government reduced its reliance on old institutions of planning and instead expanded the financial instruments and regulatory functions of key ministries (Hall 1986, 207–214). Yet—despite strong legacies of such designs, great popular enthusiasm, and weak opposition—the Socialists' strategy for economic modernization proved short-lived and was abandoned after two years.

Rather than promoting specialized firms and niche-oriented product market strategies like its predecessor, the structural reform agenda of the Socialist government was less selective in which firms would receive state support and favored the creation of large vertically integrated production chains (*filières*). The creation of large companies through orchestrated mergers was prioritized to strengthen the reach of vertical integration and limit inter-firm competition. Publicly subsidized credit and direct aid grew as a means of encouraging particular product market strategies, and significant resources were devoted to restoring the competitiveness of troubled companies with the expectation that an infusion of new technologies would return these to profitability and growth (Ministere de la Recherche et de l'Industrie 1982). The underlying premise of this strategy was that a vertically integrated industrial landscape would help establish a tightly coupled yet diversified industry that would be well suited for acquiring competitive advantages in the advanced and high-tech manufacturing sectors.

The Socialist government expected its reform strategy to produce lasting shifts in corporate behavior across the board without having to work closely with the business community or incorporate representatives of industry and employers in structures of governance. It calculated that greater levels of economic concentration and state ownership would speed up the pace of modernization and garner support within the corporate sector through new infusions of capital and aggressive public sector support for research and development. Key to its structural reform strategy was a large nationalization program that significantly shifted the ownership structure of financial and manufacturing firms to the public sector. Two large financial holding companies and thirty-six banks were nationalized and gave the government great influence over the financial industry through its control of 90 percent of bank deposits and 85 percent of existing loans (BIRP 1983, 119). In addition, the government nationalized five major industrial groups, acquired major ownership stakes in a large number of manufacturing companies, and fully owned thirteen of the twenty largest companies (O'Sullivan 2005, 357). It also actively promoted the merger of firms into larger units and encouraged joint ventures between French and foreign companies as a means of enhancing access to new technologies. Within two years, the state had increased its ownership from 17 percent to 29 percent of industrial turnover, from 44 percent to 52 percent of industrial investment in large companies, and had raised the share of state-owned companies' exports from 12 percent to 32 percent. In the process, it became responsible for one-third of industrial investment and one-fifth of both industrial value-added and employment (BIRP 1983, 46; Tuppen 1988, 102).

Although the Socialist government saw its structural reform agenda as an internally coherent program that would modernize French firms and restore equilibrium in balance of payments, its strategy was self-undermining and retarded the expected shift in corporate strategy. In addition to being expensive and thereby greatly expanding public debt, the financial burden of nationalization grew as the majority of nationalized firms ran record deficits (Tuppen 1988, 107). Relying heavily on government sponsored loans, these and other large companies cited high levels of indebtedness as the primary reason for their low investments (BIRP 1983). The profitability squeeze was further exacerbated by the government's macroeconomic policy. As the reflationary macroeconomic policy reduced unemployment and brought modest growth, the costs of production grew and levels of inflation surpassed the OECD average (Hall 1987). Growth in budget and trade deficits had negative feedbacks effects for they limited the ability of the government to continue its support for the firms at the center of the new reform strategy. Moreover, by retaining credit ceilings and prioritizing export-oriented firms, the access to credit for firms confronting the most difficult challenge—small- and medium-sized firms and import-competing ones—was circumscribed. This further constrained the ability of large firms to restore competitiveness in key segments of the integrated production chains championed by the Socialists.

The foreign economic strategy of the Socialists reinforced patterns of adjustment within the corporate sector that stymied its modernization. They saw international market liberalization as a threat to their ambitious reform programs, sought to protect key industries, and continued the strategy of their predecessor of expanding bilateral deals with foreign, often non-European, governments for large long-term and protected public procurement contracts (Levy 1999, 36). The share of national exports to Europe declined and reached a level not seen for over two decades when the Socialists took office (Adams 1989, 178).[8] This development reinforced product market strategies among the country's large export-oriented firms that rested on exploiting existing technologies rather than significantly expanding commitments to investments that would bring greater technological sophistication and innovation potential. At the same time, rationing capital to small- and medium-sized firms and focusing on integrating these into domestic production chains rather encouraging exports also stalled structural reform in the country's smaller firms.

By early 1983, a consensus had emerged within government circles that the enhanced centralization agenda was unsustainable. The very nationalized firms that were to be the anchor for a renewed and more competitive industrial sector were highly indebted, often unprofitable, their rates of investment in decline, and no significant inroads had been made in new markets. With a rapidly deteriorating balance of payments, poor industrial performance, and heavy pressure on the French currency, the Mitterrand government reversed course already two years after taking office and embarked on an economic strategy very different from that which it had attempted to implement.

Steps toward Decentralized Governance

The economic strategy employed by the Socialist government after 1983 stood in stark contrast to previous decades and served as the basic model also for Conservative governments that followed. The proximate cause of the Socialists' volte-face in economic management was persistent difficulties in restoring equilibrium to the balance of payments. However, external constraints predetermined neither the government's macroeconomic response nor the character or outcome of reforms in other domains. Alongside a major shift in macroeconomic strategy designed to contain inflation and ensure a stable and strong currency, a set of radical reforms was introduced in several major domains of the economy. The emphasis on economic centralization was radically reduced, capital and product markets liberalized, direct and subsidized support to firms largely discontinued, and public ownership of industry and banks steadily diminished through a wave of privatization programs that began mid-decade (Zaharidis 1995; Hall 1996). Finally, in a shift with significant consequences for the trajectory of domestic reforms, governments after 1983 fundamentally reoriented France's foreign economic policy and how they resolved the design problem.

In dismantling institutions of centralized governance, French governments faced the choice of what type of decentralized system should take the place of the former. In basic terms, this was a question of whether the liberal or coordinated models of decentralized governance should be privileged. Functional replacements were needed for the role governments had played within the financial, industrial relations, and innovation systems. Privatization also meant determining how to reform the insider-model of corporate governance that had characterized France since the end of the war. Both within the two main political parties and to a significant extent within the business community, there was great skepticism over the solutions introduced in Britain after 1979 and instead broad support for the type of designs found in Germany.

Designs associated with the coordinated market economy were thought to be best suited for fostering a shift toward technologically sophisticated and higher value-added product markets within large firms and also to offer better prospects for establishing a competitive sector of small- and medium-sized firms (Schmidt 1996; Levy 1999; see also Albert 1993). A key reason for these calculations was that institutions of non-market coordination associated with the coordinated model more effectively resolved coordination problems within the business community, especially within sectors where the competitive advantage of firms were closely tied to highly specific relational investments. As the system of credit restrictions was dismantled and capital markets liberalized, new institutions for non-market coordination were attractive to governments, which looked for ways to align the interests of a growing sector of private financial and manufacturing firms. Similarly, the multiplicity of local, regional, and associational forms of governance that had historically created a dynamic sector of small- and medium-sized firms in Germany was seen as an attractive solution to how direct government assistance and control could be reduced without risking a proliferation of coordination failures within the advanced manufacturing sector (Levy 1999). Though frequent references were made to French exceptionalism, it was not the past that was the primary reference point, but designs associated with the German and Japanese versions of the coordinated market economy that had acquired that status (e.g., Albert 1993).

Although far from identical to models found abroad, designs bearing the imprint of coordinated market economies were apparent in key domains. A range of initiatives designed to foster closer relations between banks and manufacturing firms were introduced as governments dismantled the system of credit restrictions and significantly reduced financial intermediation by public authorities from 75 percent to 40 percent of total financing (de Boissieu and Duprat 1990, 54). Key to this was the creation of a system of cross-shareholdings designed to establish a "hard-core" (*noyaux durs*) of privileged owners that would foster mutual interests between the largest manufacturing and financial firms. Introduced under the conservative leadership of Jacques Chirac (1986–1988), the institutional innovations surrounding the hard-cores were complemented with constraints on the market for corporate control designed to enable major owners to combat hostile takeovers as international investors gained greater access to French markets (Schmidt 1996).

French governments also introduced new arrangements in the innovation and industrial relations domains that had traits familiar from the German system. Political authority was decentralized to regional and local levels, public research facilities were supported, and new partnerships among public bodies, banks, and small- and medium-sized enterprises were championed. A combination of political decentralization and the promotion of institutions for non-market coordination at the regional and local levels represented a marked shift in the basic structure of the innovation system (Levy 1999). Efforts to create regional agglomeration economies gained importance and direct subsidies to firms declined relative to support for research institutes. Decentralization was also a major theme in the reforms to the country's industrial relations system and had begun already in 1982. To reduce active intervention by governments in matters of wage-setting and employment conditions, the Socialist government stressed the expansion of institutions for employee representation. These were designed to aid in overcoming the fragmented nature of unions and make possible greater input from employees in the production process. Though its ideas for greater self-governance in the workplace (*autogestion*) had a tradition in French socialist thinking, the organizational principles promoted by the government had clear parallels to those that characterized the German economy (Howell 1992).

The extensive scope and complementary nature of reforms after 1983 helped resolve some of the internal contradictions that had characterized institutional reforms in the 1970s. But domestic reforms were not in themselves sufficient to overcome two of the major issues that had undermined earlier reform programs, namely uncertainties in the macroeconomic environment and limited outlets for French goods. In a major departure from the post-war era when monetary policy had represented a flexible instrument used to restore balance of payments and boost the export competitiveness of industry, the Socialist government committed itself to remaining inside the EMS while the franc was under heavy pressure in 1983. This decision came with the political costs of budget austerity and rising unemployment, but also had adaptation benefits to the business sector as it was reassured that the government was committed to containing inflation and maintaining stability in the exchange rate with Germany. Though French views on the specific nature of monetary cooperation varied from Germany, the reversal in its macroeconomic policy represented a significant convergence both on the domestic and multilateral priorities of the latter (Boltho 1996).

A policy of budget austerity and trade liberalization spelled a decline in long-term public procurement contracts and enhanced the importance of gaining access to new markets for French producers. In contrast to earlier periods when exposure to international competition was deemed counterproductive and a liability, closure and protection were now seen as more costly than greater openness and brought support for international market liberalization within the EEC and the construction of the internal market (Adams 1995). The decision to support the internal market program had several consequences for corporate strategy with significant implications for domestic reforms. New multilateral rules that entailed restrictions on direct domestic support to industry enhanced the costs of inaction to firms and gave these strong incentives to undertake major rationalizations on their own.[9] At the same time, the prospect of larger markets abroad was a fillip to the country's export-oriented firms, which now could target more specialized product markets with greater confidence.

Despite the apparent benefits of creating the internal market, there were also significant concerns within government and business circles about its consequences. Fears existed that French firms would be disadvantaged with greater market liberalization because of higher social costs than key competitors. To allay fears that such developments would create large maladaptation costs to firms and that voters would lose valuable social protections, French governments joined Germany and supported a stronger social dimension to the internal market project (Springer 1992).

Multilateral agreements in the social domain fell far short of the type of harmonized legislation that French governments had advocated in the past. But the emphasis on mutual recognition in national regulatory standards that the internal market entailed gave governments great discretion in determining the structure of domestic designs. It also reassured domestic constituencies with investments in institutions of social protection that pervasive races to the bottom would not occur within Europe. Finally, Europe's multilateral social dimension entailed a commitment to common minimum standards, which served to reduce the maladaptation costs that French firms attached to operating under national rules when firms elsewhere faced lower social standards.

The French government also formed a coalition with Germany to protect national constraints on the market for corporate control. Though less concerned about the particulars of the European Company Statute than were German governments (see chapter 6), French governments and the business community shared German concerns about the potential adaptation losses associated with a proposed Takeover

Directive (CNPF 1990). Committed to protecting strategically important firms in the hard-cores from hostile takeovers, French governments opposed proposals that would reduce national discretion in establishing constraints on the market for corporate control. The proposed directive was eventually shelved and French governments and the business sector avoided the adaptation losses associated with that initiative.

During a decade after 1983, French governments engaged in persistent pattern of institutional innovation that gave greater authority to firms in how these should adapt to new market conditions (Commissariat Général du Plan 1992). The direction and nature of these reforms met with broad support within the business community. But governments remained key in shaping the institutional environment for firms and shifts in the former's macro and microeconomic policies had a mutually reinforcing relationship that improved balance sheets and significantly enhanced firms' incentives to make long-term capital investments. This trend was facilitated in the short-term by the creation of an equity market and the establishment of blockholding arrangements that reduced firms' reliance on debt financing and by a stable and strong currency, as well as access to new markets. Though the business sector attributed improved performance to the introduction of decentralized institutions of economic governance and new multilateral commitments, several of the new domestic designs would turn out not to be sustainable for very long. Paradoxically, the new multilateral institutions that were integral in facilitating the shift from a centralized system of governance to a decentralized one in the latter part of the 1980s would eventually undermine features of that system.

Recombination and the Stability of Hybrid Governance

Like most of Europe, France was engaged in heated debates during the 1990s and 2000s about the nature of economic governance. These debates took place against a backdrop of high unemployment and extended period of sluggish growth, though in a context where the productivity and profitability of French companies had significantly improved (OECD 1999). The intensity of the debate was fueled by the expected consequences of greater international market integration that the internal market precipitated, in particular by fears over hostile takeovers of France's largest firms and a decline in social protection. Finally, discussions about the form of economic institutions were closely tied up with how best to respond to the IT-revolution. Neither the traditional structures of economic governance in France nor those introduced in the latter half of the 1980s were thought to be well-suited for making major inroads in the IT-sector (Hancké 2002; Trumbull 2004). To facilitate growth in the latter sector, both the French government and the business community moved from a focus on designs associated with the coordinated market economy to promoting institutions closely related to the liberal market economy in the financial and corporate governance domains (e.g., Goyer 2001; Schmidt 2003).

Notwithstanding the very heated nature of the debate over the form of capitalism during the 1990s and 2000s, there was a great deal of consensus among Socialist and Conservative governments about the lessons from earlier periods of industrial modernization. This consensus was particularly strong in matters of macroeconomic governance where the parties shared a view that reforms of the late 1980s had successfully resolved earlier and long-standing problems that had stymied structural change, including large budget deficits, chronic balance of payments problems, and high inflation. Maintaining a low-inflation environment and a strong and stable currency through deepened commitments to multilateral solutions were widely regarded to have been an integral part for the emergence of more competitive manufacturing and large financial services firms (Minc 2000a). The macroeconomic consensus thus spelled great continuity in the support for extending multilateral cooperation and informed France's endorsement of Economic and Monetary Union (EMU) in the early 1990s and later for the Stability and Growth Pact.[10]

The successful stabilization of the macroeconomic environment elevated the importance of reforms in other areas in governments' efforts to modernize industry. The general direction of reform was toward greater levels of decentralization, but the specific nature of reforms varied across four areas of economic governance. The coordinated market economy designs that had been promoted within the financial and corporate governance domains after 1983 were gradually transformed into closer facsimiles of those found in liberal market economies. By contrast, the innovation and industrial relations domains were characterized by greater continuity in the mode of governance. The aggregate result was that the French market economy emerged as a hybrid system of governance that combined legacies of government intervention and two diverse forms of decentralized governance. Although this hybrid market economy was by historical and cross-national standards internally less coherent, it became sustainable after governments secured support from a broad business coalition.

Switching Models of Decentralized Governance

Post-war structural reforms had consistently privileged the construction of large firms, and governments had relied extensively on financial intermediation and an insider model of corporate governance to shape company strategy. The introduction of blockholding arrangements in the form of the hard-cores in the late 1980s had aimed to substitute for the prior arrangements and sustain large conglomerates by fostering complementary interests between the financial and manufacturing sectors at a time when international competition was increasing significantly. Premised on informal networks within the context of large corporate conglomerates, the expectation was that firms would sustain their investments much longer than the legally mandated two years (Schmidt 1996, 158–159; O'Sullivan 2005, 358). However, by the latter half of the 1990s, pivotal firms in the hard-cores had reassessed the institutional advantages of the blockholding arrangements and divested themselves from major holdings. By 1998, the average ownership share in hard-cores listed on the major Paris market had declined by nearly 30 percent (Lorioux 2003, 116), and an outsider version of a decentralized system of corporate governance was emerging in place of the insider version that had been established a decade earlier.

The dissolution of the hard-cores was the outcome of a set of mutually reinforcing domestic and international trends that transformed corporate strategy and ultimately the institutional foundations of corporate governance. Reforms to securities markets originating in the 1980s were extended and along with the integration of global and European financial markets shifted the nature of company financing from heavy reliance on debt to a strong emphasis on equity in the course of the 1990s. Stock market capitalization as a share of GDP increased fivefold in the decade, a rate of growth that eclipsed that of other major industrialized countries, including Britain, Germany, and even the United States.[11] Though investments were primarily national in origin, a very significant expansion occurred in foreign investments that amounted to roughly 40 percent of the major Paris stock exchange in the early 2000s (Goyer 2006, 407). The internal market brought access to larger sums of foreign capital while the EMU regime facilitated lower transaction costs and risk premiums in international financial markets.

Together with greater international competition and the prospect of significant growth in new financial services and high-tech markets, these developments led firms heavily invested in the hard-cores to reassess the value of the status quo. Large financial firms and a growing number of manufacturing firms came to see the status quo as entailing high maladaptation costs and preferred arrangements that were more liberal in nature and that entailed fewer constraints on the market for corporate control. To these firms, maintaining the conglomerate structures that had been supported by the hard-cores entailed opportunity costs for they forced strongly performing parts to subsidize poorly performing ones (Goyer 2001; Clift 2007). In a context of intense competition and dividend demands by shareholders, the hard-cores become self-undermining as firms limited the reinvestment of profits in other parts of the hard-cores.

Greater stock valuations also meant that the value of shares invested in the hard-cores rose and made feasible a more targeted emphasis among financial services and innovation-intensive firms on developing their core competencies (Culpepper 2006; O'Sullivan 2005).[12] In short, in the new business environment that domestic and multilateral reforms had produced in the course of the early 1990s, the opportunity costs of maintaining a diversified corporate profile increased because it meant forgoing the chance of using resources to acquire companies with competencies that directly complemented a firm's core product markets. This was not a cost firms willingly accepted and, with no legal limits on their discretion, spurred large sales of shareholdings by strategically important firms alongside a major wave of mergers and acquisitions.[13]

By the late 1990s, the system of corporate governance had acquired characteristics of an outsider model in which ownership was highly dispersed and large equity markets replaced the emphasis on blockholding from a decade earlier. The median size of the largest voting block for listed French companies was now much closer to that found in Britain than that in Germany (Enriques and Volpin 2007, 119).[14] The increase in foreign ownership, principally by British and U.S. investors, contributed to significant changes in the norms guiding corporate behavior and reporting, to the extent that those associated with the liberal market economy were said to be "total" in France (Morin 2000, 37). Yet, despite great similarities with the liberal model, some important differences persisted. With the decline of the hard-cores, French governments invoked a tradition of company law that gave greater weight to the public interest as a means of retaining constraints on the market for corporate control (Clift 2007). Particular attention fell on mechanisms that could be used to protect French firms from hostile takeovers such as multiple voting shares and poison pills. These were opposed by the financial industry (AFG 2008), but they enjoyed extensive support within the manufacturing sector, which framed the potential end of such practices as a significant adaptation loss (AFEP-MEDEF 2003). Because it constituted a larger and more integral part of the government's reform agenda, the latter enjoyed the upper hand in the domestic arena. However, the ability of governments to sustain constraints on the market for corporate governance could not be guaranteed through domestic means alone.

The manner in which French governments resolved the design problem proved crucial in preserving distinct features to its system of corporate governance and limiting the wholesale convergence on a liberal model. Anchored in efforts to achieve the goals of an integrated capital market, the European Commission put forward a set of proposals over two decades that had potentially transformative consequences for national systems of corporate governance, including proposals for common takeover rules and corporate voting structures. In France, many features of these proposals were thought to entail large adaptation losses to big shareholders and potentially also to others with large investments in the country's social model (Hopt 2002; Clift 2009). Commission proposals were strongly opposed by French governments, which were vulnerable to charges that they were sanctioning a multilateral arrangement that would allow hostile takeovers to undermine conglomerate alliances.

French governments successfully defended several key constraints on the market for corporate takeover during negotiations over common EU rules. They managed to block a 1989 proposal for common takeover rules and to secure compromises to a 2004 follow-up proposal that protected the ability of companies among other things to seek alternative partners (called "white knights") in combating hostile takeovers (Callaghan and Höpner 2005). Commission proposals a year later that aimed to enforce an EU-wide one-share-one-vote principle directly targeted practices in France, described by officials as "protectionist" (McCreevy 2005). These proposals were vigorously opposed by the French government, which with the aid of Sweden and Spain, pushed the Commission to undertake a study of whether its practices in fact distorted the European market for corporate control. The Commission's report concluded that privileged voting structures like those used in France did not significantly affect the European market for corporate control and lead the one-share-one-vote proposal to be shelved (Commission of the European Communities 2007). In France, this outcome was welcomed by large manufacturing firms who had argued that European rules must ensure that the French system of double voting rights be "recognized and respected" (Pernod-Ricard 2006, 4).

The manner in which French governments resolved the design problem during the 1990s and 2000s in the financial and corporate governance domains enabled them to build strong support within both the financial services industry and among large manufacturing firms for a radical reform agenda. By more closely aligning national practice to the European norm in the financial domain, governments virtually eliminated the disadvantages that these sectors associated with earlier practice in France. This development was particularly welcome within the financial services industry, but also among large manufacturing firms that gained access to new forms of financing. Reforms to the corporate governance system similarly enjoyed strong support in the two sectors as national designs became more closely aligned to practices in liberal market economies. This development reduced the maladaptation costs that large firms in these sectors attached to maintaining older designs. However, to secure long-term support among large firms in the manufacturing sector that continued to attach significant value to preserving their conglomerate structure, governments had to assure firms that the design problem was resolved in ways that limited adaptation losses in some specific areas of corporate governance. They did so successfully by preventing proposed EU directives from limiting national discretion in matters governing defensive practices like poison pills and narrow reciprocity clauses in the case of hostile takeovers, as well as by retaining the right of French companies to employ privileged voting arrangements as a means of stabilizing long-term investments in conglomerates.

Extending and Entrenching Designs

The small size of the French IT sector and high levels of unemployment generated intense debates during the 1990s and 2000s about reforms to the country's innovation and industrial relations systems. Reforms in these areas were characterized by greater levels of decentralization and some features associated with liberal market economies. However, there remained a strong emphasis on the type of decentralized institutions of non-market coordination that had been promoted during the 1980s.

The post-war innovation system had been credited with establishing large competitive firms in the advanced manufacturing sector and to some extent in high-technology product markets. Yet it was considered ill-suited for the structural transformation that more knowledge-intensive production entailed (Minc 2000b).

Major elements of the old innovation system were framed as liabilities. That system was said to have fostered an environment of low risk taking that stymied growth of firms in radical innovation markets and to have privileged large enterprises at the expense of growth in the small- and medium-sized sector.[15] However, in facilitating a structural transformation of industry, French governments faced constraints in the type of assistance they could use to substitute for the reduction in public support. Most of these were due to multilateral agreements that prohibited direct assistance to firms. France's commitments to the internal market program, its acceptance of more active enforcement of European competition rules, and new World Trade Organization rules meant that governments could not award direct subsidies to select industries or employ overtly discriminatory public procurement policies (E. Cohen 1996). They had instead to rely on non-discriminatory aid programs when supporting economic modernization. As these were smaller and budget austerity imposed by governments seeking to meet the EMU convergence criteria limited the prospects of future funds even for such programs, changes to the innovation system entailed adaptation losses to the country's manufacturing firms that had benefited from the older system.

Constraints on government support for industry and greater levels of international competition increased the costs of inaction for large established firms in particular. These responded to the reduction in direct state support through a multifaceted strategy that reinforced a trend toward corporate strategies targeting firms' core competencies. Greater resources were devoted to investments in joint ventures, mergers, and acquisitions with foreign companies as a means of obtaining new technologies (Goyer 2003). French industry both attracted very high sums of foreign direct investment, as well as recorded significant investments in Britain and the United States as a means of incorporating technologies and practices that were slow to emerge domestically (Amable and Hancké 2001). At the same time, large firms restructured their relationship with small- and medium-sized enterprises.

As the more profitable firms with stronger links to foreign markets and responsible for about two-thirds of R&D spending, large companies exercised great leverage over smaller firms. Using a combination of strong-arm tactics and collaborative programs that forced the latter to rationalize and significantly upgrade their spending on R&D, large firms created a more tightly integrated production chain in the course of the 1990s and expanded the share of small- and medium-sized firms that served as suppliers (Hancké 2002). This was a significant development for it facilitated the emergence of a stronger and more competitive sector of small- and medium-sized firms, a development that reforms in earlier decades had largely failed to achieve.

The growth of the small- and medium-sized enterprise sector was also aided by new and dedicated government programs. Investments made in new education and training programs by public authorities were now designed to benefit a broader range of firms, including smaller ones and recent start-ups (Culpepper 2006). The type of regional and local institutions of non-market coordination that had been promoted in the late 1980s were extended and adapted to the knowledge-intensive industries (Crespy, Heraud, and Perry 2007). In addition, two sets of complementary programs were designed to compensate for adaptation losses associated with shifts in the nature of government support.

To reduce gaps in financing, governments introduced national programs that gave firms access to publicly funded risk capital through open competitions (Ministère de l'Industrie and Ministère de l'Économie 1995). Because these were not directly discriminatory and designed to be of a pre-competitive nature, they were not in violation of multilateral rules and effectively reduced adaptation losses. These programs were complemented by a shift in France's support for multilateral aid programs themselves. After a long history of calling for large European industrial policies designed to benefit its large firms and national champions, the period after the mid-1990s was marked by strong French support for European public institutions such as advanced research centers and new programs supporting smaller firms (Mustar and Larédo 2002). These initiatives were considered integral by the business community as a means of facilitating a quicker transition to more knowledge-intensive innovation (MEDEF 2002).

Governments and large firms also played key roles in shaping the trajectory of the industrial relations system in the 1990s and 2000s. There was broad partisan consensus and support within the business community for a significant decentralization of economic governance in this area. Based on reforms that began during the 1980s, the post-war industry-level collective bargaining system made way for one in which firm-level bargaining was the norm, where social partner autonomy was significantly expanded, and where much greater levels of flexibility existed in employment contracts (Lallement 2006; Howell 2009). But there were also initiatives that were greeted with intense hostility by the business community. The Auroux (1982) and Aubry laws (1998, 2000)—which extended company-level employee representation and included constraints on employment contracts—encountered the fiercest opposition of any economic reforms in the post-war period (Howell 1992; Woll 2006). Employers charged that reforms exacerbated already high maladaptation costs and would undermine efforts to establish new arrangements of decentralized coordination among employers and the French workforce (Seillière 2005). By the mid-2000s, however, changes in company strategy and government accommodations had produced the conditions under which designs central to these legislative packages had become self-enforcing without the repeal of the controversial innovations contained in the new laws.

The Auroux laws were the first major legislative reform package in the industrial relations area since the end of World War II. They entailed major changes to one-third of the labor code and aimed to create greater parity between employers and employees at the firm level through the construction of new forms of employee representation such as works councils and by establishing mandatory rounds of collective bargaining (Howell 1992). These reforms were strongly opposed by French employers who saw them as counterproductive to their goals of enhancing company autonomy (CNPF 1987). However, within a decade of their introduction, those very institutions were seen to have facilitated the transition from an industry-based collective bargaining system to a firm-based one (Coffineau 1993). With more intense international competition and demand for more specialized products, institutions of workplace representation had gradually became an asset to employers who sought to design firm-specific employment contracts in an environment of weak and fragmented unions.

Record levels of unemployment during the 1990s lessened opposition among employers to new institutions of workplace representation. These had gradually taken on micro-corporatist features familiar from coordinated market economies, and for both employers and employees new designs lent legitimacy to firm-specific arrangements outside the traditional channels of negotiating with unions (Howell 2009). New designs were attractive to employers and employees alike because with multiple unions active within single firms and corporate adjustment affecting these unions differently, joint and lasting agreements were more difficult to reach. More important, new forms of employee representation had became effective vehicles for implementing government-sponsored programs designed to reduce the burden of adjustment for firms, including early retirement and training schemes, and eventually also exceptions to constraints on working time (Amable and Hancké 2001; Levy 2005).

However, as illustrated by earlier periods with significant labor strife, rising unemployment by itself is not a sufficient condition for reducing demands for greater compensation. Critical to the equation that reduces demands for large wage increases are employees' expectations about the value of current levels of compensation over time. Here, the EMU regime played a crucial role for it reassured employees of governments' intentions of ensuring relative stability in the value of compensation. In the new institutional environment that EMU brought, the incentives for employees to demand higher wages and adopt conflictual bargaining strategies were reduced. At the same time, the value of new institutions of workplace representation increased both for these and for employers as they entailed opportunities for firm-specific solutions that would benefit a company's competitiveness (Amable and Hancké 2001). Paradoxically, by the mid-1990s, the Auroux laws that employers had said would foment class conflict and EMU, which employee organizations often lambasted with similar rhetoric, had contributed to less conflict within French enterprises. In this area, then, national reforms and multilateral designs had a complementary relationship and entailed adaptation benefits that enhanced the attractiveness of existing designs over those associated with liberal market economies.

More controversial than the Auroux laws were the Aubry laws, which included a mandate for a thirty-five-hour workweek for companies with more than twenty employees. Originally an initiative that had been aborted in the early 1980s, the Socialist government of Prime Minister Lionel Jospin made the reduction of working time a key part of its legislative agenda of social modernization (*loi de modernisa-*

tion sociale). It reasoned that a shortened workweek would reduce unemployment and shore up its political support during a period when corporate restructuring increased redundancy risks for employees. However, from the vantage point of employers, remarked the head of the French Business Confederation (MEDEF), the government's agenda was an "absurdity" (EIRO 1998). The business community held up the thirty-five-hour workweek as the key example of what it saw as the large maladaptation costs associated with national designs by comparison to those found in liberal market economies (Woll 2006).

The Socialist government sought to reduce maladaptation costs by crafting EU rules that would establish more similar national standards. As it held the presidency of the European Council in 2000, the Jospin government declared that the first of its main priorities was "reconciling modernization of the economy with strengthening of the 'European social model'" (French Presidency 2000). It proposed greater harmonization of national rules, including in matters governing working conditions. In addition to reducing maladaptation costs for employers, the government's multilateral initiative aimed to reassure unions and the broader public that the EU did not represent a threat to national forms of social insurance and protection. However, other governments saw French proposals as incompatible with the goals of the EU's Lisbon agenda that stressed greater flexibility in labor markets and privileged national discretion over greater harmonization. Because the proposal by the French government met with great hostility from other member-states (see Shelley 2000), the only realistic venue by which it and future governments could secure support for their domestic agendas was through national reforms that would reduce maladaptation costs.

Support within the business community, especially large firms, was crucial for the consolidation of the decentralization agenda in the industrial relations domain because it involved a reduction in the role of governments without a corresponding increase in the organizational capacity of employers and unions (Lallement 2006). In the wake of some modest changes by the Jospin government, Conservative governments after 2002 introduced a series of laws and new practices designed to broaden support within the business community, including exemptions from the original version of the thirty-five-hour workweek and state-supported tax incentives. These initiatives, along with a growing realization among firms that the Aubry laws had helped enhance labor productivity during the decade (Hayden 2006), reduced the maladaptation costs that employers had attached to original designs. Albeit without enthusiasm, incremental reforms had led employers to accept even controversial aspects of earlier reforms by the late 2000s and contributed to a self-enforcing decentralized system of industrial relations.

The Sustainable Hybrid

The mixture of radical and incremental reforms that characterized the French market economy in the 1990s and 2000s produced a hybrid system of governance. This system was both a departure from the centralized model of governance with which France is so commonly associated, as well as the type of decentralized model of economic governance that had been pursued in the latter part of the 1980s. Although the system was more similar to a liberal market economy in the financial and corporate governance domains than to its own post-war past, there was no complete convergence on the British model. For example, the relative importance of stock markets remained smaller in France and more constraints existed on the market for corporate control. Moreover, designs introduced in the innovation and industrial relations domains during the latter part of the 1980s that were more closely related to the coordinated market economies were consolidated during the 2000s.

Questions have been raised whether hybrid systems are inherently unstable (Hall and Soskice 2001a; Campbell and Pedersen 2007). The issue is whether economic groups that play the role of contractual pivots in one domain may confront high opportunity costs from incentive incompatible designs. French reforms in the 1990s and 2000s show that this is not always the case—if a process of recombination produces domain-specific institutional equilibria, then a hybrid system can be stable. Large manufacturing and financial firms had no significant investments in the designs from the period before the mid-1980s and declining attachments to those that came after 1983 due to shifts in the international economic and institutional environments. Thus, their commitments to radical reforms in the financial and corporate governance systems were motivationally credible during the 1990s and 2000s. By contrast, in the innovation domain where manufacturing firms had more significant investments, relative continuity prevailed in the designs of the late 1980s, though a multiplicity of new designs were introduced to compensate for the loss of direct government support. Finally, in the industrial relations domain where large firms had sought extensive reforms, governments were able to reduce maladaptation costs by facilitating a process of institutional conversion that expanded the discretionary authority of employers within the existing system of industrial relations.

France's institutional trajectory in this period was not the outcome of a large integrated reform agenda like that of early post-war governments. Rather it was a disjoint trajectory characterized by patterns of institutional recombination in which governments responded to changing international economic and institutional environments that gradually created the conditions for sustainable reforms in major economic domains. The manner in which governments resolved the design problem was significant in shaping this trajectory. The 1990s and 2000s were busy periods of multilateral institution-building, and French governments were active agents, if only sometimes successful, in promoting multilateral designs that would help consolidate domestic reforms.

France's commitments to the internal market had strong support within the business community (e.g., MEDEF 2006). Together with the EMU, the implementation of the internal market increased support within the financial sector and among many large manufacturing companies for targeted reforms at the domestic level. Although these sectors supported radical shifts in the financial and corporate governance systems that had characteristics familiar from liberal market economies, some of their reservations were eliminated only after governments successfully reduced adaptation losses by limiting the scope of multilateral rules in matters relating to constraints on the market for corporate control. In the case of the national innovation system where firms confronted greater adaptation losses, French governments compensated domestic firms for the loss of support these faced from new external constraints by promoting a major expansion of large non-discriminatory EU innovation programs devoted to new knowledge-intensive products. Finally, because governments were unsuccessful in limiting maladaptation costs to employers through greater levels of harmonization at the EU level, they pursued an incremental domestic reform agenda that gradually reduced such costs and helped consolidate controversial reforms.

Conclusion

The institutional architecture of French capitalism was radically altered in the post-war period with major consequences for the country's industrial structure. In the early post-war period, a centralized system of governance was consolidated that covered all major areas of economic governance. It contributed to transforming the economy from one composed of a diminutive industrial sector made up mainly of small companies into a big industrial economy in which a few large, advanced, and often publicly owned manufacturing firms were the economic engine. By the early twenty-first century, a second transformation had taken place. By this time economic management was much more decentralized and the economic structure had become one in which large private banks and manufacturing firms, along with a robust sector of small- and medium-sized companies were defining features.

Neither transformation was quick or inevitable; each transformation entailed ambitious institutional agendas that included major domestic reforms and shifts in France's multilateral commitments. Typically, the first transformation is explained with exclusive reference to national legacies of centralized governance while the second is understood as the combined consequence of economic globalization and legacies of earlier reforms. However, neither temporal nor domain-specific variations in the consolidation of national designs can be explained by reference to national legacies alone, nor as automatic consequences of greater exposure to international markets.

Both the conditions that enabled firms to credibly commit to product market strategies associated with the centralized governance agenda in the early post-war period and to the decentralized one in the 1990s were shaped by the manner in which French governments integrated national reforms with a set of multilateral designs. As the centralized model was put in place, domestic reform was closely linked to the construction of the European Coal and Steel Community, while the

EEC was key to consolidating, if only temporarily, the reform strategy of the 1960s. In the 1990s and 2000s, governments' commitments to the internal market program and EMU preceded the significant growth in economic globalization and were key to ensuring credible commitments by the business sector to the domestic decentralization agendas. Conversely, during the 1970s and early 1980s, as well as in the early 1990s in domains like corporate governance, the policy of French governments in multilateral settings, principally the EU, reinforced the self-undermining characteristics of domestic reforms and contributed to major shifts in the structure of the French market economy.

The findings presented in the chapter have implications for two common interpretations of economic governance in post-war France. A growing literature highlights the effort by French governments to replicate key features of their domestic reform agendas at the multilateral level in the early post-war period (e.g., Lynch 1997; Hitchcock 1998). The chapter adds to this literature by underscoring that the relationship between domestic reforms and European integration was, when viewed over a longer historical period, not a one-way street where French governments persistently succeeded in establishing those multilateral designs they thought best suited for domestic purposes. In many instances, French governments were unable to establish the type of multilateral institutions they preferred.[16] Moreover, multilateral constraints had in some cases long-term negative feedback effects that eventually forced governments to reform domestic designs integral to their structural reform strategies.

Notwithstanding some successes where French governments shaped the particular form of multilateralism, the chapter shows that they often failed to secure their preferred multilateral designs. Indeed, between the late 1950s and early 1990s, multilateral designs were closer to the minimalist solutions sought by French governments than to what may be understood as their maximalist preferences. From their unsuccessful efforts to harmonize social standards, establish European-level industrial policies with discriminatory features, impose restrictions on capital markets, and skew competition policy in ways that would foster domestic objectives, French governments were often unable to ensure that their preferred multilateral designs prevailed. These failures meant that external maladaptation costs were high for parts of the industrial sector and that the consolidation of domestic reforms became more difficult as that sector deepened its dependence on international commerce. Though French governments successfully resisted some specific multilateral designs after the early 1990s and were able to protect valued national institutions, that period was generally marked by a direction of reform in which domestic institutions were adapted to multilateral ones. This shift had political consequences for some governments who were accused of accepting multilateral designs detrimental to the interests of French citizens. Yet this shift also proved important to governments in securing a broad base of support within the business community for reforms during the transformative decades of the 1990s and 2000s.

The chapter also makes contributions to debates about the evolution of French capitalism that center around the role that historical legacies owing to an interventionist state tradition, a weakly organized business sector, and fragmented unions have for the consolidation of different forms of decentralized governance. That debate has centered on the role governments played in reforms during the 1980s that targeted designs associated with coordinated market economies and designs familiar from liberal market economies during the 1990s and 2000s (e.g., Levy 1999; Schmidt 2003; O'Sullivan 2005; Culpepper 2006). This chapter complements findings in this debate by showing that governments' foreign economic policies and multilateral strategies played key roles in shaping the nature and sequence of domestic reforms. Specifically, it finds that multilateral designs were key in sustaining reforms through the 1990s and 2000s that were associated with the coordinated market economy in the industrial relations and innovation domains, as well as in consolidating reforms to the financial and corporate governance domains during the 1990s and 2000s that had significant similarities with the liberal market economy.

The evolution of the French market economy has been impacted by the foreign economic policies of its governments. During a period lasting some six decades, the national economy developed from a largely closed system of governance to an open system in which the ability of governments to successfully implement their economic reform agendas was greatly influenced by how they mediated the domestic impact of the country's multilateral commitments. French governments both failed and succeeded in their efforts to mold multilateral designs in ways compatible with preferred national designs. The outcome was a national economic system in the 2000s that was, much like the European Union, better characterized as a hybrid than one that was a close facsimile of the paradigmatic models of advanced capitalism that French politicians and society have debated since 1950.

Chapter 6

Germany

*Stability and Redesign in a
Coordinated Market Economy*

The reconstruction of the German economy and its superlative performance in the decades after World War II have been widely attributed to the institutional foundations of its national economic system. A great deal of attention has been given to the domestic origins of a macroeconomic regime devoted to price stability and a set of social and regulatory institutions conducive to long-term contracting among economic groups in fostering a major expansion of the advanced manufacturing sector. The internal coherence of the economic model is regularly identified as a key factor in helping governments secure support from a broad business coalition for the structural reforms that established the country as one of the most successful post-war industrial economies (e.g., Katzenstein 1987; Streeck 1992; Hall and Soskice 2001b; Hall and Gingerich 2009).

Although domestic institutions were the foundation on which structural reform was achieved, neither the early consolidation of the designs giving that model its internal coherence nor the factors that contributed to greater levels of coherence during the 1970s and 1980s were the product of national action alone. Constitutionally constrained in their ability to stimulate demand through macroeconomic means, establishing the conditions under which disparate parts of the business community could credibly commit to capital-intensive investment strategies hinged on the implementation of an open economy strategy. Specifically, it depended on a foreign economic policy that stabilized firms' long-term expectation with respect to their access and exposure to international markets. However, assurances to the corporate sector about the benefits of adopting capital-intensive product market strategies could not be provided simply through a combination of a unilateral open trade policy and high international demand. It required a set of international agreements that assured German firms of their long-term access to foreign markets and that regulated terms of competition, including what discretion German governments had in shaping the national business environment.

Unlike Europe's other large economies, German governments sought early on in the post-war years to provide firms with assurances about their access to international markets by supporting an encompassing set of multilateral institutions that protected free trade. Frequently presented as a means to gaining political legitimacy following the war, Germany's support for multilateral designs was neither indiscriminate, nor merely oriented toward accommodating the wishes of the Allied powers. In matters pertaining to the economy, Germany's support was informed by a distinct institutional rationale that promoted forms of multilateralism that would reinforce the domestic strategy of economic reconstruction. This institutional rationale led German governments to often promote more ambitious and less discriminatory arrangements than those sought by the Allied powers and to oppose initiatives they thought would undermine key features of domestic structural reforms. Though often forced to compromise with other states, German governments successfully secured multilateral institutions that allowed them to resolve the design problem during the 1950s and 1960s in ways that created a broad business coalition, which helped sustain ambitious agendas of structural reform.

Innovations in the multilateral domain championed by German governments were also central to how the business community responded to the international economic crisis of the 1970s and facilitated a trajectory of institutional specialization in which the internal coherence of the post-war model increased during the following decade. With a strong emphasis on European solutions, German governments secured new multilateral designs in the monetary and trade domains that increased firms' incentives to maintain product market strategies that exploited the institutional advantages of the post-war model. Governments also negotiated a set of multilateral institutions that reduced the prospect that domestic designs would be undermined by statutory authorities vested in international organizations or through regulatory races to the bottom. This enabled German governments to reinforce the post-war model during a period when most other European governments were undertaking radical reforms in their national systems of governance.

By contrast to the earlier periods, German governments were less successful in the 1990s and 2000s in resolving the design problem in ways that sustained the post-war business coalition. The very institutions that had been credited for Germany's *Wirtschaftswunder* (economic miracle) were now identified as the primary reasons for Germany being a "wirtschafts-blunder" and for being poorly equipped to make a transition to knowledge-intensive and high-technology product markets (Hall and Soskice 2001b; Sinn 2003).[1] Moreover, rather than designs that contributed to stability in the German model, multilateral institutions associated with the European Union were now widely seen to be undermining the internal coherence of that model and to be fostering a gradual move toward the liberal market economy (e.g., Streeck 1997; Höpner and Schäfer 2010).

The effects of greater levels of international market integration owing to economic globalization and the internal market program of the European Union for domestic reforms created unprecedented divisions within the business community. But the aggregate trajectory of the coordinated market economy was not one of wholesale collapse, much less systemic convergence on the liberal model. Instead, it was a trajectory of institutional recombination in which the scope of reform varied across major areas of economic governance. Fundamental reforms were successfully implemented in most aspects of the financial and corporate governance areas, but there were also some notable continuities in these areas and especially in the industrial relations and innovation systems.

Rather than uniformly undermining national institutions associated with the post-war model, multilateral designs related to the EU served both to facilitate the consolidation of radical reforms in targeted areas and frequently aided governments in preventing more far-reaching reforms in areas where they sought to protect domestic designs. The process of institutional recombination created a domestic system that was internally less coherent by the late 2000s than had been the case during most of the post-war period. Yet, this system was more stable than widely predicted a decade earlier when many speculated about the full unraveling of post-war designs (e.g., Giersch, Paqué and Schmiedling 1992; Hall and Soskice 2001b). The hybrid system became stable because it facilitated continued strength in the traditional product markets of German industry as well as inroads in high-technology markets where it struggled in the 1990s.

Table 6.1 summarizes the direction, scope, and dominant features of reforms to the institutional architecture of the German economy after 1950. The following pages analyze how German governments managed the process of reforming key features of that architecture, how they built support within the business community, and how successful they were in creating the conditions under which different parts of that community adopted complementary product market strategies during periods of structural reform.

Consolidating the Coordinated Market Economy

German industry had suffered extensive damage during the war, but large parts remained intact and there was a significant backlog of technological innovation that could be exploited for commercial purposes (Reich 1990; Eichengreen 2007). The principal question was thus not whether, but how the industrial capacity of firms could be harnessed. A broad consensus emerged among the Allied powers and the new German elite that peace and stability in Germany and Europe depended on a strong economy. However, what particular form that economy should take and what relationship it should have to international markets were subjects of much controversy.

In contrast to Britain and France who favored arrangements that mirrored their domestic agendas and encouraged the nationalization of major industries, the United States promoted a decentralized model of economic management in Germany. That model corresponded with the general preferences of the new German political elite who saw a decentralized system of economic governance as the best means of preventing a return to the *Wirtschaftsstaat* of the 1920s when business was

TABLE 6.1
Institutional developments in the German market economy

	1950–1973	1974–1991	1992–2008
Direction	Coordinated model (decentralized network based coordination)	Coordinated model (decentralized network based coordination; regulatory expansion)	Mixed: liberal and coordinated designs (greater market coordination)
Scope, mode, dominant features	Comprehensive	Selective	Comprehensive
	Finance Banking system rebuilt; public and private credit; limited risk capital	*Finance* Incremental: banking system stable; limited expansion of risk capital	*Finance* Radical: expansion of investment-oriented banks and equity markets; reform of public savings banks
	Corporate governance Codetermination; blockholding; significant constrains on market for corporate control	*Corporate governance* Incremental: expansion of codetermination and blockholding	*Corporate governance* Radical: major reductions in blockholding and constraints on market for corporate control; codetermination intact
	Industrial relations High autonomy for social partners; collective bargaining; stable employment contracts	*Industrial relations* Incremental: social partnership autonomy and employment contracts stable; some expansion in collective bargaining	*Industrial relations* Incremental: social partnership autonomy high; departures from collective bargaining; enhanced flexibility in employment contracts
	Innovation Limited subsidies to firms; cooperative relations between large and small firms; extensive support for public research	*Innovation* Incremental: closer relations between large and small firms; expansion of support for public research	*Innovation* Incremental: cooperative relations between large and small firms strong; expansion in public support for research
Aggregate outcome	Consolidation	Specialization	Consolidation (early 1990s) Recombination (stable hybrid after late 1990s)

heavily involved in the management of the economy. The model also provided a way to avoid the centralized model of governance that characterized the country during the era of National Socialism. Finally, the model favored by early post-war governments was presented as an alternative to the economic planning model of the Soviet Union and the German Democratic Republic and to strong versions of laissez faire liberalism (e.g., Nichols 1994).[2] Termed the social market economy (*soziale Marktwirtschaft*), the particular version of the coordinated economy model that was adopted was seen by its core architects as an "irenic" synthesis between a system of unfettered markets and one with high levels of coordination between the state and organized social groups (Müller-Armack 1948a).

Between the end of the war and the late 1950s, the social market economy went from a highly contested model to one enjoying broad support across the major political and economic cleavages in Germany. This outcome was not inevitable. In addition to attempts by some Allied powers to push the German economy in a different direction, the Conservative government that implemented post-war reforms faced heavy criticism from the Social Democratic opposition and had to overcome a set of serious economic crises in the 1950s. Also the German manufacturing industry, which was seen as the foundation for economic reconstruction, rejected central elements of the designs championed by the first post-war government. Yet, despite opposition and skepticism, the social market economy would go from a contested model in the late 1940s to one enjoying the support of both major political parties and an encompassing coalition of diverse business interests.[3] The process that created such broad support was one that entailed significant institutional reform at home as well as a major departure in the country's foreign economic policy, in particular its commitments to the institution of multilateralism.

Domestic Foundations

The architects of the social market economy introduced a comprehensive set of domestic reforms that aimed to ensure a stable macroeconomy, dynamic product market competition, and industrial specialization. A stable macroeconomy was a major priority because of experiences with high inflation in the 1930s that had devastated household savings, radicalized politics, and undermined the incentives for firms to make long-term investments in people and plant. The success of the social market economy, remarked Ludwig Erhard, its chief political patron, "*is inconceivable without a consistent policy of price stability*" (1957, 15). To avoid the politicization of monetary policy and provide a stable foundation for long-term investment, the central bank was insulated from political influence through a statute that gave it autonomy and a narrow mandate to ensure price stability.[4] This innovation placed significant constraints on the German government and prevented it from adopting the type of pro-growth macroeconomic strategies widely used in post-war Europe. However, it served as an effective mechanism in ensuring a propitious environment for long-term capital investment and was greeted favorably by the manufacturing industry (BDI 1958, 44).

Constitutional limits were also placed on political influence in the domain of competition policy. The collusion of large firms in pre-war Germany had given large business cartels great control over the industrial infrastructure of the economy, and they were deeply implicated in the armament industry. Limiting economic concentration, therefore, became a political priority both to the United States and to the champions of the social market economy. As the long-serving Minister of the Economy Ludwig Erhard (1949–1963) and his supporters argued, collusion among firms undermined competition with the effect of retarding the growth of small- and medium-sized enterprises and reducing firms' innovative capacity. Against the strong opposition of Germany's large industrial companies but with the support of the small- and medium-sized enterprise sector, Erhard pushed through the Law against Restraints on Competition (GWB) and established the Federal Cartel Office in 1957 (Berghahn 1985, 152–179).

The new competition regime placed significant constraints on the government's ability to undertake the type of structural reform strategy championed in Britain and France after the war. It could not create large national champions through nationalization programs, nor could it bring about company mergers in the same way that British and French authorities could. State-level governments would assume significant responsibilities, including in developing a public banking system to support industry, as well as in the promotion of human capital, research and development, and technology diffusion. But the primary responsibility of the federal government was to oversee and develop a set of broad framework regulations (*Rahmenbedingungen*). These were intended to protect product market competition and to ensure a strong and dynamic sector of small- and medium-sized companies (*Mittelstand*) alongside large firms.

A system stressing decentralized governance presents potential problems for economic reforms that aim to boost the growth and competitiveness of advanced manufacturing. Decentralized governance is often associated with extensive market and coordination failures, in particular in supply-side domains where cooperation among economic groups is crucial to ensuring long-term specific investments in people and plants. To overcome these problems and to build a broad coalition in support of the post-war model, German governments encouraged the creation of a dense system of institutions for non-market coordination and retained many pre-war designs that had been the product of extensive coordination among economic groups. The goal of the former, described in terms of a "formed society" (*formierte Gesellschaft*), was to boost the organizational capacity of social groups (Erhard [1965] 1988). In addition to creating many para-public organizations that entailed representation by economic groups, the formed society was promoted through the delegation of statutory authority to business associations and unions of functions held by public authorities in other countries (Katzenstein 1987).[5]

For a structural reform agenda centered on advanced manufacturing, high levels of social coordination offered several institutional advantages that shaped corporate strategy. The costs of social contracting were comparatively low and encouraged cooperative adaptation among economic groups, which in turn facilitated specialized long-term relational investments among diverse members of the business community, organized unions, and employees. Effective monitoring and enforcement functions vested within business associations also reduced the costs of complex contracting between firms and gave these strong incentives to develop relationally specific investments in each other and adopt complementary product market strategies. This helped the business sector develop integrated production and innovation chains that linked firms of all sizes. It also facilitated the resolution of collective action problems related to the diffusion of technology and the supply of human capital and long-term finance (Streeck 1992; Soskice 1997).

In implementing their reform program, governments restored and adapted many pre-war institutions to which German firms attached great value. Key among these were institutions that coordinated relations between banks and the manufacturing sector.[6] Dating to the nineteenth century, the financial system and its emphasis on universal banking assisted the manufacturing sector in gaining access to long-term capital with which to finance corporate strategies targeting capital-intensive production (Deeg 1999, 29–72; Fohlin 2007). This led Germany's commercial banks to acquire significant stakes in the success of large advanced manufacturing firms and to adopt product market strategies that were complementary with the long-term goals of the manufacturing sector. At the same time, a system of public sector banks was established that provided small- and medium-sized enterprises with access to long-term debt capital on highly favorable terms through public guarantees.[7] Given incentives by governments to direct long-term credit to the manufacturing sector, commercial and public sector banks became integral and committed partners in promoting growth in manufacturing firms of all sizes.[8]

Post-war governments also encouraged the establishment of a cooperative industrial relations system and extensive collective bargaining among organized employers and unions at the sectoral level. By delegating the responsibility of determining wages, working time, and many benefits to organized employers and unions and giving agreements among these groups legal force (*Tarifautonomie*), governments played a less direct role in Germany than in other European countries in determining wages and more generally in managing employment contracts. This system of relative autonomy for employers and unions gave the two sides mutual stakes in negotiating agreements that enhanced the long-term competitiveness of individual firms (Thelen 1991; 2001). Moreover, through the institution of collective bargaining and a norm whereby large export-oriented manufacturing sectors set targets for new wage contracts that were diffused to other sectors, the sector-based system contributed to moderate wage growth.

Complementing the cooperative wage determination system was a feature of corporate governance known as *Mitbestimmung*, or codetermination. Based in pre-war conceptions of how collective interests could be promoted, codetermination became a formal part after the war and gave employees representation in corporate boardrooms. Championed by members of the government and originally supported by employers as a means of co-opting unions and limiting the Allied powers' agenda of dismantling conglomerates in the coal, iron, and steel industries, employees were given equal representation in supervisory boards in these sectors. In other industries, employees were granted one-third of seats on supervisory boards under a 1952 law. Codetermination included employee representation on supervisory boards and works councils at the firm level and contributed to a cooperative relationship between employers and workers that reduced industrial strife and the need for direct government intervention during periods of structural reform. To employers who generally opposed initiatives in this area, codetermination entailed constraints, some of which in Wolfgang Streeck's (1992) words would have "productive" effects on company strategies targeting high value-added segments. Against the backdrop of constraints on easy layoffs in periods of declining demand, codetermination provided firms with an effective means of implementing productivity enhancing strategies in collaboration with unions, including upskilling of workers and even the gradual introduction of labor-replacing technologies.[9]

A second major feature of the post-war model of corporate governance was a dense system of networks held together by extensive cross-shareholdings and inter-locking directorates between banks and the manufacturing sector. Formalized through a two-tier board system dating to 1870 in which large shareholders enjoyed seats on supervisory boards, this arrangement promoted the formation of extensive blockholding arrangements, entailed modest protections for minority shareholder and major constraints on the market for corporate control. The German system thus represented a classic example of an insider model of corporate governance in which multiple stakeholders shaped corporate strategy and managerial autonomy was significantly constrained (La Porta et al. 2000; O'Sullivan 2000). Between the early 1960s and mid-1980s, non-financial firms held about 35 percent of shares in German companies (Edwards and Fischer 1994, 180–182). Though banks owned a much smaller share, they played an integral role in the network-coordinated system as guardians of proxy votes. By the early 1970s, banks held nearly 20 percent of the seats on supervisory boards in the manufacturing sector and controlled on average about 60 percent of votes at general meetings (Deubner 1984, 508).

Through its emphasis on network coordination, the corporate governance system offered several institutional advantages to German firms. The absence of threats of hostile takeovers gave firms strong incentives to make major investments in assets that had long-term returns, such as vocational training, research, and development. It also made it easier for firms to absorb the costs of restructuring during periods of lower demand without threats of imminent divestment. Stable coalitions among a firm's major stakeholders made it feasible for firms to target large market shares with small profit margins. Finally, the corporate governance system offered firms in distress greater access to long-term financing by giving banks enhanced influence in the management of the company through membership on the supervisory board (Höpner and Jackson 2001, 12).

The long-term sustainability of the broad business coalition that underpinned the post-war model depended on strong demand for the industrial products of the manufacturing sector. To manufacturing firms themselves, strong demand was essential to accepting compromises with unions and agreeing to relatively high contributions to social programs. For the financial sector, which in the early post-war period was heavily oriented toward domestic markets, the expansion of the manufacturing sector was critical for its own solvency and growth. Although domestic demand was strong in the early post-war period, limits on the ability of German governments to increase demand through the macroeconomic means employed by other Western European countries made the long-term success of its structural reform program heavily dependent on stability in external markets. For these reasons, the key architects of the social market economy attached particularly great importance to securing access to international markets and actively embraced the institution of multilateralism as a vehicle by which to reduce the uncertainties surrounding such markets.

The Multilateral Dimension

Both in the very early stages after the war and after Germany regained full sovereignty in 1955, international institutions and organizations played an integral role in helping governments secure broad support within the business community for their industrial strategies. The Marshall Plan enabled German firms to practice what Erhard (1954, 149) described as "investment nationalism" and to be relatively certain that domestic consumers would help clear the market for manufactured goods. Also crucial in the early post-war stages was the European Payments Union (EPU), which restored currency convertibility and enabled an expansion of international trade at a time when domestic demand by itself would have made long-term expansion unlikely (Eichengreen 1993). In addition, Erhard undertook a large number of trade missions designed to establish bilateral treaties that would give German firms access to overseas markets, in particular in Latin America and Asia (Neebe 2004, 233–240).[10]

Because the Marshall Plan and the EPU were temporary initiatives and bilateral treaties did not secure sufficiently large or stable markets, none of these arrangements represented the type of mechanisms that could ensure the long-term success of the domestic reconstruction project. Numerous bilateral trade agreements that existed among European countries after the war were also seen as potential obstacles to long-term growth by the German government for they entailed a great deal of uncertainty over the long-term prospects of non-discriminatory access to foreign markets. As a country lacking full sovereignty until 1955 and constrained in its ability to sign international treaties without the approval of the Allied powers, the architects of the social market economy stressed the importance of participating in the establishment of multilateral institutions at the global level.

Erhard and his supporters championed the principles of the Havana Charter and actively campaigned for free trade agreements that would establish a global order of open trade and capital markets (Neebe 2004). After the failure of the International Trade Organization, they saw the multilateral principles associated with the General Agreement on Tariffs and Trade (GATT) as potentially "provid[ing] a long-term and evidently solid contractual basis for trade, ensuring us of the chief advantages which would result from an extensive network of classical [i.e., bilateral] treaties" (Erhard 1954, 264–265). But GATT by itself was not thought to be sufficient to secure stability in external markets in the early post-war period, in particular as it lacked effective enforcement mechanisms in cases of overt discrimination and violations of the most favored nation principle. Creating an integrated European free trade order therefore gained importance, especially as intra-continental trade was expanding and the United States actively pushed Germany toward closer relations with its immediate neighbors.

Germany's support for European integration is often described as a political project by post-war governments to overcome the legacies of nationalism and military aggression during World War II (e.g., Markovits and Reich 1997; Banchoff 1999). Although the political imperative of regaining sovereignty was central in shaping its foreign policy, Germany's multilateral strategy was neither unconditionally nor indiscriminately in favor of European integration. For the supporters of the social market economy, considerations of political legitimacy were important, but not what motivated their preferences over the structure of international economic cooperation or their strategy in negotiations with other European states. Their strategy was explicitly informed by an institutional logic that generated support for initiatives that secured open trade and that resisted economic discrimination or the harmonization of national regulatory structures.

During the negotiations for the European Coal and Steel Community (ECSC) and the European Economic Community (EEC), a major cleavage existed within the government between Chancellor Adenauer and the Foreign Ministry, and the Ministry of Economics dominated by the key figures behind the social market economy. The former group favored reconciliation with France and willingly accepted a "small Europe" centered on the six countries that became the original members of the ECSC and EEC. The latter group preferred free trade agreements with larger numbers of members and reluctantly accepted organizations with limited membership as a step toward a larger and ideally global free trade order (Erhard 1957, 301; Küsters 1990; Brenke 1994).[11] The Adenauer side prevailed in determining which European organizations were established and which states became members, but the Erhard side exercised great influence in shaping the particular form that new multilateral economic institutions took.

For the architects of the social market economy, the fact of establishing multilateral institutions was as important as the form these took. With Adenauer primarily concerned with establishing the political foundations that would restore sovereignty, Erhard and his supporters concentrated on ensuring that European designs would take a form that would help consolidate domestic reforms. Erhard (1957, 301) described international cooperation in general as a matter that could be measured through its "quantity." But he also emphasized that European integration had to be understood in terms of the "quality" of its institutions. A major concern was to secure stable multilateral agreements that minimized adaptation losses to domestic constituencies to make the long-term sustainability of the social market economy a reality. For this reason, Erhard and his supporters stressed that European integration must grant member-states significant discretion in designing national institutions and underscored that "Europe is not a stew that can simply blend together all nations . . . Europe's value is a function of keeping its diversity alive without gambling away her unity" (Erhard 1966, 255). In promoting this type of arrangement, Erhard had a great deal of support within the manufacturing sector whose chief leader echoed the same sentiment: "[w]e can only accept [European] solutions that are congruous with the considerations, interests and responsibilities that relate to individual countries" (Berg 1960, 1).

The priority given to securing European designs that were compatible with domestic programs was evident in several areas to which the government attached great weight. During the EEC negotiations, the French government pushed for a set of provisions that would harmonize social policies. A plan for the *ex ante* harmonization of a broad set of social policies was presented that would lead to similar labor costs across member-states. To Erhard, the French proposal entailed the prospect of significant adaptation losses and represented a major threat to a foundational element of domestic reform, namely the constitutionally protected right of employers and employees to autonomously negotiate compensation. Rather than embracing a vehicle that would bring about a convergence in labor costs and national employment contracts, the Erhard coalition emphasized the importance of maintaining flexible conditions under which employers and unions could agree on the nature of compensation. French demands for harmonization were described as "illogical" and "spurious" by the Scientific Council at Erhard's Ministry, which encouraged the Foreign Ministry to ensure that the issue "as quickly as possible be removed from negotiations" (BMWi 1956). To the relief of the business community (BDI 1959), Erhard's position prevailed in negotiations with France and the Treaty of Rome entailed no strong mandates in matters relating to the social costs of production.

The government was also greatly concerned with maintaining the integrity of the domestic economic model by preventing activist and discriminatory industrial policies, including proposals for European-level instruments of economic planning and a multilateral competition statute it thought was incompatible with domestic reforms. Erhard had failed to prevent instruments of economic planning from informing the ECSC, but he was intensely committed to ensuring that other sectors not be governed by supranational authorities. His efforts to prevent economic planning from becoming a dominant feature of the EEC were successful, as were his efforts to shape the nature of competition policy in ways that did not undermine the domestic program. The Treaty of Rome, which established the basic principles of competition policy, endowed the European Commission with significant powers in regulating industrial subsidies, monopolies, and mergers. *Ex post*, these provisions were not "particularly constraining" on member-states as the Commission lacked the ability to prevent national authorities from awarding subsidies and monopoly and merger restrictions applied only at the European level (Moravcsik 1998, 149). However, before negotiations were concluded, the German government was deeply concerned about potential adaptation losses and about multilateral competition rules being incompatible with its domestic reform agenda.

Negotiations over the Treaty of Rome were taking place around the same time as the German government was pushing through the contentious Law against Restraints on Competition. Fearing that the European designs preferred by France would undermine the system of product market competition that was such a central pillar of the social market economy, Erhard sought multilateral rules that would constrain the ability of German firms to create large European conglomerates that could potentially lead such firms to circumvent national rules. The Federation of German Industry (BDI) made no secret that it opposed national restrictions, which it thought placed large firms—its chief constituency—at a competitive disadvantage vis-à-vis other European producers (e.g., BDI 1956, 16).

The Federation argued that restrictive national rules entailed maladaptation costs because these would force large firms to compete internationally under more restrictive conditions than their foreign competitors. However, reducing those maladaptation costs was not the primary concern of the German government. Rather, it was concerned with ensuring that it retained discretion in shaping national rules in ways that prevented potential adaptation losses for the small- and medium-sized enterprise sector. The final agreement on the EEC's competition rules did not limit the ability of national governments to award subsidies in practice. It did, however, retain discretion for German authorities in designing national merger and monopoly rules in ways that enabled them to build a dynamic sector of small- and medium-sized firms and thus sustain a key feature of their structural reform agenda.[12]

Sustainable Designs

Even with some early skepticism and strong opposition to key reforms by pivotal sectors of the business community, the German government had by the late 1950s secured support from a broad business coalition for an economic reform agenda centered around the designs of the social market economy. Though an exaggeration, the declaration by the head of the BDI that "the organization of the social market economy was from the beginning our own" (Berg 1959, 3) underscores that the most pivotal sector to Germany's reconstruction came to support the economic architecture that was put in place during the 1950s. Its support for that model was intimately linked to a foreign economic policy that stabilized firms' access to foreign markets and gave strong incentives to exploit the institutional advantages of the coordinated market economy. In particular, the prospect of steady access to international markets entailed large adaptation benefits and encouraged firms to establish close relations with banks and the Mittelstand for the purposes of sustaining large capital-intensive investments in plants and people.

But German governments also attached great weight to resolving the design problem in ways that avoided externally induced adaptation losses in crucial areas to their reform agenda, including rules governing competition, industrial support, and social compensation. Like the BDI, which insisted that the form of multilateralism "not only takes into account the autonomy of individual business decisions, but that also takes account of differences in the character of national economies" (quoted in Bührer 1992, 249), the government made it a priority to ensure that the structure of multilateral institutions was compatible with national reforms. In some cases, however, sustaining the type of broad business coalition on which its structural reforms would be successful meant not promoting the narrow interest of large firms, but to protect those of small- and medium-sized enterprises. In the case of competition rules, for example, limiting the potential adaptation losses for the Mittelstand was more important to governments for the sustainability of economic reforms than reducing the potential maladaptation costs for large firms. Because the latter costs were dwarfed by the broader adaptation benefits of how governments integrated national and multilateral designs, large firms' commitments to domestic reforms remained credible. At the same time, those of the Mittelstand were reinforced. In this manner, governments successfully established and broadened support within the business community and established the conditions under which the social market economy was consolidated.

The Politics of Institutional Specialization

European governments faced a very different economic situation during the 1970s and 1980s than during the Golden Age, including lower levels of growth, significant labor unrest, and great uncertainty in the international economic environment. In Germany, the prospect of sustained growth was reduced by the saturation of domestic demand in the major product markets of its manufacturing sector and by constitutional constraints on expansionary policies. Moreover, with instability in international currency markets, a major international energy crisis, and the emergence of new competitors in Germany's traditional markets, concerns were raised that the export-oriented growth strategy that had anchored domestic reforms was "reaching [its] limits" and would make the post-war model unsustainable (Kreile 1978, 292).

Governments elsewhere responded to similar challenges through fiscal expansion and significant innovations in several areas of economic governance, including radical changes in some cases. However, German governments adopted a reform strategy that stressed incremental adjustments to the post-war model.[13] They amended and extended the designs of previous decades and the internal coherence of the coordinated market economy model gradually increased, giving the country new monikers such as Modell Deutschland and Deutschland AG. Sustaining a trajectory of continuity, much less one of institutional specialization in which levels of internal coherence increased, required that a variety of industrial sectors adopted complementary product market strategies and framed domestic designs as superior to feasible alternatives. But new international market conditions and a set of controversial domestic reforms created distributional conflicts that exposed cleavages within the business community and threatened to weaken the broad-based business coalition on which governments had relied.

Particularly controversial were two sets of reforms to key pillars of the post-war model that were opposed by large manufacturing firms. In the early 1970s, a new set of constraints was introduced to the Law against the Restraint on Competition in the form of a new merger statute that exposed a cleavage within the manufacturing sector. Considered "the strictest in the world" (Gerber 1998, 327) and intended to benefit the small- and medium-sized enterprise sector, large companies argued that new rules constituted a "particularly difficult barrier" for structural reform and a hindrance to their ability of competing successfully with multinational companies in their traditional product markets (BDI 1971a, 1). The same sector also strongly opposed the extension of codetermination rights through two legislative acts and went as far as bringing their grievances to the Federal Constitutional Court. This conflict pitted large employers against unions and created a division between the two sides that had rarely been seen in the post-war period. As in the case of merger rules, large firms favored the status quo and argued that the expansion of post-war designs entailed maladaptation costs that would threaten their ability to adjust to new market conditions.

Yet, despite external challenges and great controversy over new government initiatives, the broad business coalition remained intact. Indeed, the ties between different sectors deepened in the course of the 1970s and 1980s. In both the case of large enterprises and the Mittelstand, firms responded to greater levels of competition by investing in machinery and skills that fostered increases in productivity and a move toward more specialized forms of production. Large firms moved to higher value-added goods by upgrading the quality and variety of goods to mitigate price competition and reduced demand in mass markets, and the Mittelstand expanded its reliance on such forms of production into mass markets (Kern and Schumann 1984; Streeck 1992). The result was the creation of a large number of beneficial alliances based on complementary product market strategies between large and smaller firms. Facilitated by dense forms of business organization at the local level and strong regional agglomeration economies, closer ties between the two sectors became apparent as larger firms continued to integrate smaller firms into their production and innovation chains to meet the challenges posed by competition from East Asia (Piore and Sabel 1984).

Though the relationship between unions and employers had become more contentious during the 1970s and 1980s, levels of cooperation between the two sides remained noticeably less conflictual than in other countries, especially Britain. Employers' concerns with specific designs of the industrial relations and corporate governance systems such as constraints on employment contracts and codetermination were considerable, but they did not produce a preference for a radical transformation of the larger systems associated with the post-war model. Concerned with maintaining autonomy in wage setting and avoiding new legislation in matters governing strikes, employers continued to frame the industrial relations system as an efficient means to cooperating with unions in implementing productivity enhancing practices and limiting wage growth (Thelen 2000; Wood 2001). Furthermore, because new constraints in the corporate governance and industrial relations domains encouraged firms to treat labor as a fixed cost and enhanced their incentives to collaborate with unions and work councils, large employers' commitment to the basic structure of the post-war model was also reinforced.

Finally, though not a matter of controversy for the private sector as much as for the public, the ties between the manufacturing sector and banks were also strengthened during the 1970s. With the prospect of growth elsewhere limited and government policies encouraging long-term lending to domestic enterprise, the institutions of cross shareholding and inter-locking directorates led commercial banks to increase their stakes in the manufacturing sector during a period of corporate restructuring in the 1970s. Indeed, it increased to such an extent that the government convened a commission designed to explore the role of the universal banking system and whether banks had acquired too large a role in shaping the corporate landscape. However, rather than framing such developments in negative terms, the report concluded that the extant financial and corporate governance systems were sound and constituted essential elements in helping firms enhance their international competitiveness (BMF 1979). Meanwhile, for large commercial banks and the manufacturing sector, the deepened alliance generated a shared stake in steady productivity and export growth within the latter.

The ability of German governments to resolve the distributional conflicts associated with domestic reforms and to ensure stability in the post-war model in this period has been attributed to the good "fortune" that there existed strong international demand for its manufactured goods (e.g., Kitschelt and Streeck 2003, 2–3). Such external demand may have been necessary to sustain a broad business coalition at home, but it was not a sufficient condition to ensuring the long-term viability of the post-war model. Nor was stability in external demand something that existed in the absence of actions by German governments.

In responding to the economic uncertainties that had become apparent, the business community emphasized that governments "must consider national measures in the context of the European framework" (BDI 1970, 41). In particular, with a structural reform agenda heavily oriented toward capital-intensive investments, governments had to reduce the uncertainties surrounding the value of the Deutsche mark and secure access to international markets on non-discriminatory terms that entailed the prospect of continued growth in exports. The former concern led them to support major multilateral innovations in matters governing exchange rates, while the latter concern generated attempts to revitalize GATT and eventually support for the European internal market program. Moreover, as multilateral trade initiatives took root, sustaining national designs integral to the post-war model meant that German governments had to actively protect national discretion in matters that directly affected the integrity of that model.

Macroeconomic Stability and Multilateral Innovations

A commitment to price stability was central to the institutional blueprint of the social market economy and also a necessary condition for convincing firms to make long-term investments of the sort that defined the structural reform agenda of German governments. The architects of the social market economy ensured the constitutional independence of the Bundesbank and established a system of cooperative industrial relations that delivered moderate wage settlements as a means to containing inflation. They also underlined the importance of establishing "external economic underpinnings" to domestic policy by means of institutionalized international cooperation (e.g., Erhard 1954, 151; Tietmeyer 1999, 175–192). During the Golden Age, the Bretton Woods exchange rate regime constituted those underpinnings, stabilized investment incentives, and boosted the export performance of German industry by contributing to an undervalued currency.

However, toward the end of the 1960s there were price disparities within the EEC and substantial upward pressure on the mark. This raised concerns in Germany that the economic policies of its key trading partners would generate inflationary pressures and gradually undermine the price competitiveness of its exports. To contend with this scenario, the Advisory Council of the Economics Ministry proposed in 1967 that the German government initiate negotiations with members of the EEC and potentially beyond for a "community of stability" (*Stabilitätsgemeinschaft*). The Council's ideas were reflected in a formal proposal for a European economic and monetary union in 1970, but differences among potential member-states over the conditions for participation and the responsibilities of European authorities prevented an agreement.[14] The collapse of the Bretton Woods exchange rate system in 1971 renewed the urgency of formalized cooperation within Europe and the German government took a leading role in developing new multilateral designs to stabilize exchange rates.

The government, the export-oriented manufacturing sector, and banks alike saw a stable European exchange rate system as essential to sustaining the post-war economic strategy. A regime of floating exchange rates was framed as a threat to domestic goals because it was expected to cause the appreciation of the mark and to reduce the competitiveness of German industry. Meanwhile, a return to a stable exchange rate system was viewed by the manufacturing sector as a matter of "the highest priority" (BDI 1971b, 1971c). The coordinated market economy was centered around a set of domestic institutions that sustained a great deal of non-market coordination and that contributed to competitive advantages based on the capacity of firms to sustain high-quality production. Without a stable macro-economic environment, the incentives for firms to undertake capital-intensive investments in plants and people would be significantly undermined. The urgency of establishing a new international framework for monetary stability was great, especially because German governments were constitutionally constrained from matching the practice of competitive devaluations used by other governments.

In the 1971 Smithsonian agreement, the world's leading industrial economies agreed to a system in which national currencies would fluctuate within narrow bands against the dollar. A similar arrangement (known as the Snake) was established in Europe to ensure stability in inflationary expectations and currency values. The Smithsonian agreement ended after two years, but European designs lasted for nearly a decade and were characterized by frequent realignments and changes in membership. From German vantage points, these arrangements were insufficient to guaranteeing long-term stability and generated demands for a more stable system in which exchange rate realignments would occur less frequently. In 1978–1979, German and French governments cooperated in establishing the European Monetary System (EMS) and brought greater stability in the nominal value of exchange rates. Moreover, by placing the onus of adjustment on other governments, the EMS reduced fears in Germany that its currency would appreciate and served to establish a new set of multilateral "underpinnings" that strengthened firms' commitments to making large capital-intensive investments.[15]

Market Liberalization and External Adaptation

Stability in international currency markets was necessary if insufficient to ensuring that German firms' would pursue higher value-added specialized manufacturing markets. More than anything, the credibility of German firms' commitments to the social contracts that sustained post-war designs was contingent on their access to foreign markets. However, between reduced international demand following the energy crises of the 1970s and increasing levels of competition from producers in East Asia in several of the major product markets of European producers, there were strong demands for greater protection and state support in many countries. Because the federal government was constrained in awarding significant industrial subsidies, it was particularly worried that a trend toward protectionism in Europe, now constituting half of German exports, would have detrimental effects on its own manufacturing sector (BMWi 1988). This led Conservative and Social Democratic governments alike to continue Germany's opposition to proposals for European industrial policies and other potentially discriminatory practices and instead to support multilateral market liberalization programs. Again, GATT was seen as an important but inadequate foundation to securing access to foreign markets, and it led German governments to strengthen their support for market liberalization and enlargement of the EEC.

By the mid-1980s, the government, export-oriented manufacturing industry, and the banking sector had become strong supporters of the European single market program. Though that program would substantially increase levels of competition for German firms, the government's embrace of the internal market enjoyed enthusiastic support in the business sector with 90 percent of companies expecting benefits relative to maintaining the status quo (Adam-Schwaetzer 1988, 539). The majority of firms viewed the internal market program as a way to secure access to their primary product markets at reduced transaction costs and as a means to strengthen their competitive position vis-à-vis non-European producers. Meanwhile, the multilateral status quo was framed as a significant liability that would prevent German industry from enjoying higher level of economic growth (BDI 1988; BMWi 1986; DIHK 1988). The export-oriented sector in particular antici-pated that market liberalization in Europe would help it gain further advantages from specialization that would offset its lack of price-competitiveness with Asian producers. Although acknowledging the importance of a larger and more integrated European market for the competitiveness of industry, BDI's president underscored that the size of that market was by itself not the only factor, and that "its [institu-tional] quality is of decisive importance" (Necker 1988, 252).

The internal market program presented challenges for the German govern-ment, in particular when it came to maintaining support for key features of the na-tional industrial relations and corporate governance systems. The government was particularly concerned that a single European market governed by the principle of mutual recognition would promote regime competition (*Systemwettbewerb*) within Europe and generate a race-to-the-bottom dynamic that would undermine its abil-ity to sustain domestic designs over time. One solution to the threat of regime com-petition that enjoyed wide support in Germany, especially among unions, was the promotion of upward harmonization on German standards among members of the EEC. It has been suggested that German business also supported such a strategy as a means of equalizing the costs of production to offset comparatively high levels of regulation at home (e.g., Huelshoff 1993, 312). However, this was not the case. While upward harmonization would have been a way to level the playing field for German firms since they did not expect to see a rollback in national standards, it was strongly rejected for having detrimental long-term effects. It was thought that upward harmonization would cause the closure of companies in countries with lower levels of industrial productivity, which in turn would force the German state to contribute greater sums to the European budget and thus generate higher taxes for firms at home at the same time as demand abroad would decline (BDI 1996; see also Deregulierungskommission 1991, 147).[16]

But the principal reason business was opposed to upward harmonization was the eventuality of externally induced adaptation losses because harmonization could potentially eliminate the flexibility firms had in negotiating with unions about specific solutions to economic challenges. Common European standards would be the product of intergovernmental agreements, which would not only undermine the benefits German firms enjoyed under the institution of Tarifautonomie, but it would also make institutional reforms over time more difficult because member-states would have to agree on the nature of such reforms (BDA 1989). Because the institutional infrastructure that had characterized the post-war era was perceived by the business sector to be superior to alternative models of governance, European agreements that threatened the ability of German employers to work within the existing system represented potentially significant adaptation losses and were therefore strongly opposed. At the same time, however, German firms did not support the total absence of a social dimension because they worried that such an arrangement could place them at a competitive disadvantage in the long-term vis-à-vis producers in countries where social standards were lower (e.g., Heinzemann 1994; Demmler 1995).

Competing demands from unions and employers placed the German government in a position of having to resolve the design problem in a way that assured the former that their investments in national institutions would be protected, and the latter that their stakes in national designs would be preserved without the introduction of new constraints. It addressed this challenge by promoting two sets of solutions to the design problem that minimized potential adaptation losses to the former and potential maladaptation costs to the latter. First, the government promoted and ensured the adoption of multilateral rules that prescribed common *minimum* standards in social matters such as working and employment conditions. Such standards reassured unions that egregious forms of social dumping would not radically reduce social standards in Germany.[17] At the same time, common minimum standards reassured employers that national discretion in matters relating to the workplace would persist and that externally induced maladaptation costs would be minimal and that upward harmonization would not take place.

Second, the German government sought to ensure that multilateral rules would not undermine the long-term sustainability of institutions integral to the post-war model such as those associated with the system of corporate governance. In the case of the European Company Statute (ECS), an old initiative that was renewed for the purposes of creating a European legal identity for publicly owned companies, concerns were focused on codetermination. Germany's minister for work and social affairs argued that the success of German industry was "not achievable without codetermination." He claimed that although his government promised to liberalize domestic labor markets, codetermination was an "unrenounceable" institution (Blüm 1989). However, an agreement on the ECS could potentially undermine codetermination if German companies could transform their legal identities into European ones and there was no mandate on employment representation.

German industry had a long record of supporting the ECS, but it had objected to an agreement that mandated codetermination for companies incorporated under the Statute (BDI 1972). As attempts to reach an agreement on ECS were renewed in the mid-1980s during negotiations over the internal market program, the government was unwilling to accept a Statute that would let companies convert their legal identities into European ones in ways that enabled them to circumvent national rules governing employee representation.[18] For that reason, the government was unwilling to agree to proposals that included no protection of existing national practice. However, as long as national autonomy was preserved in this area and governments could limit the discretion of employers to overturn the institution of codetermination, it was willing to accept an agreement that did not mandate codetermination in other countries. In other words, the government was not concerned with having companies elsewhere observe the same rules as did domestic ones, but rather to prevent multilateral rules from imposing domestic adaptation losses on constituencies that were supportive of codetermination. However, with other member-states (chiefly Britain) worrying that forms of codetermination may eventually find their way into national legislation or be mandated for their companies that merged with firms in countries with such mandates, an agreement could not be reached. For the German government, non-agreement was unproblematic as it preserved the status quo and thus did not impose any adaptation losses.

The government's efforts to ensure a compatible relationship between national and multilateral designs in this period also covered competition law, which gained a great deal of attention in the 1980s as European firms were under pressure from producers in East Asia. The combination of higher levels of international competition and amendments to the Law against Restraints on Competition in 1973 led Germany's large manufacturing companies to renew their opposition to national rules governing competition, especially those relating to mergers.[19] Having failed both in the 1950s and early 1970s to prevent the adoption of stricter national rules, these firms turned their attention to the European level in the hope that less stringent multilateral rules may help loosen national constraints. To the government, this prospect was worrisome as new domestic merger rules were designed to strengthen the Mittelstand that was such a key element of its structural reform agenda (Gerber 1998, 301–316). However, its stricter view on multilateral merger rules stood in contrast to most other member-states who sought more liberal standards. In the process of negotiating an agreement, the German government was able to secure a special arrangement and rare departure from the governance of European competition law. Known as the "German clause," the government gained the right to request that the European Commission refer cases with national consequence to national authorities (Niederleitinger 1990). In this manner, German governments limited the prospect that multilateral rules would undermine aspects of a key pillar in the social market economy.

Self-Reinforcing Designs

Germany's post-war economic model and the reforms that enhanced its internal coherence during the 1970s and 1980s may have been defined by its national designs, but its sustainability was heavily dependent on governments actively redesigning the country's engagement with multilateral institutions. To give assurances to large and Mittelstand manufacturing firms that continued long-term investments in plants and people would be rewarded, German governments spearheaded the creation of new forms of international monetary cooperation that limited the appreciation of the German currency and that contributed to macroeconomic stability during a period of unprecedented turmoil in post-war global financial markets. They also worked actively to maintain and expand multilateral institutions designed to encourage international market liberalization, in particular the European internal market program, which helped governments assure firms of their access to export markets on non-discriminatory terms. These assurances helped governments sustain broad support within the manufacturing sector, as well as from commercial banks that had expanded their stakes in the German manufacturing sector.

New multilateral initiatives promoting international market integration also opened the door that some institutions integral to the post-war model would be undermined unless forms of multilateral market regulation limited externally induced adjustment costs. Therefore, German governments devoted significant attention to several initiatives they feared could undermine national designs, including proposals for new multilateral rules in the corporate governance, industrial relations, and competition domains. Contrary to common perceptions of Germany as a country intent on establishing a mirror image of its domestic model at the European level, governments were not motivated by attempts to export national designs to the European level. Such a strategy was not deemed feasible given different traditions of economic governance in other member-states. Rather, German governments sought to protect national discretion and limit the prospect that international rules would entail large adaptation losses and gradually erode features integral to the post-war model. In some cases like that of working and employment conditions, this strategy was a matter of securing common minimum standards. In other cases such as the European Company Statute it meant preventing agreements that could eventually undermine core designs such as codetermination; and in the case of competition policy it meant securing special departures from the typical form of multilateral regulation.

German governments resolved the design problem in ways that reinforced the incentives of a broad set of business sectors to deepen their investments in each other and their commitments to product market strategies that exploited the comparative institutional advantages of the coordinated market economy model under a new set of international conditions. In this way, their foreign economic policies contributed to making a domestic program of reform that followed a trajectory of institutional specialization sustainable in a period when post-war designs were self-undermining in many other industrialized countries and where governments found themselves embarking on radical reform agendas.

The Politics of Institutional Recombination

During the 1990s, Germany was immersed in an intense debate explicitly framed in institutional terms centered on whether the post-war model remained a viable foundation for a competitive industrial economy. Known as the location debate (*Standortdebatte*), discussions focused on whether Germany was able to maintain and attract investments, produce jobs, keep the costs of production in check, and generate simultaneous growth in traditional advanced manufacturing markets and in new high-technology ones. In all these areas, performance was generally poor in historical and cross-national comparison. Private capital formation had declined in most industrial domains, and Germany recorded the largest deficit in foreign direct investment among member-states of the European Union. Unemployment surged throughout the decade and reached double digits in the late 1990s. Productivity growth was declining and the costs of unification and of meeting the EMU criteria brought few reductions in non-wage labor costs for employers as the federal government prioritized a balanced budget. Finally, growth in traditional export markets was sluggish, and the high-tech sector remained small and grew at a modest rate in comparison to that of other industrialized countries, in particular liberal market economies.[20]

In broad terms, the location debate was one between those supporting incremental adjustments to post-war designs and those supporting more radical changes in the direction of the liberal market economy. Every major building block of the post-war model became the subject of close scrutiny. The financial system was criticized for being risk-averse, backward-looking, and for failing to provide sufficient risk capital for industries targeting new markets in the high-tech sector. The corporate governance system was blamed for perpetuating an insider model in which large firms and banks sustained industrial conglomerates in traditional markets and for preventing firms from forming new international alliances and raising foreign capital. In a similar vein, an innovation system geared toward incremental innovation in platform technologies and toward the advanced manufacturing sector was said to be ill-equipped to meet the challenges posed by the rapid advancements made by U.S. and British firms in the booming computer software, biotechnology, and high-end service industries. Finally, the industrial relations system was charged with protecting the interests of entrenched unions rather than with assisting firms in making the transition to new product markets targeting greater technological content.[21]

Initially, German governments sought to address competitiveness concerns through an incremental reform agenda. This agenda had begun in the 1980s, but accelerated after the unexpected reunification of the two Germanys in 1989 when demands for more far-reaching reform intensified (Streeck 2009, 207–218). Governments sought to boost the performance of its traditional industrial backbone, the advanced manufacturing sector, while gradually facilitating inroads into new markets in the high-tech and financial sectors. This strategy quickly presented governments with an institutional dilemma that had distributional consequences within the business community. Many of the very institutions that were assets to the advanced manufacturing industry were deemed detrimental to growth in the high-tech sector. For example, the financial and corporate governance systems that had constituted institutional advantages to firms benefiting from access to patient capital were framed as liabilities by firms who sought to raise risk capital and by commercial banks who feared the loss of market shares with the liberalization of international financial markets (Beyer and Höpner 2003; Lütz 2000). Another example was the industrial relations system that had secured modest wage increases to the benefit of large advanced manufacturing firms in exchange for relatively high compensation. It was now seen as undermining the incentives of workers to acquire new skills and for preventing the emergence of the type of flexible and high compensation employment contracts that were associated with growth in the information technology and high-end financial services industries.

Resolving the new distributional conflicts through incremental means in ways that sustained the historic business coalition proved unworkable to German governments. Sectors that held pivotal positions in several institutional equilibria framed incremental reforms as insufficient given high maladaptation costs and thought it feasible that superior designs could be established through a strategy of defection. In anticipation and in response to the changing interests of firms in those sectors, German governments embraced a more radical reform agenda in the financial and corporate governance domains and gradually built sufficient support to consolidate that agenda. In contrast, a greater level of institutional continuity prevailed in the industrial relations and innovation domains where pivotal sectors did not experience profound changes in their preferences, maladaptation costs were comparatively low, and the political feasibility of reform was more heavily constrained.

By the mid-2000s, the mixture of radical and incremental reforms had produced a hybrid system of governance that was distinct from the post-war model as well as from that found in other countries in the same period. Though this system was internally less coherent than in the past and the business coalition more fractured, those sectors that were pivotal to sustaining domain specific equilibria supported new designs and contributed to making the hybrid system stable. This outcome was a consequence, in part unanticipated, of how governments had resolved the design problem in the previous period and the manner in which they adapted domestic reforms to new multilateral designs during the 1990s and 2000s when major innovations occurred within the European Union.

Domains of Transformative Reform

Key features of the post-war financial system were gradually undermined in the 1990s. Big commercial banks were unwilling to pursue corporate strategies that would have served to reproduce the core features of the banking system. Perceiving large maladaptation costs from maintaining the post-war status quo, these banks sought reforms that would more closely align national designs to the emerging European norm, which was more directly associated with the liberal market economy. This process had begun in the 1980s when commercial banks started to sell significant shares in non-financial firms and lessened their dependence on loans to large manufacturing firms and began to more actively pursue securities markets and investment banking (Deeg 1999, 95–99). Financial services liberalization in the wake of the internal market program enhanced the attractiveness of this strategy. Increased international supply of capital in domestic markets squeezed profits for banks while the gradual introduction of the Euro during the 1990s reduced the advantages commercial banks had enjoyed in their home markets by virtue of avoiding the risks and costs of currency exchanges. Together, these developments produced a radical shift in the institutional preferences of commercial banks who now sought a fundamental transformation in the post-war financial system in the direction of liberal market economies.

The government responded to the challenges faced by its commercial banking sector with an extensive set of reforms to rules governing banks, securities markets, and the market for corporate control. Capital standards were reformed and efforts were made to create a dynamic system of stock markets that could compete with such markets elsewhere, especially in London. The basic purpose was to attract foreign investment and increase the number of financial instruments at the disposal of German companies in order to make possible an expansion in traditional product markets and especially to encourage investments in the IT sector. With Britain outside EMU, the government and the banking sector sought to position Frankfurt as the center for innovative banking and foreign investment. Reforms did not meet ambitious targets in terms of stock market capitalization. However, they assisted in enhancing the international competitiveness of banks by enabling a shift away from long-term low-yield corporate loans to a stronger emphasis on higher returns from investment banking and new financial services (Vitols 2001b; Deeg 2005). This process was facilitated by the expansion of global markets, as well as by the emergence of new markets in Central and Eastern Europe that made it possible for commercial banks to expand their international presence and address domestic profitability problems.

The same developments in the international economic and multilateral environments that spurred commercial banks to push for radical reforms in the private banking pillar of the post-war financial system also played integral roles in pushing these to challenge features of the public sector bank pillar. Because regional savings banks (*Landesbanken*) were backed by public guarantees, including liability and bail-out provisions, they enjoyed premier ratings and were able to make loans on more favorable terms than commercial banks.[22] As large commercial banks faced greater competition, they became more vociferous in their criticism of the advantages public savings banks enjoyed and sought an end to the latter's public guarantees. In the late 1990s, the Association of German Banks (BdB) abandoned its efforts to bring about reforms through domestic means and instead invoked European competition rules to argue that regional public savings banks enjoyed unlawful competitive advantages. The decision by commercial banks to pursue this route met with great criticism at home as the changes they sought entailed substantial adaptation losses for public savings banks that constituted a major asset to both regional governments and the Mittelstand.

In 2002 it became clear that regional savings banks would fail to defend their interests in the European Court of Justice and they lost the special protections that had been a major source of their competitive advantage. After the lifting of state guarantees, all public banks that had Triple A ratings lost that standing (Council of Economic Experts 2004, 63), a reality that was seen as a potential death knell to the competitiveness of public sector savings banks and a major challenge to the Mittelstand. But the long-standing and close relationships between these banks and the Mittelstand, together with accommodations by the EU, ensured a gradual transition to new market conditions for these banks that contributed to significant continuity in their basic practices after the court's final ruling (Smith 2001; Vitols 2005). But losing access to those institutions that had been a source of their competitive advantages pushed some public savings banks into new areas outside their traditional core competencies, including risky securitized debt transactions that generated major losses in 2007–2008. The latter process precipitated consolidation in the sector and great uncertainty about the long-term financing model on which the Mittelstand had historically relied.

To facilitate the structural transformation of industry toward a more knowledge-intensive economy, German governments introduced a set of complementary reforms to the corporate governance system. These reforms brought about levels of corporate transparency and accountability far beyond what had existed and were welcomed by the business community (BDI 2001c). With the 1998 Corporate Sector Supervision and Transparency Act (*KonTraG*), management was no longer required to take the interests of employees into account, which had been the practice since the 1930s. The act, which included the introduction of a one-share-one-vote model, ushered a transition to a shareholder model that, while not identical to that found in Britain, was more similar to liberal market economies than the post-war model found in Germany (Lütz 2000; Beyer and Höpner 2003; Goergen, Manjon, and Renneboog 2005).[23] Constraints on hostile takeovers were also significantly reduced and became fewer than in most other European countries.

Reforms overseen by a conservative government in the early part of the decade were extended under a government led by Social Democrats. Among the most far-reaching and radical reforms undertaken by the new government was a law that eliminated capital gains taxes on large blockholdings (Höpner 2001). Introduced in stealth-like manner by a government that had long championed blockholding as a key institution of the coordinated economy model, the law spurred a large number of firms and banks to sell their stakes in each other to meet a short deadline set by the government. By removing the statutory constraints that had ensured long-term cross-shareholdings and by giving companies tax incentives to divest themselves from stakes in other companies, the laws of the late 1990s significantly weakened the blockholding system that had long existed and created a more open market for corporate control (Beyer and Höpner 2003; Vitols 2005).

Throughout this period, the German government actively sought to resolve the design problem in ways that would help consolidate the domestic reform program. From having been strongly opposed to multilateral takeover rules in a liberal vein for decades, the government became a major champion of a 2001 proposal for an EU directive on takeovers. That directive had originally been modeled on British practice, and in a major volte face from its position a decade earlier, the German government now modeled its domestic reforms on the EU directive as a means of reinforcing domestic reforms and minimizing external maladaptation costs (Cioffi 2002). However, to some members of the business community and even more so among labor unions, the government's multilateral agenda was too far-reaching. Framing the issue as one where "[n]o directive is better than a bad directive" (Seyppel and Sell 2001, 7), opponents to the EU directive underscored that the status quo was more attractive than the more liberal prescriptions of the EU proposal because the latter entailed adaptation losses. In particular, aligning national designs with proposed multilateral ones would reduce the means firms had traditionally employed to deter hostile takeover bids. Describing it as "grotesque" for entrenching a domestic regime that would afford German companies fewer defensive means than firms in some other countries, major business leaders in the traditional manufacturing sector opposed EU's proposed Takeover Directive (Wiedeking 2001, 11).

To gain support from a broader base within the business community and to accommodate German members of the European Parliament who had mobilized to defeat the directive, the government eventually endorsed a new 2003 version of EU's Takeover Directive that left intact the ability of national authorities to give firms recourse to a range of defensive mechanisms (Callaghan 2008).[24] This arrangement reduced the external adaptation losses that some members of the business community and German labor unions perceived. It also more closely aligned national practice with multilateral norms in ways that eliminated the maladaptation costs that the business community associated with earlier national designs. By resolving the design problem in this fashion, the government was able to successfully secure broad support within the business community for what in historical terms was a radical agenda of institutional reform in the national system of corporate governance.

By contrast to the Takeover Directive where the goal was to consolidate recent reforms, the German government approached multilateral initiatives affecting the institution of codetermination with the goal of protecting historic designs. With the business community seeking extensive reforms in the area, the government was concerned that multilateral rules would enable large employers to jettison post-war domestic practice and gradually undermine a key feature of the country's corporate governance model. Because the European Works Council Directive was based in labor law, the real potential threat to codetermination came from initiatives to expand company law at the European level. Throughout the 1990s, German governments insisted that any agreement on the European Company Statute entail strict constraints on the ability of German companies to convert their legal identities into international entities in ways that would enable them to easily exit from the post-war social contract that was the foundation of codetermination. The final 2001 agreement ensured that German companies could not easily circumvent established national practice and thus allowed the government to give assurances to those supporting codetermination practices that multilateral and national designs were incentive compatible (Fioretos 2009).[25]

Although multilateral agreements relating to matters of codetermination ensured continuity at the national level, a decade of ambitious reforms to the corporate governance and financial systems aligned these more closely with emerging European norms and brought transformative changes to post-war practice in Germany. Major reforms to the banking structure, equity and credit markets, shareholding arrangements, and long-existing constraints on the market for corporate control undermined the statutory foundations of the close-knit relationship between banks and large firms in the course of the 1990s and 2000s. Instead of an economic model where commercial banks and large manufacturing firms had highly specific relational investments in each other, a market-based system emerged in which cross-shareholdings were less common and where the product market strategies of commercial banks bore more resemblance to those traditionally found in liberal market economies than in post-war Germany. However, the shift in the corporate strategies of large manufacturing firms was not nearly as radical as might have been expected after the decline in blockholding and long-term financing. Such firms continued to rely heavily on retained earnings to finance major investments in new technologies and used their new access to foreign direct investment and new equity markets to consolidate their traditional strengths and make gradual inroads into lucrative high-end innovation markets.

Governments played key roles in bringing about the conditions under which both the financial services industry and the large manufacturing industry could credibly commit to the reforms of the 1990s and 2000s. They responded to a large number of the reform demands by these industries, often took the lead in pushing through legislative changes, and developed a set of complementary transformations in the financial and corporate governance domains that reduced the maladaptation costs that large parts of the business community associated with the status quo ante. They also paid close attention to aligning domestic innovations with European designs in ways that largely corresponded to the preferences of commercial banks and the manufacturing sector. Furthermore, they played key roles in ensuring that some designs such as codetermination were preserved and that the systemic convergence on the liberal market economy was not complete.

Domains of Relative Continuity

Long heralded as major sources of successful corporate adjustment, both the post-war industrial relations and innovation systems became the subject of extensive debate on how costs of production could be reduced and how firms could become more flexible and make inroads in new knowledge-intensive product markets. Yet, despite the emergence of major cleavages within the business community that threatened to undermine the broad post-war business coalition and intense preferences for radical changes in some sectors, reforms in both domains took on incremental features and divisions were eventually bridged. Governments played key roles in rebuilding a broad business coalition and ensured stability in new designs through a set of domestic and multilateral reform programs that over time made incremental changes more attractive than wholesale transformations to a broad constituency within the business community.

A significant profit squeeze in the 1990s and high levels of unemployment made reforms to the industrial relations a major priority for both German business and governments (Streeck and Hassel 2003). The business community and the major political parties were in agreement that continuity should prevail in the decentralized nature of governance in matters concerning the negotiation of wages, working time, and benefits between employers and unions. But there was a division within the business community over institutions governing collective bargaining and individual employment contracts.

In the eastern part of the country, large numbers of employers found the transfer of post-war designs from the western part burdensome and opted not to observe the agreements of the Confederation of German Employers' Associations (BDA). At the same time, a small but growing high-tech sector decided to form new employers' associations as a means of securing a more flexible system. Also the Mittelstand that was located in the western part of the country and invested in traditional product markets questioned the benefits of a system in which wages were set by large export-oriented manufacturing firms that were less sensitive to such costs. The Federation of German Industry, which traditionally had been the voice of large firms, became a major champion for the Mittelstand and promoted radical reforms that would bring about significant changes in institutions governing wage bargaining. Meanwhile, the BDA, whose members were bound by the institution of collective bargaining and saw it as a means of securing modest wage growth, sought less radical changes (Silvia 1997; Hassel 2007). By post-war standards, the asymmetry in the institutional preferences of the two business associations represented a major departure from earlier periods.[26]

The reference points employed by different sectors and the manner in which they framed their historical investments in institutions of collective bargaining help explain why a division emerged within the business community over collective bargaining. Because smaller firms were more sensitive to relative labor costs, their maladaptation costs from maintaining historic designs rose more quickly than for large firms as levels of international competition increased. The urgency for reform was exacerbated for the Mittelstand as large firms could credibly threaten that they would relocate production to newly opened markets in Eastern and Central Europe where the costs of production were significantly lower. Meanwhile, firms in the eastern part of Germany had no actual historic investment in the post-war designs of the coordinated market economies and were thus more likely to reject these designs.

German governments employed a number of domestic initiatives to bridge cleavages within the business community and sustain an incremental reform trajectory. They facilitated greater levels of firm-level flexibility by encouraging negotiated departures between employers and unions from collective bargaining norms and matters pertaining to working hours and other dimensions of the employment contract. Government initiatives such as informal tripartite meetings enhanced the legitimacy of negotiated departures from previous norms and were crucial in reducing the maladaptation costs of not achieving more radical reforms to those firms that had sought transformative changes (Hassel 2007). In time, these actions facilitated a process of institutional conversion in which the formal structures of governance remained relatively intact, but where the norms guiding contracts changed and allowed greater flexibility in the scope of collective bargaining. This reduced the incentives for companies to call for radical reforms and contributed to reproducing post-war designs.

The consolidation of the EMU regime gradually served to bridge the cleavage that had emerged between large firms and the Mittelstand during the early 1990s. By stabilizing the European macroeconomic environment, EMU increased the relative value large employers attached to domestic institutions of collective bargaining as these were effective in containing wage inflation. In the decade after EMU's introduction, Germany was the only Eurozone country that experienced a steady decline in relative wages and where a significant improvement in the cost competitiveness of firms was apparent by the mid-2000s (Council of Economic Experts 2006). Meanwhile, small- and medium-sized firms concluded that monetary union helped shield the Mittelstand from fast growth in labor costs and from currency appreciations, which they thought would have been inevitable without the Euro (DIHK 2007). EMU thus served to reinforce the traditional product markets strategies of large firms and the Mittelstand and gave these incentives to make large investments in new technologies and skill development (Hancké and Hermann

2007). The outcome was that in the course of the 2000s, the motivational credibility of firms' commitments to the post-war architecture increased despite relatively dire economic circumstances and the early perception that retaining national designs entailed maladaptation costs and that the liberal market economy model would have been a superior means to ensuring price competitiveness.

Because EMU only served to reduce maladaptation costs after an extended period of time, German governments also sought to actively manage adjustment costs with the help of other programs. Domestic constituencies saw different merit in new multilateral rules. Unions sought to protect their stakes in national designs by expanding multilateral statutory protections, including the addition of a separate chapter to EU treaties devoted to employment, and employers saw multilateral designs as an opportunity to hasten domestic reform by encouraging greater levels of labor market liberalization throughout the EU. For German governments grappling with high levels of unemployment, the competing demands required a resolution of the design problem that reassured both sides. Its solution was to support the so-called Luxembourg process and programs like the European Employment Strategy (EES) that encouraged greater levels of labor-market flexibility through multilateral cooperation but that stressed national discretion in the particular solutions used (BMWi 2006).

Rather than relying on international statutory means to bring about domestic reform or promoting greater levels of labor market liberalization as was for example the case in financial services, new EU programs in the social policy domain such as the open method of coordination stressed peer-review, best practice, and national discretion (Zeitlin and Pochet 2005). Scholars have differed in their conclusions on the effectiveness of these programs in lowering unemployment and transforming national labor markets (see, e.g., Citi and Rhodes 2007), but the underlying political consequences of such programs are not in doubt. By not legally mandating domestic reform of a particular kind while actively encouraging the development of new solutions that were compatible with national practice, initiatives such as the Luxembourg Process provided unions with assurances that post-war designs would neither be immediately transformed in ways that entailed large adaptation losses, nor die a slow death through neglect. At the same time, these multilateral initiatives assured employers that the German government was committed to a process of incremental change rather than defending the status quo and also that EU-level authorities lacked statutory powers that could alter domestic practice (BDA and BDI 2001, 4). In other words, multilateral programs in this area imposed neither significant adaptation losses to unions nor new maladaptation costs to employers. As such, they served to reinforce national discretion and thus continuity in the type of negotiated arrangements between employers and unions that had been central to how German firms had adjusted in the post-war period.

Like in the case of the industrial relations system, Germany's innovation system experienced significant levels of continuity despite some extensive criticism and major cleavages within the business community. Particular attention was directed at the scope of public support to industry and the nature of collaborative relations between large and smaller firms. The post-war system was characterized by extensive public support for research institutes and beneficiaries of that system feared that economic constraints and temporary aid to declining industry in the eastern part of the country following unification would reduce their ability to make significant progress in new high-tech segments. German authorities reaffirmed the temporary nature of state aid to declining industry and expanded attention both to basic research in areas that would benefit the advanced manufacturing sector and to new programs that would benefit radical innovation industries (BMBF 2000; BMF 1999). In addition, facing domestic budget constraints, German governments became stronger backers of multilateral programs designed to assist firms in overcoming comparative institutional disadvantages associated with the national system of innovation. For example, with the strong backing of the business community, German governments supported new multilateral programs that encouraged higher levels of cooperation across national borders in the IT industry. To the country's large firms as well as the Mittelstand, these initiatives were much welcomed and helped ease domestic distributional conflicts owing to scarce government resources (BDI 2005; DIHK 2005).

By the early 2000s, the integrated production and innovation chains that had linked large manufacturing firms with the Mittelstand came under new criticism. Germany was described as a "bazaar economy" (Sinn 2004) in which large manufacturing firms engaged in little innovation, imported crucial supplies, and focused on the assembly for export at the expense of the long-term viability of industrial innovation. The manufacturing industry found some criticisms valid, but generally defended Germany as a location for innovation (BDI 2006).

The essence of the business community's defense of the German innovation system was that though the production chain had been partially disaggregated through the outsourcing of labor-intensive segments, high value-added segments that required advanced research and development remained within the country. Large firms argued that sustaining competitiveness required more resources, and that the emphasis be placed on incremental reforms to national designs (BDI 2008). Studies by federal ministries and the independent Council of Economic Experts concurred with the business community that descriptions of Germany as a bazaar economy were ill-founded. They pointed specifically to the growth in high value-added production and continued export growth in the advanced manufacturing sector as evidence of the continued viability of integral features of the innovation system (e.g., Council of Economic Experts 2004, 354–364).

The focus by large firms on investing more in their core competencies and outsourcing those parts that entailed lower levels of value-added production complemented the government's strategy of strengthening the Mittelstand as a means of encouraging employment growth and boosting the technology and information-intensity of German industry.[27] Like large firms, the Mittelstand emphasized that its success in a more globalized economy depended on maintaining their access to national institutions, especially those relating to innovation (DIHK 2005).[28] The strategies of large and smaller firms had become less tightly coupled in the course of the 1990s, but toward the end of the next decade both sectors endorsed the basic designs characterizing the innovation system. The enlargement of EU's internal market was important in this respect for it entailed significant adaptation benefits by allowing large firms to outsource some parts of the production chain without significant cross-national transaction costs and to concentrate more resources in high value-added segments. Over time, this transition encouraged a transformation also in the innovation intensity of firms in the Mittelstand and reinforced the trend toward higher levels of knowledge-intensive production throughout the product chain of the advanced manufacturing sector.

A Sustainable Hybrid

Scholars debate whether the erosion of central pillars in the post-war financial and corporate governance systems would end the coordinated market economy as a whole (e.g., Hall and Soskice 2001a; Berghahn and Vitols 2006; Streeck 1997, 2009). After more than a decade of reforms in these domains, it was apparent that a fundamental systemic transformation did not occur. Rather than becoming a facsimile of a liberal market economy, the German market economy underwent a process of institutional recombination that eventually produced a stable hybrid system of economic governance. The institutional complementarities that existed in the past were loosened, particularly those that became apparent during the 1970s and 1980s. But the commitments by pivotal sectors of the business community to the core designs of individual domains were credible and thus ensured a set of self-enforcing designs. Although institutional complementarities may contribute to strengthening firms' commitments to a range of institutions, they are neither a sufficient nor a necessary condition to maintaining domain-specific institutional equilibria. Because economic groups engage in mental accounting and evaluate the costs and benefits of alternative arrangements first in domain-specific and only secondarily in systemic terms, particular institutions can remain stable. That can occur even under declining levels of internal coherence in a system of governance as long as those groups pivotal to sustaining particular designs frame the former as more attractive than feasible alternatives.

German governments played a major role in ensuring that the hybrid arrangement was characterized by stability rather than systemic collapse. In key areas of the financial and corporate governance systems where the aspirational reference point of firms shifted radically in the early 1990s and maladaptation costs were large, governments initiated significant national reforms that closely mirrored the preferences of pivotal sectors in the business community. By the early 2000s, that reform agenda had become self-enforcing as the majority of firms in the commercial banking and manufacturing sectors concluded that recent reforms offered them a better foundation on which to meet global economic challenges than did alternatives.

In other areas such as the industrial relations and innovation domains, as well as the institution of codetermination, a combination of incremental reforms at home, which reduced internal maladaptation costs, and foreign economic policies, which limited externally induced adaptation losses, served to gradually mute demands for more fundamental reform and ensured a set of self-enforcing equilibria.

With an economic upswing after the mid-2000s credited to reforms in the preceding decade, both governments and the business community invoked the benefits of reforms after the late 1990s. These benefits were regularly presented as contingent on developments within the EU. The expansion of the internal market and the stabilization of the macroeconomic environment through the EU had increased the incentives of the manufacturing sector to support continuity in several key domains and the incentives of commercial banks to develop the domestic financial market. By the mid-2000s, the largest employer association was describing the European Union as having "existential importance" to the private sector (Hundt 2007). The ubiquitous calls for radical reforms from a decade earlier had given way to preferences for incremental reform. With the government insisting on "staying the course" (BMWi 2008) and the largest business association defining its "overall reform concept" (*Gesamtreformkonzept*) as one devoted to the consolidation of recent reforms (BDI 2004), German governments had successfully established the necessary conditions for a stable system of hybrid governance by the late 2000s.

Conclusion

Germany's first annual economic report of the new millennium has been described as a "milestone" in economic policymaking because it made explicit references to what lessons the country could draw from other countries and because it dealt directly with the role of European-level multilateral designs in national economic policy (BMWi 2000; Dyson 2001, 137). Though the report is noteworthy in many respects, including in its defense of a "new" social market economy, this chapter underscores that neither comparisons with other countries nor attention to European multilateralism were in any way novel features to economic policymaking. Comparisons with alternative models of governance and how to embed domestic reforms within a fabric of multilateral institutions were consistent themes from the earliest moments of the social market economy after the war. The difference between the recent period and earlier decades was in the nature of the conclusions reached by German governments and the business community. Both governments and a growing and diverse set of constituencies within the business sector concluded in the 1990s that several designs integral to the post-war model constituted liabilities and that multilateral institutions were vehicles to ensure stability in domestic practice but also means to initiate and consolidate radical reforms in targeted areas of the post-war economic architecture. The millennial report was therefore not as much a milestone in terms of an end to a closed system of governance, but rather a new marker in how governments sought to reconcile domestic reforms with multilateral innovations.

The German market economy at the end of the first decade of the twenty-first century looked institutionally very different than it did two decades earlier. Core pillars of the post-war model such as the financial and corporate governance system experienced profound changes and had more in common with liberal market economies than with their own past. There were partial exceptions such as the continued presence of a large public banking sector, the institution of codetermination, and some constraints on the market for corporate control that illustrate that even in domains that underwent major change there were still areas with legacies of early post-war designs. For the most part, however, market-based forms of economic coordination had replaced the network-based arrangements that had existed in the financial and corporate governance systems. In other domains such as the industrial relations and innovation systems, the general picture was reversed; though significant change occurred here also, incremental reform and high levels of continuity were the defining features in these domains. The aggregate outcome of the differentiated process of institutional development was a hybrid system of governance that was distinct from the internally coherent system of governance that characterized Germany for the larger part of the post-war period.

How German governments aligned domestic and multilateral designs proved crucial during the 1990s and 2000s. After the defection during the 1990s of pivotal business sectors such as commercial banks and large manufacturing firms from the social contracts that sustained core features of the national financial and corporate governance systems, German governments embraced a reform agenda that aligned national designs with emerging European norms. This process served to reinforce the credibility of firms' commitments to domestic reforms and helped consolidate what in post-war terms was a radical set of changes. In other domains such as the industrial relations and innovation system, as well as select aspects of the former two domains, governments were able to facilitate a mixture of incremental reforms and protect national designs by securing multilateral ones that limited external maladaptation costs. In this manner, firms' incentives to defect from national institutions were reduced and their commitments to domestic designs remained motivationally credible.

Because the post-war system decentralized political power and economic governance, it is often argued that the nature of reform in Germany is determined by the ability of key groups like unions or regional governments to oppose change (e.g., Shlaes 1994; Heinze 1998; Sinn 2004; Phelps 2007). Although the ability of strategically located groups to prevent or slow down a process of change is apparent in many instances, neither unions nor regional governments were uniformly opposed to reforms. Furthermore, in several cases continuity was a function of the business community actively endorsing processes of incremental change over radical transformations. In other cases, however, such as designs integral to the financial and corporate governance systems, the transformation of preferences within the business community was the critical factor that undermined the sustainability of designs, which was a process that occurred despite the opposition of interest groups who have been said to have veto power in matters of economic governance.

This chapter underscores that the federal government played an active role in shaping the conditions under which different business sectors were able to credibly commit to adopting the type of product market strategies that would make the former's reform agendas sustainable over time. Governments frequently anticipated and often quickly responded to demands for major reforms as well as for the protection of designs integral to the post-war model. Though many of their actions were controversial and there were periods in which there were significant cleavages within the business community, a pattern of proactive government behavior ensured high levels of stability in the economy's architecture and contributed to the conditions under which stability returned quickly after transformative reforms. A key means by which governments ensured such outcomes was through a foreign economic policy that promoted forms of multilateralism that were compatible with domestic reform agendas.

By detailing the institutional logic behind governments' multilateral strategies, this chapter makes contributions to the literature addressing the origin of German support of international cooperation after 1945. It is commonly argued that the reason Germany has been strongly committed to European multilateralism was due to efforts of the business community and government to be perceived as "good Europeans" and that these willingly sacrificed material benefits to secure political acceptance (e.g., Bulmer and Patterson 1987; Huelshoff 1993; Cowles 1996; Banchoff 1999). Although the pursuit for political legitimacy has unquestionably influenced Germany's view of multilateral agreements, exclusive attention to such factors has limits when exploring developments in the economic area. For example, a political legitimacy argument would expect the importance of historical memory to recede over time and thus lessen the intensity with which Germany would support multilateralism. Yet Germany's commitment to multilateralism has gained strength with time. Furthermore, the political legitimacy thesis offers no clear answer to why German governments and the business community have preferred particular kinds of multilateralism, or why, for example, the centralization of multilateral regulatory authority has been supported in some domains whereas greater national discretion has been sought in other areas.

By highlighting the interdependence between domestic institutional reforms and the multilateral strategy of governments, this chapter complements arguments that focus on the material interests of German governments and economic groups in European integration (e.g., Moravcsik 1998). Such arguments correctly underscore that material interests were key in shaping Germany's foreign economic policy, but they do not articulate why particular forms of multilateralism were pursued or how governments reconciled competing demands for institutional reform within the business sector. For example, the chapter shows that in some cases governments supported European designs that were opposed by large manufacturing firms because such designs were deemed integral to sustaining the type of broad business coalition governments considered necessary to sustaining the social market economy. Thus, although economic interests were the engine that propelled support for European integration in general, it was domestic institutional considerations that steered governments to support particular forms of multilateralism.

The consolidation of the social market economy and its changing character in recent decades has been as much a function of domestic reforms as it has been one of the multilateral context within which post-war governments embedded national reforms. German governments have consistently used the institution of multilateralism, in particular within Europe, as a tool for creating the conditions under which the compromises and commitments associated with the social market economy were politically and economically sustainable over time. In recent years the European Union has been seen as a potential threat to that model and in some cases has occasioned even radical domestic reforms. However, it continued to be an integral anchor that served to preserve core features of the post-war model, including a stable macroeconomic environment and a social model that made an open economy strategy feasible over time. Peter Katzenstein (1997) notes that Germany and the EU have a greater institutional affinity than do other large economies. This chapter documents the evolution of that affinity in economic matters and underscores that it has not been accidental. German governments actively created the multilateral conditions under which domestic reform agendas and economic priorities have been realized. They have also, when unable to secure their preferred multilateral designs, adapted national designs more closely to those of the EU. Both practices have been integral features in the implementation of industrial strategies since the 1950s and have helped governments secure broad support within the business sector during moments of structural reform that exposed major differences within German society over the desirable form of economic management.

Chapter 7

Lessons from Capitalist Diversity and Open Governance

The evolution of the modern market economy in Europe was profoundly influenced by post-war innovations in the institution of multilateralism. The structural and institutional transformations that characterized Europe's largest economies were not a product of domestic histories and designs alone. They were integrally linked to a history of international cooperation and an expanding set of multilateral institutions that promoted international trade, exchange rate cooperation, and a set of common rules that regulated markets and permissible forms of government intervention. In the process the institution of multilateralism not only reshaped politics between nations, it also redefined economic management within nations.

A large comparative capitalism literature treats national economies as closed systems of governance. Significant parts of that literature recognize the importance that exposure to international markets has in shaping economic performance and distributional conflicts within states, but the institutions that mediate those effects are understood nearly always in exclusively national terms. It is often assumed that because multilateral designs have promoted greater levels of market integration, their effects are synonymous with those of the latter. That assumption obscures the independent effect that multilateral designs have and also that they are frequently devised as a means of regulating international markets in ways that make their effects more palatable with domestic objectives.

Previous chapters placed the design problem at the center of analysis and studied the consequences of relaxing the assumption of national economies as closed systems of governance. They treated economies as open systems of governance in which the actions of governments and economic groups—the corporate sector, in particular—are shaped by the joint and evolving constraints of national and multilateral designs. The broader implication of the design problem is that the degree to which institutions at the national and multilateral levels are incentive compatible affects the long-term willingness of domestic groups to support the national economic reform agenda of governments.

The case studies underscored that the institution of multilateralism helped protect some features of national models of capitalism, but also that it periodically undermined key features of domestic reform programs. In three paradigmatic cases of advanced capitalism—Britain, France, and Germany—in four areas of economic governance across six decades, the case studies showed that no government was consistently successful in resolving the design problem in ways that delivered only benefits to those economic groups on whom they depended to successfully implement their reform agenda. Multilateral commitments invariably entailed different types of adjustment burdens for domestic groups, and governments sought to minimize both losses and maladaptation costs to those groups whose support was critical to sustain domestic reforms. Identifying when and why these effects of multilateralism varied across time, in distinct areas of economic systems, and in different national models is key to accounting for the evolution of European market economies.

The Findings

How governments mediated the domestic distributional consequences of multilateral institutions had significant implications for their ability to build societal coalitions that could sustain their domestic reform programs. The broader conclusion that emerged from the case studies was that when governments aligned national and multilateral institutions in ways that were incentive compatible and ensured that adaptation losses were small and maladaptation costs low for pivotal sectors of the business community, they were able to construct sufficiently broad coalitions within that community to successfully implement their economic reform agendas. However, the relative success of governments in producing these conditions varied significantly across countries, time periods, and areas of economic governance.

In the early post-war period, governments in Britain failed to create such a broad coalition, while French governments were successful despite pursuing a more comprehensive program. By remaining outside the EEC during the 1960s, which hosted its fastest growing markets, British governments were unable to secure broad support within the business community because firms' incentives to undertake the type of strategic shifts sought by the government were undermined. The business coalition also remained narrow because the financial industry, which was heavily invested in overseas markets owing to the imperial period, was unwilling to significantly redirect its attention toward domestic modernization given modest prospects for growth. By contrast, support for multilateralism by French governments helped them sustain a business coalition that enabled the consolidation of a new system of governance stressing economic centralization.

The two cases stand in contrast to developments during the 1980s. A liberal reform agenda in Britain became sustainable after a domestic liberalization program was accompanied by strong support for a new set of multilateral programs stressing market liberalization, but French governments' attempts to enhance levels of economic centralization failed. In Britain, the manner in which governments resolved the design problem facilitated the emergence of a broad business coalition that encompassed the financial industry as well as large and small companies in the manufacturing industry. By contrast, French governments were able to create only the conditions under which domestic designs were sustainable after a radical shift in national forms of governance that aligned these with multilateral ones.

The manner in which the design problem was resolved in Germany also had significant consequences for domestic reforms. German backing for multilateralism was not simply informed by efforts to regain political legitimacy after the war. Rather it was shaped by an institutional rationale that generated support for some and strong opposition to other multilateral designs. Throughout the 1950s, government officials and the business community stressed the importance of ensuring that both national macroeconomic and microeconomic institutions would not be undermined by multilateral commitments and that, ideally, the latter would reinforce the former. Governments were successful in maintaining support from a broad business coalition during the 1970s and 1980s by promoting a new set of multilateral designs, including in the monetary and trade domains that helped preserve the incentives of the business sector to make large capital investments in their productive capacity. This coalition fell apart in the 1990s as pivotal sectors perceived large maladaptation costs from maintaining the post-war status quo in the financial and corporate governance domains. Only after governments undertook fundamental changes to the institutional structure in these domains and more closely aligned them with the multilateral norm did they create the conditions under which a sustainable model of governance was re-established. That model, however, lacked the internal coherence of earlier decades. Instead it combined features of the post-war model with dimensions familiar from liberal market economies.

In all three countries and across three post-war periods, governments actively sought to secure potential adaptation benefits and limit potential adjustment burdens associated with multilateral institutions. Although not always successful in either endeavor, they were frequently able to secure forms of multilateralism that reduced domestic adaptation losses. They did so through a variety of strategies, including blocking agreement on specific multilateral initiatives such as rules affecting industrial support, corporate takeovers, and industrial relations. They also successfully reduced maladaptation costs in many instances by protecting national discretion in domestic financial, innovation, and corporate governance systems.

The varied success that governments had in securing adjustment benefits and limiting adjustment costs had diverse consequences across economic domains. These were particularly pronounced in national industrial relations and innovation systems, but they became less significant in national financial and corporate governance systems during the 1990s and 2000s. In the latter two areas, French and German designs gradually adopted features more closely associated with liberal market economies. With some exceptions such as changes in Germany's public banking sector, most of these shifts were not legally mandated by the European Union. Rather, they were the outcome of transformations in the preferences of the financial sector and large manufacturing firms following what they perceived to be large maladaptation costs from not more closely aligning national designs with the multilateral norm. These transformations were radical by post-war standards, but they did not represent a complete convergence on the liberal market economy. The reason rests in the success with which German and French governments secured multilateral agreements that protected some nationally distinct features in each of these domains, including codetermination in Germany and constraints on the market for corporate control in the two countries.

Disparities in the timing and scope of the consolidation of liberal designs in the three countries in the financial and corporate governance domains were tied to variations in how firms framed the merits and liabilities of employing alternative designs as the nature of international markets and multilateral institutions evolved. In the 1980s, British firms framed alternatives to liberal designs as liabilities, had few investments in post-war designs, and saw liberal designs as superior because they offered comparatively lower costs of governance in sectors that faced higher levels of international competition.

France was the second country to experience a significant turn toward liberal market economy institutions. The failure of previous reforms meant that adaption losses were limited in France and that firms often saw larger opportunity costs from rejecting liberal designs than corresponding firms did in Germany. Finally, by the mid-1990s, the maladaptation costs that German banks perceived from maintaining the status quo had grown and eventually produced preference transformations that brought radical changes as governments adopted a reform agenda that closely aligned national designs with the multilateral norm.

In contrast to the financial and corporate governance domains, there was greater continuity in national forms of governance in the industrial relations and innovation domains. In the British case, the sustainability of an industrial relations system characterized by comparatively low levels of social protection and high levels of flexibility in employment contracts was contingent on preventing efforts by other EU member-states to raise common standards. British governments did so successfully, including by securing special opt-outs from some EU rules. Meanwhile, in both France and Germany where the post-war industrial relations systems came under heavy criticism during the 1990s, governments undertook a series of domestic reforms that reduced maladaptation costs for firms and lowered the business sector's incentives to seek radical changes. The consolidation of the EMU regime also played a role in this context. German and French producers were more productive than their counterparts in other EU member-states; thus EMU had adaptation benefits to firms in these countries by improving their relative price competitiveness. Demands for radical reforms in the industrial relations era gradually dissipated over time, though calls for incremental reforms remained steady.

Changes in national designs were less radical in national innovation systems despite criticisms in both Germany and France that these systems were poorly equipped for undertaking a transition to more knowledge-intensive forms of production. Governments reduced demands for radical changes by promoting new multilateral programs in areas where these countries had difficulties in making quick inroads. The EU significantly expanded its commitments to support research and development in high-tech industries, a process that helped governments reduce domestic distributional conflicts between sectors invested in traditional product markets and those seeking to develop their radical innovation potential. The enlargement of European markets during the 1990s and 2000s was also key in this context for it provided new opportunities for firms in the former sector to expand their productive capacity, thereby reinforcing their support for continuity in the basic structure of national innovation systems.

Would national trajectories have taken the same form had multilateral institutions not been a major feature of economic governance and had governments not actively sought to shape those institutions in ways that served domestic goals? Answers to these and other counterfactual questions have been addressed both directly and indirectly in specific cases in the preceding chapters. Multilateral institutions were not always more important than historic national designs in shaping the preferences of national business communities, and governments were not always successful in securing their preferred designs. Indeed, there is little historical evidence to suggest that those with significant stakes in how the design problem was resolved expected domestic reforms to take the same form in the absence of multilateral institutions or active attempts to shape the form of those institutions.

Whether multilateralism served to reinforce domestic designs for long periods of time or undermine these slowly or suddenly, post-war political battles over the nature of advanced capitalism were fought both at the national and multilateral levels because governments and societal groups expected designs at both levels to have consequences for their ability to achieve their respective goals. Due to historical legacies, shifting assessments of the relative attractiveness of alternative national designs, and the evolving character of multilateralism, the outcomes of these battles were not uniform. They varied as national varieties of capitalism were periodically reconstructed and in ways not feasible had the institution of multilateralism not been an integral feature of economic governance after 1950.

Implications

The preceding chapters focused on the contributions of behavioral institutionalism, a modified version of historical institutionalism informed by behavioral economics. By overcoming some commonly identified limitations in standard historical institutionalist models, the modified version specified the conditions under which governments are able to secure domestic support for their economic reform agendas as economic and institutional environments evolve. Behavioral economics complements historical institutionalism by providing the microfoundations that give nuance to how the manner in which economic groups frame alternatives affects the credibility of their institutional commitments over time. Because potential losses loom larger in the calculations of social actors, behavioral institutionalism expects preference reversals to occur with greater frequency than suggested by typical contributions to historical institutionalism. At the same time it acknowledges that such transformations occur more rarely than do standard rational choice institutionalist models.

A standard historical institutionalist model expects preferences to be relatively static over time and to favor continuity when positive feedback effects are present. Conversely, a behavioral model suggests that when the benefits from change outweigh the premium firms attach to extant designs, preference transformation occur relatively quickly. Even in cases where positive feedback effects are present and strong, firms' commitments to existing designs will lack credibility if alternative designs are significantly more attractive. In other words, although established institutions often hold great value to firms who employ them to resolve difficult coordination problems and to secure relationally specific investments, firms may jettison these if alternatives offer the prospect of long-term advantages.

Behavioral institutionalism has implications for debates in comparative and international political economy. It underscores that historical legacies are important in shaping national reform trajectories, but that the latter are rarely as path-dependent as some accounts suggest. Neither historic forms of capitalism nor political institutions that give groups extensive veto powers have served to keep countries from deviating significantly from historical trajectories. The effects of history are often contingent on whether societal groups choose a part of their own or some else's history as the reference point and whether changes from such reference points are framed as gains or losses. Variations in such assessments are significant for they shape the degree and direction of reform that societal groups will support, and thus the conditions under which historic or novel features of economic governance are sustainable over time.

Behavioral institutionalism also speaks to an issue frequently explored in the varieties of capitalism literature, namely the relationship between the internal coherence of economic models and their stability over time (e.g., Crouch et al. 2005; Höpner 2005; Hall and Gingerich 2009). By examining how those parts of the business community integral to sustaining particular institutions framed the costs and benefits of alternative reforms, it underscored that domain-specific considerations take precedence over systemic ones. The members of that community typically evaluate the costs and benefits of reform in different domains separately and not in terms of a comprehensive package, a practice that has become more apparent over time in Europe as international competition and liberalization increased the potential costs that business associated with maintaining the status quo. Behavioral institutionalism thus explains why national patterns of specialization and hybrid governance are sustainable in the same time period although countries face common external constraints.

The institutional turn in the comparative and international political economy disciplines has been about exploring the microfoundations behind the choices and behavior of political actors. The extensive use of well-established theories from economics and sociology in these areas has contributed to significant disciplinary maturation in these fields through the promotion of rigorous and common standards of scientific inquiry and the use of concepts that are common across the social sciences (Katzenstein, Keohane and Krasner 1998; Lake 2002 and 2006). Behavioral economics, which finds itself at the intersection of economics and psychology, offers the potential for more disciplinary progress, especially in the study of institutional reform that is often characterized by large distributional conflicts.

Robert Gilpin remarks that "it has become increasingly clear that the role of domestic economies and the differences among these economies have become significant determinants of international economic affairs" (2001: 148). Yet the international political economy discipline employs relatively crude theories of the ways in which differences in national economic systems shape economic affairs between states. Governments' choices are not motivated by enduring logics of what constitutes the superior or "rational" design for joint economic governance (Koremenos, Lipson, and Snidal 2001, 781). Governments assess the consequences for international cooperation of their choices at significant length and are often influenced by new ideas of appropriate forms of economic governance (e.g., Abdelal 2001; Green, Caporaso, and Risse 2001). Moreover they have historically approached the issue of what form multilateral economic institutions should take with particular attention to the national distributional conflicts among economic groups whose support was deemed integral to sustaining domestic reforms. Because the stakes of such groups in domestic designs have varied over time and across areas of economic governance as they have reassessed the merits of historic and alternative types of economic institutions, governments' perspectives of what constitutes the "rational" or "appropriate" form of multilateralism have been mixed across time and countries.

By grounding a theory of why governments promote particular forms of multilateralism in how variations in domestic groups' national institutional investments affect their preferences over the form of international cooperation, behavioral institutionalism moves from general statements about national preferences over multilateral designs to context-specific and conditional accounts of why governments promote different types of multilateral institutions across a range of economic domains. Such a move helps, for example, to resolve why countries like Britain that are typically described as Euroskeptics have supported high levels of integration in certain domains and periods, while countries like Germany and France described as Europhiles have resisted greater levels of cooperation in other areas and periods.

In the theoretical landscape of political science where the motivations of governments and political groups are often viewed as following enduring logics over time and where analytical parsimony is prized, the additional considerations introduced by behavioral institutionalism may be discounted by those who see merits in maintaining the trade-offs in extant approaches. Yet, in analytical terms, behavioral institutionalism merely introduces the proposition that political actors respond to potential gains and losses differently and in situationally contingent ways. This proposition holds a key to a finer understanding of preferences and thus for more dynamic and nuanced accounts of the politics of institutional reform. When used to complement theoretical traditions such as historical institutionalism, behavioral economics may contribute to disciplinary progress in the political economy sub-fields through a negligible surrender of theoretical parsimony in exchange for a potentially large increase in substantive nuance.

Finally, this volume contributes to the multilevel governance research agenda (e.g., Hooghe and Marks 1999; Kohler-Koch and Eising 2002) with which it shares theoretical affinities and which explores the intersection of comparative and international politics. By embracing open systems analysis, the book extends the scope of the multilevel governance literature by explaining how overlapping institutions shape trajectories at a particular level of governance instead of focusing on the trajectory of the totality of governance. One of its findings is that open governance helped countries undertake partial reforms at home without risking that national systems would quickly and fully unravel. Schumpeter once remarked that "[f]or just as the existence of an efficient opposition is a requirement for the orderly functioning of democratic government, so the existence of economic forces that resist institutional change may be necessary in order to keep the speed of this change within the limits of safety" (1950, 452). In the contemporary market economy, multilateral institutions have in many instances played similar countervailing functions as does a strong opposition in democracies.

The countervailing function of multilateral institutions may not be permanent because supranational authorities such as courts and regulators may eventually interpret intergovernmental mandates differently than anticipated by governments (Höpner and Schäfer 2007; Scharpf 2010). But they can play significant roles in the short- and medium-terms during the implementation of contentious reforms. The generalized principles of conduct that the institution of multilateralism involves mean that individual governments are often unable to undertake quick and comprehensive domestic reforms in ways that do not involve coordination with other states. This reality may be a liability in some cases and prevent individual countries from designing what they consider to be the optimal adjustment strategy in the short-term. However, the extensive presence of multilateral institutions reduces uncertainty in periods of crises and encourages a steady level of incremental adjustment. In cumulative terms, the latter has often brought significant reform over time, but it has done so in ways that have kept, in Schumpeter's language, "the speed of change within the limits of [political] safety." In other words, though a multilevel governance system in Europe is not always the most efficient means of resolving a crisis for individual governments, it is a practice that often produces collectively more stable solutions than would be the case in the absence of a dense fabric of multilateralism.

Lessons for and Beyond Europe

The structure and evolution of Europe's largest economies are often said to have unique characteristics that cannot be replicated elsewhere in the world. But the lessons that Europe holds for institutional reform beyond its borders lie not in its particular history and whether a specific European model of capitalism or form of multilateralism should be emulated elsewhere. Rather, the lessons from post-war Europe are found in the conditions under which a set of diverse countries successfully resolved the design problem, an international governance dilemma that confronts all open economies. In particular, Europe offers lessons for how to sustain and expand mutually beneficial exchange through common multilateral designs without undermining national designs that are highly valued by domestic constituencies.

The case studies of Britain, France, and Germany underscore that domestic groups' investments in historic designs have major implications for their support of governments' reform agendas, including the multilateral commitments of the latter. When such investments are threatened by multilateral designs, there may be significant political costs to governments from supporting international institutions. Governments, therefore, have supported diverse forms of multilateralism depending on their domestic objectives and have sought to minimize the particular external adaptation losses and maladaptation costs domestic groups' anticipate and experience from different solutions to the design problem. This generates a potential problem in international negotiations, as governments may find that the zone of potential intergovernmental agreement is too small in areas where domestic groups are strongly invested in protecting domestic institutions.

In the early stages of European integration, the European Commission sought to expand the zone of intergovernmental agreements by promoting the harmonization of many national regulatory designs. Such efforts proved unsustainable because governments found it domestically too costly to support that agenda. In a process characterized by trial and error and in part by unintended consequences, European governments instead came to adopt a set of mechanisms that accommodated diverse forms of capitalism while expanding the scope of multilateralism. In the course of adopting these mechanisms, they were able to reduce domestic adjustment burdens from distinct multilateral initiatives and created the foundations for a set of diverse and sustainable models of open governance. The key mechanisms that the EU has came to rely on in accommodating a diverse set of national models have been mutual recognition, subsidiarity, variations on the concept of variable geometry, and the open method of coordination. These mechanisms allow governments to retain significant discretion in determining what national institutions will define distinct domains and to mitigate domestic adjustment burdens while ensuring high levels of international market integration.

Though the principle of mutual recognition and the use of directives—rather than regulations—have brought high levels of regulatory competition, it has given member-states flexibility in the type of designs they use domestically to achieve common objectives. In combination with common minimum standards, mutual recognition has allowed governments to devise strategies that reduce adaptation losses and maladaptation costs to key domestic constituencies. Subsidiarity has ensured that member-states have retained authority in major parts of economic governance unless there is explicit reason and common agreement to delegate functions to supranational authorities. Thus, in areas deemed particularly sensitive to the sustainability of an economic system's comparative institutional advantages, governments have successfully invoked the principle of subsidiarity to limit domestic adjustment burdens. Used in ad hoc fashion, variable geometry has been a means with which members of the EU has enabled the collective of member-states to extend short-term transition waivers and long-term opt-outs to some members. This has been done to ensure that common goals have not been undermined by national vetoes when key domestic constituencies have expected large adaptation losses. Finally, although the effects of the open method of coordination for domestic economic performance has been debated, it is an innovation that has preserved government discretion in the management of the national economy while furnishing the prospects of enhanced coordination at the multilateral level.

The four mechanisms have given governments the room to reduce externally induced adaptation losses as well as to reduce maladaptation costs while expanding the scope of international cooperation. They underscore that the EU is far from a multilateral organization that embraces a one-size-fits-all answer to the question of what system of capitalism countries should employ. The expansion of EU's membership to twenty-seven states, including many formerly socialist economies, further illustrates that it remains an organization of diverse market economies. The newest members had to meet stringent criteria to join an organization devised by advanced capitalist economies (e.g., Vachudova 2005; Epstein 2008). Like older member states, these countries have adopted diverse national designs to sustain open economy strategies. To wit, as in the cases of France and Germany that have become hybrid systems of governance, many new member-states have undergone a process of institutional recombination that has brought a variety of distinct rather than uniform models of capitalism (e.g., Stark and Bruszt 1998; Orenstein 2001; Nölke and Vliegenthart 2009).

The coexistence of diverse systems of national economic governance within the EU holds important lessons for other parts of the world that have moved toward becoming open systems of governance. The reforms that were associated with the Washington Consensus failed to be sustainable in many countries because of popular opposition and because pivotal domestic groups were unable to credibly commit to the type of reforms championed by their governments following the priorities of organizations like the World Bank and the International Monetary Fund (e.g., Rodrik 2007a; Serra and Stiglitz 2008). Consequently, governments in several developing countries have actively campaigned against the principles of economic governance associated with the major global multilateral organizations and instead have opted to pursue bilateral and preferential trade agreements with select countries as a means to minimizing external adjustment costs. There are potentially large opportunity costs from such strategies in terms of forgone economic growth (Bhagwati 2008). As behavioral institutionalism would expect, such opportunity costs are underweighted and it is therefore politically more palatable to pursue such strategies.

The European cases hold two lessons for how an expansion of multilateralism can be made sustainable for a diverse set of market economies. First, they illustrate that quick transitions in structures of governance was not the norm and that governments instead were given significant leeway in developing their own economic strategies at speeds that were politically and economically sustainable. Economic liberalization has been a leitmotif of European integration over the past several decades, but it has not been the type of a rapid process experienced by many developing economies since the 1990s. Instead, it was an incremental process in which governments had significant room to creatively address domestic distributional conflicts. An important lesson is therefore that instead of encouraging governments in developing countries to quickly embrace reforms that align domestic designs with multilateral ones devoted to extensive liberalization, governments should have the discretion to gradually reform national designs in ways that allow domestic groups to retain their investments in historic designs. As behavioral institutionalism underscores, gradual reforms tend to have more lasting success because political groups are more likely to normalize small losses than large ones. This means that groups are more prone to accept incremental reforms that eventually produce radical results than they are to support quick wholesale reforms.

Dani Rodrik (2007b) notes about the contemporary era that "[t]he greatest risk of globalization lies in the prospect that national governments' room for manoeuvre will shrink to such levels that they will be unable to deliver the policies that their electorates want and need to buy into the global economy." Though the EU is frequently seen as an organization that forces governments to adopt unpopular liberalization agendas, it has also facilitated incremental national reforms and served to protect national designs that have been key to political sustainability. It has been an organization that has prevented protectionist impulses during economic downturns, thus sustaining open markets. Moreover, the EU has embraced international programs to compensate domestic losers from economic liberalization and openness. These include social insurance programs as well as support for large research and innovation programs that have replaced an earlier national emphasis on discriminatory aid to specific industries.

The European cases hold another lesson pertaining to the role of employing several layers of multilateralism. The EU is foremost a regional organization composed of multilateral institutions that are designed to help governments stabilize their national economies and ensure predictability and openness in international markets. As many countries in developing countries have supported international liberalization, they have often sought to meet global commitments without developing significant regional institutions. Although there is no reason to copy the EU model, there is reason to consider the general functions played by the European example. The EU and its precursors served to provide a set of regional public goods such as relative economic stability that would have been lacking in its absence. For example, it has ensured economic openness during periods of relative turmoil and when governments have been tempted to adopt protectionist measures. It has also sustained a steady expansion of international markets when global trade liberalization initiatives have stalled.

Rather than examining whether regional organizations divert from greater levels of global trade, the relevant consideration here is how regionally specific forms of multilateralism can be expanded to sustain national economic models while at the same time ensuring that global forms of multilateralism remain strong. Here Europe offers lessons, though it should be recalled that it is the mechanisms by which it has enabled a diverse set of national responses to coexist that is most important, and not the particular national designs that have existed.

The role played by the expansion of the EU's social dimension in sustaining support for market liberalization is instructive in this context. The members of the EU steadily expanded its social dimension as a means of ensuring domestic support for international liberalization. This process did not undermine the coordinated market economy model as is often suggested by those who focus on the potential consequence of regime competition. Nor did it impose the type of high standards associated with these economies on liberal market economies that have been reluctant to implement such standards. Rather, the expansion of the European social dimension helped sustain key aspects of both the coordinated and liberal market economy during crucial periods of international liberalization; the former by assuring domestic constituencies that their national investments in social institutions were protected, and the latter by avoiding high common standards.

A similar set of solutions does not presently exist in other multilateral contexts. For example, instead of incorporating a social dimension into a coherent system of governance or within multilateral organizations such as the World Trade Organization, the social dimension at the global level is either neglected or delegated to bodies that lack the ability to assure domestic groups that market liberalization will not impose significant adaptation losses. The European case suggests that countries wishing to increase their participation in international markets should consider an expansion of the social dimension of multilateral bodies at the regional level or attach such dimensions to existing global organizations as a means of improving the prospects that strategies of economic openness are sustainable over time.

If the past is prologue, the world will continue to be defined by a diverse set of national economic systems that are traveling at different speeds of change. The critical question for Europe and beyond, then, is not how to perfect a particular model of capitalism. Indeed, as development economist Pranab Bardhan reminds us: "[t]o proclaim the universal superiority of one coordination mechanism over another is naïve, futile, and ahistorical" (2005: 500). Rather, the lessons from Europe for beyond its borders are found in how to create international forms of governance that accommodate differential speed of reform and capitalist diversity.

Appendix

The Bases of Diverse Preferences Orders

Chapter 3 explored the implications of global, embedded, and behavioral rationality models for how firms rank institutional alternatives. This appendix details the origin of these rankings, or preference orders. Figure 3.1 was central to the chapter for it detailed how the context in which firms are situated affects their incentives to rank some institutional designs over others. It explained how the relationship between the specificity of firms' relational investments (a proxy for their sectoral profile) and what system of governance is in place (a proxy for national economic system) determine the costs of sustaining a social contract.

Based on figure 3.1, table A lets the costs of contracting (c) when employing a particular form of governance (x) at a specific moment in time (t) be positive and variable such that $0 < c(x)_t^k \leq 1$, where k indicates in what sector a firm is active depending on its degree of asset-specific relational investments. The table lists the high and low levels of governance costs associated with each level of asset specificity in the three alternative system of governance (x: L, E, C), where L represents a liberal market economy, E a centralized one, and C a coordinated market economy.[1] Firms are assumed to retain their sectoral identity (i.e., they are characterized as $k1$, $k2$, $k3$, or $k4$ firms), and market integration is operationalized as the opportunity to engage in institutional arbitrage and to move from the high to the low end within the parameters of a given sector. If the opportunity to exit is captured graphically by the prospect of a jump between lines between two moments in time, the same action may be represented in table A as an opportunity to move from the high end of an interval of k to the lower end of an alternative interval of k.[2]

The global, embedded, and behavioral rationality models posit that firms' preferences are a product of different utility functions. Let a represent the status quo institution, b an institutional alternative, t the moment at which evaluations are made, $t+1$ a moment in the future, and $t-1$ a moment in the past. Global rationality model posits that firms rank alternatives based on which alternative is associated with the lowest governance costs in the future: $U^k (a_{t+1} - b_{t+1})$. Embedded rationality model proposes that firms weigh the balance of costs and benefits from engaging in radical reform currently with how maintaining the status quo compares with past designs: $U^k ((a_{t-1} - a_t) - (a_t - b_t))$. Finally, behavioral model suggests that firms rank alternative after calculating the potential benefits of incremental reform at a future point versus the potential benefits of radical change at the same moment: $U^k ((a_t - a_{t+1}) - (a_{t+1} - b_{t+1}))$.

Tables B, C, and D represent the preference orders of the three models based on table A and the three utility functions. Table B specifies the preference orders of the global rationality model. It shows that firms' preferences will converge across economic models depending on their levels of relational asset specificity. Table C lists the preferences of firms according to an embedded rationality model and shows that firms prefer extant designs. Alternatives are assumed to be ranked according to which is associated with lower governance costs, though strict models of embedded rationality offer few answers to how alternatives are ranked beyond the status quo. Finally, table D lists the preference orders derived by the behavioral rationality model. The table underscores that preference orders do not converge as often as in table B or as rarely as table C.

If firms' preferences were a function only of where they were located and whether market integration presented opportunities to engage in institutional arbitrage, the preference orders detailed in the tables B, C, and D are sufficient to identify empirical expectations. If, however, these preferences also are influenced by the nature of external multilateral institutions, then their preferences may take different forms. Multilateral designs may be dimensionalized in similar ways as national ones. Typologized in such ways, the combination of national (x) and multilateral institutions (y) generate nine hypothetical cases of open governance (xy): LL, LE, LC, EL, EE, EC, CL, CE, CC.

Given the nine forms of open governance and four different sectors to which firms may belong, there are thirty-six hypothetical scenarios of how firms in different sectors will respond to alternative solutions to the design problem. Based on the figures in table A, the costs of contracting under situations of open governance may be calculated as $c(xy) = c(x) + Rc(y)$, where R is an interaction variable representing the extent to which national and multilateral designs jointly shape the behavior of economic groups, such that: $-1 \leq R \leq 1$. When national and multilateral forms of governance are incentive neutral (LC; CL), $R = 0$ and the costs of contracting remain unchanged. If national and multilateral institutions are incentive compatible (LL, EE, CC), R acquires a negative value that serves to reduce the comparative costs of governance. (This suggests that there are potential adjustment benefits from open governance.) However, should national and multilateral incentive structures be incompatible (LE, EL, EC, CE), R has a positive value and contributes to an increase in the comparative costs of contracting.

Table E adjusts the value of R for the purposes of comparing scenarios under which multilateral institutions play smaller or larger roles in shaping the costs of contracting in the national setting. It details the costs of sustaining social contracts in different national contexts under three scenarios of open governance: when the intensity of interaction (R) is low ($\pm.25$), medium ($\pm.5$), and high ($\pm.75$).

Tables F and G report the preferences according to the global and behavioral rationally models. (Because it is unclear in the embeddedness model what are the preferences of firms beyond the national status quo, there is no separate table for that model.)

TABLE A
Costs of contracting under alternative forms of governance

$0 < c(x) \leq 1$				
	Asset specificity (k)			
Form of governance (x)	$k1$	$k2$	$k3$	$k4$
L	.175–.400	.400–.525	.525–.750	.750–1.00
E	.500–.505	.505–.525	.535–.575	.575–.600
C	.325–.400	.400–.450	.450–.575	.575–.700

TABLE B
Global rationality model

Type of firm	Preference orders
$k1$	L>C>E
$k2$	C>L>E
$k3$	C>E>L
$k4$	E>C>L

TABLE C
Embedded rationality model

Type of firm	Location of embeddedness		
	L	E	C
$k1$	L>C>E	E>L>C	C>L>E
$k2$	L>C>E	E>C>L	C>L>E
$k3$	L>C>E	E>C>L	C>L>E
$k4$	L>C>E	E>C>L	C>E>L

TABLE D
Behavioral rationality model

Type of firm	Location of embeddedness		
	L	E	C
k1	L>C>E	L>C>E	L>C>E
k2	L>C>E	C>L>E	C>L>E
k3	L>C>E	C>E>L	C>L>E
k4	L>C>E	E>C>L	C>E>L

TABLE E
Contracting costs under open governance

		Low interaction intensity ($R: \pm.25$)		
		y =		
k=	x=	L	E	C
k1	L	.131–.300	.219–.500	.175–.400
	E	.625–.631	.375–.379	.500–.505
	C	.325–.400	.406–.500	.244–.300
k2	L	.300–.394	.500–.656	.400–.525
	E	.631–.656	.379–.394	.505–.525
	C	.400–.450	.500–.563	.300–.388
k3	L	.394–.563	.656–.938	.525–.750
	E	.656–.719	.394–.431	.525–.575
	C	.450–.575	.563–.719	.388–.431
k4	L	.563–.750	.938–1.25	.750–1.00
	E	.719–.750	.431–.450	.575–.600
	C	.575–.700	.719–.875	.431–.525

		Medium interaction intensity ($R: \pm.5$)		
		y =		
k=	x=	L	E	C
k1	L	.088–.200	.262–.600	.175–.400
	E	.750–.758	.250–.252	.500–.505
	C	.325–.400	.487–.600	.162–.200
k2	L	.200–.263	.600–.787	.400–.525
	E	.758–.788	.252–262	.505–.525
	C	.400–.450	.600–.675	.200–.225
k3	L	.263–.375	.787–1.125	.525–.750
	E	.788–.863	.262–287	.525–.575
	C	.450–.575	.675–.862	.225–.287

TABLE E—cont.

		Medium interaction intensity $(R: \pm.5)$		
		$y =$		
$k=$	$x=$	L	E	C
	L	.375–.500	1.125–1.50	.750–1.00
$k4$	E	.863–.900	.287–.300	.575–.600
	C	.575–.700	.862–1.05	.287–.350

		High interaction intensity $(R: \pm.75)$		
		$y =$		
$k=$	$x=$	L	E	C
	L	.044–.100	.306–.700	.175–.400
$k1$	E	.875–.884	.125–.126	.500–.505
	C	.325–.400	.569–.700	.081–.100
	L	.100–.131	.700–.919	.400–.525
$k2$	E	.884–.919	.126–.131	.505–.525
	C	.400–.450	.700–.788	.100–.112
	L	.131–.188	.919–1.313	.525–.750
$k3$	E	.919–1.001	.131–.144	.525–.575
	C	.450–.575	.788–1.001	.112–.144
	L	.188–.250	1.313–1.75	.750–1.00
$k4$	E	1.006–1.050	.144–.150	.575–.600
	C	.575–.700	1.001–1.225	.144–.175

TABLE F
Global rationality model under open governance

$R: \pm.25$

Type of firm	Order of alternatives
$k1$	LL>LC>LE>CC>CL>EE>CE>EC>EL
$k2$	LL=CC>EE>CL=LC>LE=CE>EC>EL
$k3$	CC>LL>EE>CL>LC=EC>CE>EL=LE
$k4$	EE=CC>LL>EC=CL>EL=CE>LC>LE

$R: \pm.5$

Type of firm	Order of alternatives
$k1$	LC>CC>LC>EE>LE>CL>CE>EC>EL
$k2$	LL=CC>EE>CL=LC>EC>LE=CE>EL
$k3$	CC>EE>LL>CL>LC>EC>CE>LE>EL
$k4$	EE=CC>LL>EC=CL>LC>CE>EL>EL

TABLE F—cont.

R: ±.75	
Type of firm	Order of alternatives
k1	LL>CC>EE>LC>LE>LC>EC>CE>EL
k2	LL=CC>EE>LC=CL>EC>LE=CE>EL
k3	CC>LL=EE>CL>LC=EC>CE>EL>LE
k4	CC=EE>LL>EC=CL>LC>CE>EL>CE

TABLE G
Behavioral model under open governance

Low interaction intensity (R: ±.25)		
Firm	Location of embeddedness	Order of alternatives
	L	LL>LC>LE>CC>CL>EE>CE>EC>EL
k1	E	LL>LC>LE>CC>CL>EE>CE>EC>EL
	C	LL>CL>CC>LE>CL>CE>EE>EC>EL
	L	LL>LC>CC>LE>EE>CL>CE>EC>EL
k2	E	LL=CC>EE>CL=LC>EC>LE=CE>EL
	C	CC>LL>CL>EE>LC>CE>LE>EC>EL
	L	LL>LC>LE>CC>EE>CL>EC>CE>EL
k3	E	EE>CC>LL>CL>EC>LC>CE>EL>LE
	C	CL>CC>LL=EE>CE>LC=EC>EL=LE
	L	LL>CC=EE>LC>CL>EC>LE>CE=CE
k4	E	EE>CC>EC>LL>CL>EL>CE>LC>LE
	C	CC>EE>CL>CE=LL>EC>EL>LC>LE
Medium interaction intensity (R: ±.5)		
Firm	Location of embeddedness	Order of alternatives
	L	LL>LC>LE>CC>EE>CL>CE>EC>EL
k1	E	LL>CC>LC>EE>LE>CL>CE>EC>EL
	C	LL>CC>LC>CL=EE>LE>CE>EC>EL
	L	LL>CC>EE>LC>CL>LE>EC>CE>EL
k2	E	LL=CC>EE>CL=LC>EC>CE=LE>EL
	C	CC>LL>EE>CL>LC>EC>CE>LE>EC
	L	LL>CC>EE>LC>CL>LE>EC>CE>EL
k3	E	CC>EE>LL>CL>EC>LC>CE>EL>LE
	C	CL>CC>LL=EE>CE>LC=EC>LE=EC
	L	LL>CC=EE>LC>CL=EC>LE>CE>EL
k4	E	EE>CC>LL>CL>EC>LC>CE>CL>LE
	C	CC>EE>LL>CL>EC>CE>LC>EL>LE

TABLE G—cont.

	High interaction intensity ($R: \pm.75$)	
Firm	Location of embeddedness	Order of alternatives
	L	**LL>LC>LE>CC>EE>CL>EC>CE>EL**
k1	*E*	**LL>CC>EE>LC>LE>CL>EC>CE>EL**
	C	**LL>CC>EE>LC>CL>LE>CE>EC>C**
	L	**LL>CC>EE>LC>CL>LE>EC>CE>EL**
k2	*E*	**LC=CC>EE>LC=CL>EC>LE=CE>EL**
	C	**CC>LL>EE>CL>LC>EC>CE>LE>EL**
	L	**LL>CC>EE>LC>CL>LE=EC>CE>EL**
k3	*E*	**CC>EE>LL>CL>EC>LC>CE>EL>LE**
	C	**CC>EE>LL>CL>CE>LC=EC>LE>EL**
	L	**LL>CC>EE>LC>CL=EC>LE>CE>EL**
k4	*E*	**EE>CC>LL>EC>CL>LC>CE>EL>LE**
	C	**CC>EE>LL>CL>EC>CE>LC>EL>LE**

Note: Boldface indicates cases where the costs of governance under open governance are less than under closed governance.

Notes

Chapter 1

1. "Anglo-Saxon capitalism" is a common synonym for liberal market economy.

2. For summaries of the debate, see Berger (2000); Guillén (2001); and Drezner (2001).

3. The distributional consequences of institutions and the political realities associated with their change are detailed in Knight (1992) and Pierson (2004).

4. On variations in incremental reforms, see Streeck and Thelen (2005b) and Mahoney and Thelen (2009).

5. The average economic openness of EU members, measured by exports and imports as a share of gross domestic product, increased five-fold in the six decades since 1950 to approximate 100 percent (author's calculation based on Heston, Summers, and Aten 2006). From 1957 to 2008, enforceable international legal mandates associated with the European Union and its precursors (regulations and directives) went from zero to reaching nearly 10,000 distinct instruments (Eur-lex 2010).

6. The periodization in this book stresses economic parameters that affected all countries discussed. The first period begins in 1950 during significant if uncertain economic expansion. It ends in 1973, a date around which there is broad consensus that the so-called Golden Age of post-war capitalism was over. The second period, 1974–1991, is marked by international economic crises and responses to these crises that included major multilateral initiatives like the European Economic Community's internal market program that targeted 1992 as the date of completion. The year 1992 represents the beginning of the third period, also marked by the signing of Treaty on European Union, and ends with the onset of the global economic crisis of 2008.

7. For discussions of criteria for contextualized comparisons, see George and Bennett (2005, 151–180).

8. Multilateral rules associated with the European Union impact terms of competition, the structure of capital markets, industrial relations, social regulations, and a host of other areas with direct relevance for corporate strategy. For general developments in these and other domains, see Hooghe and Marks (2001, 187–188); Hix (2005, 20–21); and Sandholtz and Fligstein (2001).

9. Partial equilibrium analysis, which characterizes much of the comparative and international political economy subfields, holds variables at one level constant while examining changes at a different level. For example, studies examine how changes in international rules affect responses at the national level, or how different national regimes affect the construction of international rules. By contrast, general equilibrium analysis examines how changes in variables at both levels affect the stability of institutions over time.

10. What in 1991 became known as the European Union (formally becoming operational in 1993) has historical origins in other organizations. When referring to precursor organizations, the narrative uses period-appropriate names.

11. Society-centered theories of political economy in which interest groups shape national reform agendas often imply that such groups (directly or indirectly) determine government choices. This volume makes no claim about what role such groups play in leading governments to pursue a particular set of reforms. Rather it focuses on how successful governments are in sustaining support for their reforms over time after choices have been made. Although the ability of societal groups to shape government agendas may have bearing on whether they later supported the reforms championed by governments, the latter dimension is treated here as an open empirical question.

12. For extended discussions on the analytical stakes in specifying the preferences of societal groups, see Frieden (1999), and Katznelson and Weingast (2005b).

13. For an overview, see Coen, Grant, and Wilson (2010).

14. Historical institutionalists debate the extent to which critical junctures transform preferences. If preferences are defined materially, for example by the distribution of factor endowments, then critical junctures like economic crises and wars would not be expected to significantly change the course of economic governance. If preferences have institutional and cognitive foundations, however, critical junctures can be expected to be more significant in altering preferences. Yet, historical institutionalists find evidence that institutional preferences often prevail across major historical junctures and that they frequently change in their absence (Thelen 2004; Streeck and Thelen 2005a). It is exactly because preference transformations are contextually contingent that the manner in which pivotal political groups frame the benefits of alternative modes of change is integral to a theory of institutional development.

15. In international relations studies, where behavioral economics features more extensively than in political economy, the focus has been on the decisions of political elites. See Levy (1992), (McDermott 2004), and Mercer (2005) for overviews. For a discussion of its potential contributions to research in political economy, see Elms (2008).

16. Scholars differ in their answers to whether historical institutionalism has unique microfoundations or if it is better subsumed under the umbrella of other traditions. Henry Farrell, for example, concludes that newer forms of historical institutionalism "do not have unique microfoundations" (2009, 1). Some subsume it under rational choice or sociological institutional traditions (Stein 2008, 215–216; Lawson 2006, 410). Others, like Peter Hall and Rosemary Taylor, argue that historical institutionalism is a distinct tradition because it incorporates the microfoundations associated with both rational choice and sociological institutionalism (Hall and Taylor 1998; Hall 2010). Turning to behavioral economics for the microfoundations of historical institutionalism represents a different perspective.

17. Multiple literatures suggest that the EU will produce progressively greater levels of convergence in economic models across its member-states. Early contributions focused on the consequences of regulatory competition (see discussions in Woolcock 1997; Sinn 2003), while later ones point to "judge-made law" through the interpretation and enforcement of legal rules and principles that favor one set of economic models over others (e.g., Höpner and Schäfer 2010; Scharpf 2010).

Chapter 2

1. Multilateralism is a generic institutional form that is the product of formal and informal international agreements among three or more states. Unlike other forms of international coopera-

tion (bilateralism, trilateralism, or universalism), multilateralism "does not analytically presuppose any particular number of countries" (Caporaso 1993, 55). Its defining characteristic is that it embodies a set of "generalized principles of conduct" that apply to all contracting parties (Ruggie 1993, 14). In the economic domain of post-war Europe, such principles were codified in specific and enforceable rules as well as in informal understandings of what constituted acceptable forms of government intervention and market regulation at the domestic and international levels. The literature on the origins of multilateralism in Europe is large, and ranges from studies of national purpose (e.g., Milward 1992), political and economic interests (e.g., Moravcsik 1998; Eichengreen 2007), normative considerations and resolutions (e.g., Checkel and Katzenstein 2009), to technical regulatory matters (e.g., Majone 1996).

2. Depending on the substantive focus of contributions to the varieties of capitalism literature (e.g., inflation, employment, innovation), research places the emphasis on different domains. A comprehensive overview of alternative typologies is found in Deeg and Jackson (2006). Table 2 represents ideal-types of the three models of capitalism that serve as reference points when making comparisons across cases. On the difference between research designs that are based on ideal-types versus variable-based ones, see Ragin and Zaret (1983).

3. Discussions about what constitutes an institution quickly become very long. In lieu of an extended account, this book understands institutions to be human constructs that constrain the behavior of political actors so that these behave in ways that constitute regularized practices. This understanding is consistent with broad ones like that of Douglass North who characterizes institutions as the "incentive structure of an economy" or as "the humanly devised constraints that structure political, economic, and social interaction" (1991: 97). It is also consistent with a more specific view such as that of Peter A. Hall and Kathleen Thelen (2009: 9) who define institutions "as sets of regularized practices with a rule-like quality in the sense that the actors expect the practices to be observed; and which, in some but not all, cases are supported by formal sanctions. They can range from regulations backed by the force of law or organizational procedure . . . to more informal practices that have a conventional character." Political actors are conceived as those public and private entities with stakes in the economic and social designs that govern interaction in variously regulated markets. On criteria for actor designation, see Frey (1985).

4. The conceptualization of self-enforcing institutions is rooted in the institutions-as-equilibria tradition. Associated with rational choice institutionalism (Shepsle 1986; Calvert 1995), a growing number of studies in the historical institutionalist tradition employ tools associated with the former tradition to examine patterns of stability and change (e.g., Hall and Soskice 2001a; Hall and Thelen 2009). Rational choice and historical institutionalism are often thought to be focused on different types of outcomes (equilibria or orders at a specific moment versus equilibria or orders over time). This is often the case, but need not be. The former's understanding of institutions as private orders that are designed to resolve enduring social dilemmas with some temporal permanence (e.g., Greif 2000, 2006) is similar to historical institutionalism's attention to the mechanisms that reproduce designs over time (e.g., Thelen 1999; Streeck and Thelen 2005; Streeck 2009). It is not their definition of institutions or the tools (e.g., game theory, archival research) used to identify when institutions are sustainable that is the primary reason for why rational choice institutionalism and historical institutionalism represent analytically distinct traditions, but different answers to so-called second-order issues. These issues concern how a theoretical tradition understands the structure and origin of preferences, conceptions of human action, and the principal constraints on human behavior. On second-order issues, see Wendt (1999, 4–6), and on the microfoundations of alternative institutional traditions, see Fioretos (2011).

5. Institutions are self-reinforcing when existing designs are more attractive than alternatives under an expanding set of conditions (Greif 2006, 167).

6. Radical change is defined here as a change in the mode of coordination in a specific institution so that the new arrangement is more similar to a different mode than to its own past.

7. See discussions in Berger and Dore (1996); Drezner (2001); Guillén (2001).

8. "The pivotal decisionmaker is that individual or group whose choices decides the outcome" (Bates et al. 1998, 235).

9. The political science literature focused on credible commitments is vast and covers all subfields. For early statements about the centrality of commitment problems in institutional analysis, see North (1993) and Shepsle (1991).

10. Defection is an act that occurs when firms behave in ways that do not reproduce institutions. Though typically intentional and following deliberation, it may be the unwitting consequence of legal actions that mandate new behavior, as well as incomplete or erroneous information that contributes to mistaken action.

11. For studies that place business at the center of analysis for similar reasons, see Hall and Soskice (2001a); Hacker and Pierson (2002); Swenson (2002); Thelen (2004); Hall and Thelen (2009).

12. The varieties of capitalism tradition's conceptualization of the role played by business in policymaking departs in several respects from other perspectives, including the structural power perspective that is associated with Charles Lindblom (1977) in which business interests directly impact public policy even if they do not actively seek to shape the latter. In the varieties of capitalism literature, no a priori assumption is made about the ability of business to shape public policy or the institutional choices of governments. Firms are instead understood to be social actors who confront multiple coordination problems, often within a set of constraints that governments have established and which they cannot easily alter. Meanwhile, governments often promote solutions opposed by powerful business interests and sometimes favor non- or narrow business interests. In other words, unlike the structural power perspective where influence runs in one direction (from business to governments), the varieties of capitalism tradition views this as a two-way relationship where diverse interests must be reconciled and where long-term institutional outcomes are contingent on several factors (see Hall and Soskice 2001a; Hall and Thelen 2009; and Hancké 2010).

13. Greif (2006) offers an extensive treatment of the differences between self-enforcing, self-reinforcing, and self-undermining institutions.

14. Structural reform is distinct from what is typically invoked by the term "industrial policy." The latter may be a part of the former, but it is associated narrowly with direct forms of intervention in industries and companies. Structural reform is here understood in broader terms to be the institutions promoted by governments for the purposes of influencing the composition and product market strategies of industry and enhancing the competitiveness of firms. Unlike the standard notion of industrial policy, structural reform may be explicitly non-interventionist and be oriented toward promoting and protecting market mechanisms.

15. On the distinction between commitments that are credible in imperative or motivational terms, see Shepsle (1991, 247) and North (1993).

16. In Schumpeter's terms, market competition "disciplines before it attacks" (1942, 85)

17. For heuristic purposes, the discussion here focuses exclusively on what the comparative economic organization literature terms first-order economizing, which pertains to preferences over structural alternatives of governance (Williamson 1991). Second-order economizing, which concerns incremental adjustments within a specific system of governance, is a common means by which firms and governments seek to reduce negative institutional differentials and informs other sections.

18. Constraints can be "beneficial" or "productive" when they encourage firms to invest in long-term capacity (Streeck 1992).

19. A large literature underscores that no model of advanced capitalism has historically been able to ensure that all types of firms across all major industrial sectors have been able to retain or enhance their relative competitiveness over time (e.g., Whitley 1999; Coates 2000; Schmidt 2002; Allen, Funk, and Tüselmann 2006). Firms specialize in particular product markets depending on the nature of the institutional environment in which they are situated (Hall and Soskice 2001a; Hancké 2010). For example, the liberal market economy offers an institutional environment that helps firms develop core competencies and competitive advantages in product markets characterized by radical innovation practices. Conversely, the liberal market economy has entailed comparative institutional disadvantages to firms competing in markets characterized by incremental innovation and highly specialized forms of advanced manufacturing. The centralized market economy has typically benefited large firms that have competed in large scale-intensive industries, but not provided much support for firms in specialized markets associated with high value-added advanced manufacturing. Finally, the coordinated market economy has been found to help firms acquire strong presence in product markets characterized by incremental innovation in the advanced manufacturing sector, but to entail some institutional disadvantages in high-tech sectors characterized by radical innovation.

Hall and Soskice (2001b: 42–43) use patent data to identify where comparative institutional advantages are found. Fioretos (2001) and Allen, Funk, and Tüselmann (2006) use measurements of revealed comparative advantage and demonstrate similar patterns to Hall and Soskice using data on firms' performance in international markets.

20. Institutional complementarities are systemic effects that exist when the presence of one design enhances the benefits associated with a different one (Hall and Soskice 2001b, 17).

21. Adjustment costs are those accrued when extant designs are modified. Because these costs may be common across all types of institutions, they do not determine whether commitments to extant designs are credible. Adjustment costs are, in James Buchanan's words, "choice-influenced." By contrast, maladaptation costs, which are the product of comparisons between the costs and benefits of extant designs and feasible alternatives and thus entail assessments of potential opportunity costs, are "choice-influencing" (Buchanan 1998, 719).

22. By contrast to maladaptation costs, which actors have incentives to encourage in some cases (especially if they expect increases to tip the balance of political power toward reforms that reduce such costs), actors do not have incentives to support scenarios that produce adaptation losses. That is, unless they take pleasure in securing alternatives they rank below their first choice or suspect such a course to be compensated with rewards in other contexts.

23. Maladaptation costs exist when economic groups perceive negative institutional differentials from sustaining the status quo. (Radical change thus entails potential benefits.) Conversely, adaptation losses are manifest when changes in the status quo (or other reference points) eliminate (or reduce) positive institutional differentials. The distinction between the two scenarios is important for in the former case a change in the status quo places economic groups in the domain of gains, while in the latter case they find themselves in the domain of losses. This difference has many implications for economic groups' incentives to mobilize in favor of one or another alternative and for the conditions under which groups can credibly commit to specific institutions. For example, in contrast to situations where maladaptation costs transform preferences and lead groups to mobilize resources to radically change existing designs, adaptation losses do not have such effects in the short term; rather, they create incentives for constituencies to devote resources to protecting existing arrangements.

24. The phraseology of luck, stuck, and pluck comes from Schwartz (2001).

25. See also Risse, Cowles, and Caporaso (2001, 7) who describe incentive compatible arrangements as situations where membership in an international organizations generates no "adaptational pressures" on national designs.

26. Since the Single European Act (1986), legislative decisions in EU's intergovernmental bodies are taken either by unanimity or by qualified majority voting. The very large majority of decisions that pertain to the internal market in products, goods, and services—including financial—are taken under the latter rule.

27. Efforts to enhance the prospect that domestic designs are preserved through common minimum standards may be temporary. As Fritz Scharpf details (2010), the European Court of Justice has at times interpreted treaty provisions in ways not anticipated by member-states and in ways that eventually had asymmetric effects across countries with respect to the conditions under which national designs could be reproduced. In particular, Scharpf notes, the EU serves to undermine social market economies. As James Caporaso and Sidney Tarrow (2009) find, however, the ECJ has in some instances lessened such prospects by embedding a social purpose within EU's regulatory architecture that reduces the prospect that social market economies are undermined.

28. Adaptation benefits are present when adjustments improve institutional differentials. The term comes from Callaway (2003).

29. Peter A. Hall describes systematic process analysis as "a very different project from the one in which most historians engage," and adds that "[I]t is focused on the testing of propositions derived from a deductive process of theory formation" (2003, 395). The advantages of the deductive elements to theory testing are enhanced when theories focus on the same political actor over time. From this perspective, it is not analytically efficient to compare theories that focus on different political actors (e.g., class interests versus inter-industry cleavages). Contemporary institutional analysis, of which systematic process analysis is partly a reflection, is focused on theorizing the foundations of the interests of the same collective over time. The assumptions that are made about the preferences of such collectives are potentially significant for they may generate more or less complete accounts of how societies resolve recurring political and social dilemmas. There are, however, potential drawbacks of systematic process analysis. If the political groups on which the emphasis falls are not consistently consequential in shaping outcomes, then the value of systematic process analysis are purely theoretical. Conversely, if the political groups at whom the primary emphasis is directed are consequential for how recurring political and social dilemmas are resolved, then systematic process analysis offers the opportunity to identify which theoretical approach is better suited to account for empirical regularities.

Systematic process analysis allows social scientists who grapple with political and social phenomena that are not easily measured to comment on the consequences, empirical and analytical, of employing alternative assumptions and operationalizations of key microlevel features, such as utility calculations or preference orders. To the extent that a successful theory is a function of its microfoundations, this advantage of systematic process analysis is significant. Here, the particular aspect of theories' microfoundations is the institutional preferences of political groups, principally members of the business sectors. If one accepts Jeffry A. Frieden's (1999) arguments about how political scientists most effectively approach the issue of the origins and structure of preferences, then there are advantages both in terms of analytical parsimony and in analytical consistency from approaching the study of preferences through deductive procedures and to focus comparisons on tested models.

Readers less set on academic debates may find the focus of systematic process analysis narrow. They would be justified. In part the narrow focus is a casualty of systematic process analysis devoting extensive attention to multiple theoretical claims and to testing these. Such exercises have their value but they also come at a cost. For example, it entails trade-offs with respect to how successfully a single study can meet both ambitions of what Theda Skocpol (2003) calls "doubly engaged" social science.

30. Global rationality models inform neoclassical theories, the economic approach to institutions, and standard expected utility theory, which have narrow disciplinary connotations that the

term "global rationality" avoids (see discussions in March and Olson 1984; Tversky and Kahneman 1991; Simon 1997; Gilpin 2001, 46–76).

31. The representation of rational choice institutionalism as a tradition closely beholden to global rationality models is a reduced, perhaps narrow representation, though one widely accepted. See, e.g., discussions in Simon (1955); Elster (1979); March and Olsen (1984); Green and Shapiro (1996).

32. See Capoccia and Kelemen (2007) for a discussion of historical institutionalism and the role of critical junctures in producing radical departures from established practice.

33. A subject of debate in behavioral economics is whether the logics of adaptation that characterize individuals can be applied to the study of groups or organizations, including firms. Kahneman, Knetsch, and Thaler (2000, 227) note that there is evidence that firms are "reluctant to divest themselves of divisiòns, plants, and product lines even though they would never consider buying the same assets." Thaler has explored the issue further (e.g., Thaler and Shefrin 1981), most notably in the context of financial firms and markets (e.g., DeBondt and Thaler 1994; Thaler 1993; see also Akerlof and Schiller 2009). These studies underscore that decision biases that characterize individuals also exist within groups and organizations and are in fact in some cases exacerbated in the latter setting.

34. What Portes and Sensenbrenner (1993) term the neo-classical model employs assumptions of global rationality.

35. Revealed preferences theory posits that the choices individuals make reflect their preferences given existing constraints.

36. For details of joint idiographic and nomothetic counterfactual analysis, see Tetlock and Belkin (1996, 6, 10–12).

Chapter 3

1. Institutions figure prominently in the open economy politics literature in aggregating preferences and mediating international market signals, but not as potential variables that shape firms' preferences over forms of economic governance. See the exchange between Frieden and Rogowski (1996) and Garrett and Lange (1996).

2. On the centrality of opportunity costs in economic models of rationality, see Alchian (1968), Becker (1976), and Buchanan (1998).

3. Paul N. Doremus, William W. Keller, Louis W. Pauly, and Simon Reich assert that a "[full] and commonly accepted definition [of globalization] refers to the . . . tendency for economic and political variables to *converge towards global norms* (1998, 151, n.2, emphasis added).

4. If a government is unwilling to promote the reforms preferred by firms, the commitments of the latter to the agenda of the former will in a global rationality model only be credible if firms' discretion to defect is constrained.

5. The goodness-of-fit hypothesis informs major studies of the EU (e.g., Duina 1999; Haverland 2000; Cowles, Caporaso, and Risse 2001). It has generally been explored in the context of how quickly and completely member-states implement EU legislation and not to theorize the conditions under which governments are able to generate support among domestic groups. This literature does not generally explore what role the goodness-of-fit has for the institutional preferences of domestic actors over time. Nor does it typically address instances where multilateral designs reinforce domestic designs by enhancing their value to political groups or cases where a misfit persists because domestic groups voluntarily accept the costs associated with poorly fitted institutions. The former case is one that makes patterns of specialization possible. In the

latter case, other institutions are not necessarily the source of continuity because groups may accept the reality of some degree of misfit as superior to a situation that involves radical changes domestically.

6. The goodness-of-fit literature focused on Europe highlights these types of institutions extensively. For a comprehensive conceptual discussion on the key issues, see Börzel and Risse 2003.

7. For extended discussions of increasing returns, see Pierson (2000), and Buchanan and Yoon (2001).

8. Granovetter (1985) offers an extended discussion of the broader implications for substantive analysis from employing global and embedded rationality models. Granovetter's thesis—that a neoclassical model, analogous to what this study summarizes as the global rationality model, treats social actors as "undersocialized" and that its alternatives treat them as "oversocialized"—informs central distinctions in this book. Although the premises embraced in this chapter are those of Granovetter, I have found the work of Oliver Williamson, whom Granovetter targets for critical attention, to offer practical solutions to identifying the expectations of the models discussed by Granovetter. Williamson's work (1991), which entailed no direct response to Granovetter (1985), offers, perhaps unwittingly, through discrete structural analysis a means to isolating analytical problems discussed by Granovetter, including identifying when small changes have transformative effects. The appendix entails one attempt to isolate instances when alternative claims of actor rationality affect empirical expectations. Specifically, it identifies when such claims generate observationally equivalent or distinct predictions about the structure and evolution of the institutional preferences of social actors operating within multiple institutional contexts.

9. Endowment effects constitute a form of loss aversion (Kahneman and Tversky 1984), which is to say that someone will attach greater value to giving something up than acquiring the same possession. Thaler (1992, 4) gives a simple illustration of the endowment effect when someone suddenly wins a pair of tickets to a championship game. Though the value of these tickets may be readily known, behavioral economics finds that individuals who hold the tickets tend to request larger sums of compensation to part with them, even if just acquired, than would be the case were they offered the opportunity to purchase the same tickets.

10. Endowment premiums are not infinite, nor are they invariable over time. Under some conditions, social actors will jettison their existing investments—even if highly overvalued. The hypothesis that emerges from a behavioral model is that firms' commitments to extant designs are credible when the endowment premium is greater than any positive institutional differential between an existing arrangement and the most attractive alternative. Conversely, if the endowment premium is smaller than the difference between extant arrangements and the most attractive alternative, firms' commitments to extant designs lose motivational credibility. In the latter case, firms are expected to favor the alternative that offers the greatest return above the endowment premium. The greater is the negative balance between the endowment premium and a particular reference point, the stronger will be a firm's preference for transformation. Conversely, the greater is the positive balance between the endowment premium and cost differentials, the stronger are firms' incentives to support extant designs and devote resources to securing them.

11. What constitutes the relevant reference point is a more open empirical question in behavioral models than standard accounts that employ global and embedded rationality models. In global rationally models, reference points are found in the future, while in embedded models it is the past or the present that serves as the reference point. Behavioral models note that reference points can, in addition to being found in the past or the present, also be aspirational in nature. The key issue in such models is how large changes in the costs and benefits associated with alternatives are with respect to the reference point employed by any given social actor in a given case (Kahneman and Tversky 1984; Kahneman, Knetsch, and Thaler 1991).

12. Williamson (1991) labels the three forms of governance markets, hierarchies, and hybrids. I adapt his terms to those more familiar in the comparative capitalisms literature. Economic systems predominantly characterized by market-based coordination are thus termed liberal market economies, those employing hierarchical modes are designated centralized market economies, and what Williamson calls hybrid systems are termed coordinated market economies.

13. As is often the case in the new economics of organization literature, the terms governance and transaction costs are used interchangeably. Williamson defines the latter as "The ex ante costs of drafting, negotiating, and *safeguarding* an agreement and, more especially, the ex post costs of maladaptation and adjustment that arise when contract execution is misaligned as a result of gaps, errors, omissions, and unanticipated disturbances; the costs of running the economic system" (Williamson 1996a, 379).

14. Bilateral dependence gives rise to asset specific relational investments (Williamson 1991).

15. The varieties of capitalism literature shows that industries that rely on highly flexible social contracts (*k1* firms), such as financial services and radical innovation industries, enjoy comparative institutional advantages in liberal market economies and exploit these to create distinct core competencies. Meanwhile, firms relying on long-term social contracts with substantial specificity (*k2* and *k3* firms)—for example scale-intensive and specialized supplier industries—are found in larger numbers in coordinated economies that are conducive to industries characterized by incremental innovation and diversified quality production. Finally, industries characterized by highly specific assets (*k4* firms) such as natural monopolies or firms benefiting from high levels of fixed infrastructure investments have often been championed as lead sectors in centralized market economies (see Hall and Soskice 2001a; Jackson and Deeg 2008).

16. The social science methods associated with Max Weber, who emphasized typological differences in social systems, stress comparisons of structural alternatives or what is termed first-order considerations. Such considerations are in Oliver Williamson's terms about "getting the basic alignments right," while second-order considerations are focused on marginal adjustments (Williamson 1991, 1996b; see also Simon 1978).

17. Two assumptions are made throughout the chapter. First, national economies are treated as structurally differentiated forms of governance and as distinct institutional equilibria (Williamson 1991; Hall and Soskice 2001a). Second, though firms' utility functions and the nature of their comparative assessments are varied according to the claims of the three models of rationality, firms are assumed to be intendedly rational actors that seek to conserve on governance costs in all models (Williamson 1985, 1991).

18. Institutional arbitrage is a process in which a firm evaluates the relative attractiveness of alternatives and pursues that which it reasons ensures the lowest costs of governance. Practices of institutional arbitrage are widely thought to be a major feature behind institutional development in open economies where firms become more sensitive to variations in the costs of contracting and where opportunities exist for firms to jettison extant design for new ones. Drezner (2001) offers an overview of the debate.

19. Potential transition costs are highly discounted in global rationality models and thus the primary source of preference transformations is found in comparisons of prospective alternatives.

20. Exercising the exit option does not necessarily mean that firms relocate to a different jurisdiction; it simply means that they withdraw their support for extant designs. It is an erroneous inference on the part of much of the globalization literature that exit threats are necessarily international in scope. In market economies, firms that rely exclusively on domestic contracts and that have limited recourse to relocating abroad are also subject to the effects of international competition and thus sensitive to institutional differentials. Unless such firms wish to see their domestic market shares gradually reduced by imports from foreign firms exploiting the institutional advantages of a different setting to be more competitive, they also have strong incentives to adopt

practices that stop reproducing extant designs if they think such actions will generate outcomes that reduce negative differentials. In the 1990s, for example, most European governments significantly expanded their attention to small- and medium-sized firms—generally thought to have relational contracts that are not easily substituted with new ones abroad—because such firms were considered integral in addressing both high levels of unemployment and promoting growth in new information-intensive industries. From the vantage point of governments managing an open economy, then, credible threats of exit from the social contracts that sustain institutions over time are not limited to firms that can relocate abroad, but include any type of firm on which governments rely to successfully implement a specific economic strategy.

Firms have relational investments in other firms and economic groups as a means of developing and maintaining core competencies and capabilities that generate competitive advantages. Thus, their decision to exit is not one they make lightly as it typically involves giving up access to valuable resources. (Relational investments are made in order to conserve on the costs of maintaining social contracts and to gain and maintain access to specialized information, knowledge, and skills, as well as to processes of production and innovation that enhance the competencies and capabilities of firms. See Williamson 1991; Hart 1995.) Albert O. Hirschman reminds us that a threat to abandon existing arrangements comes not from those who are set on giving up on their investments, but from those who seek to preserve their stakes: "The threat of exit will typically be made by the *loyalist*—that is, by the member who cares—who leaves no stone unturned before he resigns himself to the painful decision to withdraw or switch" (Hirschman 1970, 83, emphasis added). If a firm is truly committed to exit, it would seek to avoid the costs of issuing threats and simply move. "Hence," writes Hirschman, "the decision to exit will be taken and carried out in silence" (1970, 83). As Hirschman suggests, if the goal is to answer why some institutional designs are stable and others erode over time, then the primary analytical attention should not be on the terms under which firms that are pivotal to sustaining existing designs threaten to exit. Rather it should be on the conditions under which the conditions exist for them to be loyal.

21. On the role of baseline comparisons, see Tversky and Kahneman (1991).

22. Thaler (1980, 44) notes that endowment effects may be understood as the underweighting of opportunity costs. In this context, an endowment premium may be understood as the underweighting of opportunity costs in the sense that firms reason that the benefits forgone from rejecting an alternative are less than would be the case in a global rationality model. Alternatively, from the vantage point of the latter model, the premium may be understood as a surcharge in governance costs given the non-elimination of opportunity costs.

23. Because multilateral institutions in the modern advanced economy have been used to enhance market integration, the effects of multilateralism are examined solely in a context of high levels of market integration.

24. Studies of the European Union note that multilateral designs in post-war Europe have often taken on the characteristics associated with the centralized, coordinated, and liberal models (e.g., Streit and Mussler 1995; Pollack 2000; Hooghe and Marks 1999; Höpner and Schäfer 2010).

25. The underlying assumption of the multilateralism null hypothesis is that economic groups prefer incentive compatible arrangements. But just as the political economy null hypothesis exaggerates the degree of convergence across sectors, there are significant sectoral variations in firms' preferences when employing the strict conditions of the multilateralism null hypothesis (appendix, tables B and F). At higher levels of asset specificity, incentive compatible arrangements structured around coordinated and centralized designs are often associated with lower governance costs than liberal ones. Moreover, under the criteria of the multilateralism hypothesis, there are important changes in the ranking of solutions to the design problem under alternative forms of open governance when the intensity of interaction increases. Finally, if there is a large enough discrepancy in

the governance costs of national alternatives and the intensity of interaction is relatively low, some incentive incompatible agreements may be preferable to some that are compatible.

26. Paradoxically, the one case (at $R\pm.5$: $k3^L$) in which firms are embedded in liberal settings where the multilateralism null hypothesis and the endowment model differ is one in which the former predicts convergence on coordinated economy designs, while the latter expects firms in liberal settings to prefer institutional continuity.

27. This holds in all cases except those where firms rely on very high levels of asset-specific investments or when interaction intensities are low.

28. Firms could further reduce governance costs if they changed the national system of governance to a liberal one. However, they have no strong incentive to do so because they could reduce these costs further if the multilateral arrangement were to be changed at a future date to one that is congruent with the national form (CC).

29. There is one exception to this prediction. Under low and medium intensity levels of open governance, $k3$ firms in coordinated settings may also support a liberal multilateral arrangement if they can maintain the existing national form of governance, which would decrease total governance costs. This would be a rare instance of firms having a primary preference for an arrangement that is not incentive compatible.

Chapter 4

1. The rate of productivity growth in 1960 was 4.5 percent in Britain, 9.8 percent in Germany, and 7.8 percent in France (U.S. Department of Labor 2008: table 1.2).

2. The importance of gaining the support of private industry is apparent in government documents. For example, Prime Minister Macmillan (1961) noted in a memo to Chancellor Selwyn Lloyd that "it is extremely important that any attempt to enlist the co-operation of industry in a new approach to the economic problem carry real conviction." In a letter he was asked to draft and send to industry leaders, Lloyd (1961) acknowledges the importance of securing the support of industry "on whose co-operation the fulfillment of our objectives must significantly depend." Blank (1973) offers a detailed history of the relationship between government and industry in this period.

3. Support among large companies for the government's centralization program in the early 1960s, as well as the opposition among small and medium-sized companies, is evident in the substantial correspondence that took place between the office of the president of the Federation of British Industry and its members (Harrison Papers, 1961–1963).

4. By international standards productivity growth in Britain was particularly weak between 1950 and 1973, when it underperformed European countries by about 0.7 percent per year (Broadberry and Crafts 1996, 72).

5. British tariff rates remained relatively unchanged at around 30 percent from the 1950s until it joined the EEC. By comparison, rates in Germany were slightly above 5 percent in the 1950s and 1960s, and declined to half that level in the 1970s (Broadberry 1997, 139–141). Import surcharges were imposed in 1964 as an alternative to currency devaluation.

6. Within the business community, strong support was found in the mechanical engineering, electrical engineering, metals and metal manufacturing, vehicles, chemicals, and the construction industry. Only within the textiles and food and beverages industries was there mixed support (CBI 1967c). For the evolution of the business sector's support for multilateral alternatives, see Lieber (1970); Rollings (1998); McKinlay, Mercer, and Rollings (2000).

7. Citing a study from 1969, CBI argued that assessments of the costs and benefits of membership were made with reference to the situation "Britain could face in the eighties" (CBI 1975, 3).

A major study of the manufacturing industry's views on multilateral alternatives in the late 1950s used a similar time horizon (EIU 1957).

8. A government white paper justified membership in the EEC on the grounds that it would bring "substantial advantage for British industry . . . stemming primarily from the opportunities for greater economies of scale, increased specialization, a sharper competitive climate and faster growth." It also noted that these advantages were greater "than exists at present or would otherwise exist in the future" (HMSO 1970, 37, 26). A Cabinet memo stated that "The reasons for joining the Community can equally well be expressed as the disadvantages of exclusion or the advantages of being inside" (Official Committee on Europe 1966, 3).

9. Between 1950 and 1960, British exports to the EEC members doubled from 10 percent to 20 percent, while the Sterling Area saw a drop of some 15 percent to a total of roughly 35 percent. Parity in the two markets was reached in 1972 at about 25 percent; thereafter, the European market gained substantially. Unlike in the 1950s, there was no significant growth in the share of British exports going to EEC markets in the 1960s. Small increases were evident only prior to each application, but there was a corresponding decline after each French veto (based on calculations in CSO [1960–1962, 211] and CSO [1969–1970, 247]).

10. If one's historical reference point is the Victorian era, an argument could be made that what happened after 1979 was the restoration, rather than construction, of a liberal market economy (e.g., Levy, Kagan, and Zysman 1998). However, for politicians and the business community, the primary reference point was the post-war period and reforms after 1979 were therefore construed as the creation of something new, even if frequent references were made to earlier historical periods.

11. Privatization was a gradual process, which began in earnest only after Thatcher secured re-election in 1983. By the end of the decade, however, the government had divested state shares in all major industries with the exception of the nuclear energy sector.

12. Unemployment more than doubled in the 1980s to 9.7 percent of the total labor force in comparison to the 1974–1979 period when it was 4.2 percent (OECD 1997, 45).

13. In an open letter in the *Times* of London (30 March 1981), a group of 364 economists questioned the Thatcher government's macroeconomic strategy.

14. The exception to firms preferring a liberal model is found among firms with highly specific investments, which would see an increase in the costs of contracting if a switch occurred from a centralized model of governance to a liberal one. However, firms in this sector—primarily found in the nationalized industries and those that had been major recipients of government support— were sidelined politically by being privatized or forced to close due to lacking profits. Unlike previous governments that saw firms in this sector (e.g., coal, steel) as important sources of political support, the Conservative government under Thatcher opted to implement a strategy that did not rely on this sector. Instead, it built a coalition of support among small- and medium-sized enterprises, large internationally oriented manufacturing companies, and the financial services sector. Each of the latter lacked investments in old designs and each were in a position to exploit comparative institutional advantages associated with the liberal market economy.

15. During the 1980s, Britain attracted 15 percent of all incoming foreign direct investment in the OECD, while the corresponding figures were 6.3 percent in France and 2.3 percent in Germany (OECD 2004, 13).

16. In describing her government's approval of the Single European Act, Thatcher (1993) noted: "we would never have got the single market without an extension . . . of majority voting. We could never have got our insurance into Germany . . . a fair deal for our ships in picking up goods from other ports as other could pick up from ours . . . a fair deal for our lorry and transport business because lorries had to go over there full and come back empty as they were not allowed to pick up on the way back. Yes, we wanted a single market and we had, in fact, to have some majority

voting." On the response by British business to the SEA and internal market program, see Cowles (1994) and Moravcsik (1998, ch. 5).

17. Williamson (1996b, 7) distinguishes between first-order economizing behavior, which involves the choice of a model of governance, and second-order economizing, which concerns incremental adjustments within an existing model.

18. A comparison of the Labour Party's 1983 and 1996 election manifestoes underscores the major changes informing the new leadership of the party. Unlike the former that called for the re-nationalization of firms, a five-year national plan centering around agreements with trade unions, and exit from the European Economic Community, the latter accepted privatization, made no mention of national plans, and embraced European integration.

19. The reforms of the 1980s had allowed firms to significantly cut costs and to gradually narrow the productivity gap that had existed with Germany and France between 1979 and 1989. For example, labor productivity in the manufacturing sector had increased by 50 percent, and the gaps with Germany and France had been reduced from 51 percent and 34 percent, to 17 percent and 20 percent, respectively (Crafts 1994, 210).

20. Due to the more extensive hostility to EEC membership among past Labour governments, the Blair government devoted greater attention to communicating its commitment to membership in the EU than its Conservative predecessor. In addition to asserting that his government would place Britain at the "center of Europe," Blair often recounted in his defense of membership the costs the British economy had incurred from the uncertainty that characterized its prospective membership in the 1960s and 1970s (e.g., Blair 2001; 2006a).

21. Dyson and Featherstone (1999) offer a comprehensive treatment of negotiations, and Fioretos (2001) presents a discussion on why member-states varied in their views on particular designs across key areas.

22. The other side of opposition to an industrial policy was support by the Major government for a more stringent competition policy, in particular to limits on collusive practices often found in coordinated market economies.

23. In a significant departure from its predecessor, the Major government decided to take part in the Exchange Rate Mechanism of the European Monetary System in 1990 to reinforce its commitment to fighting inflation. The government expected membership to shape price expectations (including in wage negotiations) in ways that would place downward pressures on price growth. However, less than two years after it joined, speculative attacks against the British currency forced the Major government to exit the arrangements and return to a more autonomous monetary and exchange rate policy.

24. Ian Lang, the head of the Department of Trade and Industry, launched a vigorous defense of the opt-out and spoke directly about avoiding multilateral rules that were incompatible with those at home: "The British approach is one of low burdens on business and voluntarism. The continental approach is based on regulation and statutory obligation. The Social Chapter embodies the continental approach" (*Telegraph*, 1 October 1996).

25. The directive was introduced by the European Commission as a health and safety provision, thus making its passing subject to a qualified majority in the Council. The Thatcher government strongly objected to interpreting the directive in such terms, and in 1993 the Major government challenged the case in the European Court of Justice. The Court ruled against Britain after three years of deliberation.

26. Prime Minister Gordon Brown threatened not to sign the Treaty of Lisbon in 2007 unless he was assured that Britain's special status was maintained with respect to the Working Time Directive (*Financial Times*, 6 December 2007).

27. Goergen, Martynova, and Renneboog (2005) offer an overview of national differences and the main issues involved with the British case as the primary reference point.

Chapter 5

1. Based in pre-war practice and formalized in the Collective Bargaining Act of 1950, the extension procedure enabled governments to exercise great influence in tripartite contexts over wages by promoting binding agreements on companies in any sector, region, or across the economy. Though companies could individually deviate upward from wage minima, the post-war system contained wage drift because of the continued weakness of unions and through provisions that allowed management to meet statutory obligations by signing agreements with single unions (N. Parsons 2005, 7–8).

2. About one-third of the early planning commissions were composed of representatives from the business sector, which by itself was the largest economic group. As the total size of commissions grew, the relative share of the business sector remained steady and roughly twice that of civil servants who constituted the second largest membership in the commissions (Cohen 1977, 193–194). Though there was some opposition within the manufacturing sector to the emphasis on indicative planning, France's large manufacturing benefited from privileged access to scarce capital and protected markets and supported the government's commitment to industrial modernization. In contrast, small and medium-sized companies were given little attention, mostly seen as obstacles to modernization, and thus generally opposed the government's commitment to creating larger industrial conglomerates and cartels.

3. Pitman (1997) offers detailed accounts of how domestic considerations shaped French assessments of multilateral alternatives during the 1950s.

4. The same year, only 16 percent of exports went to the future members of the EEC, while 27 percent had destinations in other industrialized states (Adams 1989, 178).

5. The 1958 EEC agreement was part of a package deal that also included two other initiatives that were key to France's domestic strategy of structural adjustment. One was the Common Agricultural Policy, which offered protection to farmers and helped French governments reduce the political and economic costs of transforming its economic structure. The second agreement concerned cooperation in the area of nuclear energy, which the French government saw as essential to replacing its reliance on coal for industrial power. Moravcsik (1998, 86–158) offers a comprehensive account of this period and the relationship between national economic interests and intergovernmental negotiations.

6. B. Balassa (1981) offers an extended discussion of the economic effects of membership in the EEC.

7. Bankruptcies rose by 70 percent under the Giscard presidency, and there was a significant contraction in the manufacturing workforce (8.5%) between 1975 and 1979. A similar process occurred in other industrialized countries, but it progressed at a faster pace in France (Green 1984, 148–149).

8. The share of French exports to Europe and the original members of the EEC had reached a peak in the early 1970s at 69 percent and 50 percent, respectively, but declined gradually in the course of the decade. In 1981, the figures stood at 57 percent and 37 percent, and recorded a sharp drop of about 4 percent in each category in the preceding year (Adams 1989, 178).

9. From the perspective of the French business community, the internal market introduced a set of new and largely beneficial constraints. It significantly limited the ability of French authorities to discriminate against companies through direct support, subsidized loans, or targeted non-tariff barriers. To large export-oriented and many smaller companies, this was a welcome development as it served as insurance against a return to the interventionist strategies of the early 1980s when resources were frequently redirected to failing firms. Moreover, for the country's large firms, the loss of domestic support was in large part compensated through the introduc-

tion of a large number of major R&D programs at the European level, which gave them access to investments seven times the size of their own contributions (Moynot 1987, 273). More broadly, France was a major net-recipient of European level R&D programs to the tune of 95 million European Currency Units between 1988 and 1992 (calculations based on Peterson 1996, 236).

10. Domestic consensus did not spell international consensus. French governments repeatedly sought greater discretion for national and European monetary authorities in promoting growth, but met resistance for such designs from other member-states. Reaching an agreement meant accepting the priorities of the latter in many important areas that had practical consequences for French governments, including the adoption of more austere budgets than preferred. Dyson and Featherstone (1999) offer a comprehensive treatment of French support for European monetary cooperation.

11. Market capitalization in France rose from 26 percent to 105 percent of GDP in 1999. The corresponding figures were 22 percent and 68 percent in Germany, 87 percent and 198 percent in Britain, and 56 percent and 181 percent in the United States (Goyer 2006, 407).

12. Goyer (2001, 147) entails a list of the specific parts divested by conglomerates.

13. International mergers and acquisitions by French firms rose from 0.6 percent of GDP to a peak of 12.9 percent in 2000 (O'Sullivan 2005, 373).

14. The median voting bloc in France's largest listed companies was 20 percent of shares, while it was 10 percent in Britain, below 10 percent in the United States (5% at NYSE, 9% at NASDAQ), and 57 percent in Germany (Enriques and Volpin 2007, 119).

15. Trumbull (2004) offers an overview of the major issues in this debate.

16. The reality that French governments have often been unable to secure EU rules that would prevent the undermining of long-term domestic objectives has been a persistent preoccupation of governments, including in the recent period (e.g., Vedrine 2001; Meunier 2004; Conseil d'Etat 2007).

Chapter 6

1. The expression "wirtschafts-blunder" comes from the *Economist* (4 May 1996).

2. The architects of the social market economy saw that model as more closely aligned to the liberal alternative, but rejected a system of unfettered markets for having detrimental social consequences, for underestimating the political necessity and economic benefits from an extensive set of social policies, and for its lack of effectiveness in providing public goods. Meanwhile, the statist model was repudiated for compromising individual freedom and for generating an inefficient allocation of economic resources. Finally, both models were renounced (though for somewhat different reasons) for not actively preventing the formation of anti-competitive practices that would limit the effectiveness of the market mechanism. See Müller-Armack (1947, 1948b).

3. The social market economy was formally adopted as the institutional foundation for economic reconstruction by the Christian Democrats in their election program of August 1949. Ten years later, the Social Democrats did the same.

4. The Bundesbank inherited its core principles of monetary policy from its predecessor, Bank deutscher Länder, which was established by the Allied powers in 1949.

5. About 80 percent of firms were members of business associations, and roughly 40 percent of workers belonged to unions (Katzenstein 1987, 26).

6. Another domain where pre-war institutions played a major role was in the area of human capital formation in which employers supported designs with roots in the nineteenth century to secure adequate numbers and skilled individuals to make growth in advanced manufactured goods feasible (Thelen 2004).

7. In addition to commercial banks and public sector banks (which include savings banks and banks owned by state-level governments, so-called *Landesbanken*), a significant share of the banking sector was made of cooperative banks owned by customers (Vitols 2001a).

8. During the 1950s and 1960s, nearly 60 percent of direct liabilities among non-financial firms were in the form of loans from banks. Meanwhile, in the mid-1960s, long-term loans to the manufacturing sector constituted a quarter of all loans made by large commercial banks and public savings banks (Vitols 1995, 42–43).

9. Between 1950 and 1960, the average annual growth rate in total factor productivity was 3.36 percent in Germany, 2.23 percent in France, 1.24 percent in the United States, and −0.07 percent in Britain (Eichengreen 2007: 88, table 4.1).

10. During the 1950s, Latin America and Asia constituted about 15 percent of German exports, while the United States and Canada combined for about 7 percent, and Western Europe made up about 65 percent (Neebe 2004, 230).

11. Moravcsik (1998, 137) answers an interesting counterfactual question about what would have been the structure of the EEC had Erhard become chancellor instead of Adenauer: "If Erhard had ruled Germany, the likely result would have been an Anglo-German [free trade agreement] with no agricultural component."

12. The government enjoyed broad support among small and medium-sized firms, which championed anti-trust provisions because they would be in a better position to protect themselves against takeovers by larger companies (Müller-Henneberg and Schwartz 1963; Robert 1976; and Berghahn 1985, 152–172). The position of large firms is detailed in Arbeitskreis Kartellgesetz (1968).

13. The theme of continuity in economic governance is apparent in the first declarations made to Parliament by the two coalition governments of the period. Social Democrats under Helmut Schmidt labeled the program "continuity and concentration" (Schmidt 1974), and Christian Democrats under Helmut Kohl announced its intention of governing in "the spirit" of the previous era and that of the social market economy (Kohl 1982).

14. On divisions between member-states, see Moravcsik (1998, 241).

15. Perspectives from the business sector on the conditions affecting the competitiveness of industry in the late 1970s, including the role of exchange rate regimes, is found in Institut der Deutschen Industrie (1980).

16. Discussions in the 1980s take place against the backdrop of an expanding commitment to European structural program designed to bring greater equality in living standards throughout the EEC.

17. Specifically, there were concerns that foreign firms could establish a presence within Germany and adopt Community norms and thus potentially lessen the credibility of domestic producers' commitment to existing national structures.

18. Fioretos (2009) entails a longer discussion of this case.

19. The 1973 amendment to the law toughened the restrictions on the ability of large companies to merge, but eased the constraints on cooperation and mergers between small- and medium-sized companies.

20. Kitschelt and Streeck (2003) offer a comprehensive overview of economic performance in the period.

21. For overviews of the key issues shaping the debate, see Streeck (1997) and Siebert (2005). For the view from industry, see BDI (1993) and Henkel (2000).

22. Of eight international banks enjoying Triple A ratings in the mid-1990s by the major international rating agencies, five were German banks of which four were public banks (Sinn 1999, 31–32).

23. Formerly modest protections for shareholders were expanded significantly in the course of the 1990s and 2000s and came to exceed average levels in industrialized states (Martynova 2006, 204–206).

24. At the center of dissent was the neutrality provision, which would mandate that management boards not initiate strategies to immediately preempt or forestall unexpected hostile takeovers. Similar concerns informed opposition to a comprehensive European corporate governance code, which business saw as potentially detrimental to the consolidation of recent domestic reforms. Because they were content with domestic reforms, the decision by the European Commission not to pursue a common European code was welcomed by large manufacturing firms and commercial banks for it minimized the potential for future adaptation losses (BdB 2003, 3–4).

25. Large parts of the business community had sought solutions that would have enabled companies to reduce the constraints of codetermination. But the final version of the ECS made such strategies difficult by limiting the terms under which German firms could jettison their national legal identities and adopt European ones. More important to these firms, by not mandating codetermination and by preserving national discretion, the Statute left the door open to future reforms at the national level (BDI et al. 2001; BDA and BDI 2004).

26. A large number of firms exited the Confederation with the effect that the organizational capacity of employers declined and wage-bargaining became more decentralized through the decade. The share of employers that were members of employers' associations and that were bound to observe collective bargaining at the industry level declined to 45 percent in the western part of the country and to 23 percent in the east (Hassel 2006, 11).

27. In the early 2000s, the Mittelstand represented 98 percent of all companies, 53 percent of employment, and 37 percent of investments in the industrial sector (von Wartenberg 2004, 2).

28. DIHK (2006) reports that most small and medium-sized enterprises that expanded operations abroad also increased their investments and employment in Germany (41%), while a much smaller number reduced their employment at home (25%).

Appendix

1. The figures in table A are not derived by empirical observation or measurement. They are hypothetical, and as such they are approximations. For the purposes of discrete structural analysis, the critical issue is not whether the measurements are exact, but rather how governance costs at different levels of asset specificity and different models of governance compare to one another (Williamson 1996a, 5).

2. Because firms are expected to retain their sectoral identity, globalization is modeled here only as an opportunity to reduce governance costs to the lowest level associated with a particular sector.

References

Abdelal, Rawi. 2001. *National Purpose in the World Economy: Post-Soviet States in Comparative Perspective*. Ithaca: Cornell University Press.

Adam-Schwaetzer, Irmgard. 1988. Chancen des Binnenmarktes für Wirtschaft und Handel. *Bulletin* 55 (May 10).

Adams, William James. 1989. *Restructuring the French Economy: Government and the Rise of Market Competition since World War II*. Washington, DC: Brookings Institution Press.

———. 1995. France and Global Competition. In *Remaking the Hexagon: The New France in the New Europe*, edited by G. Flynn. Boulder: Westview Press.

AFG (Association Française de Gestion Financière). 2008. *Recommendations on Corporate Governance*. Paris.

Akerlof, George A., and Robert J. Schiller. 2009. *Animal Spirits: How Human Psychology Drives the Economy and Why It Matters for Global Capitalism*. Princeton: Princeton University Press.

Albert, Michel. 1993. *Capitalism vs. Capitalism*. New York: Four Walls Eight Windows.

Alchian, Armen. 1968. Cost. In *International Encyclopedia of the Social Sciences*. New York: Macmillan.

Allen, Matthew, Lothar Funk, and Heinz Tüselmann. 2006. Can Variations in Public Policy Account for Differences in Comparative Advantage? *Journal of Public Policy* 26 (1):1–19.

Alesina, Alberto, and Francesco Giavazzi. 2006. *The Future of Europe: Reform or Decline*. Cambridge: MIT Press.

Amable, Bruno. 2003. *The Diversity of Modern Capitalism*. Oxford; New York: Oxford University Press.

Amable, Bruno, and Bob Hancké. 2001. Innovation and Industrial Renewal in France in Comparative Perspective. *Industry and Innovation* 8 (2):113–133.

Amin, Ash, and Jerzy Hauser, eds. 1997. *Beyond Markets and Hierarchies*. Cheltenham: Edward Elgar.

Aoki, Masahiko. 2000. *Information, Corporate Governance, and Institutional Diversity: Competitiveness in Japan, the USA, and the Transitional Economies*. Oxford: Oxford University Press.

Arbeitskreis Kartellgesetz (Bundesverband der Deutschen Industrie), ed. 1968. *Das Wirken des BDI in der Wettbewerbspolitik*. Gladbach: Heider.

Associated Industrial Consultants. 1962. Enquiry into the Reasons Why Some Managements Are Unable or Reluctant to Introduce Technological Change More Quickly. Deposited in Modern Records Centre (MSS.200/F/3/p7/19/1/doc41), Warwick.

Association Française des Entreprises Privées (AFEP), and Mouvement des Entreprises de France (MEDEF). 2003. *The Corporate Governance of Listed Companies.* Paris.

Audretsch, David B., and Julie A. Elston. 1997. Financing the German Mittelstand. *Small Business Economics* 9 (2):97–110.

Balassa, Bella. 1965. Whither French Planning? *Quarterly Journal of Economics* 79 (4):537–554.

———. 1981. The French Economy under the Fifth Republic, 1958–1979. In *The Fifth Republic at Twenty.* Albany: State University of New York Press.

Balassa, Carol Levy. 1978. *Organized Industry in France and the European Common Market: Interest Group Attitudes and Behavior.* Ph.D. dissertation, Johns Hopkins University.

Banchoff, Thomas. 1999. *The German Problem Transformed: Institutions, Politics, and Foreign Policy, 1945–1995.* Ann Arbor: University of Michigan Press.

Bardhan, Pranab. 2005. Institutions Matter, But Which Ones? *Economics of Transition* 13 (3):499–532.

Barro, Robert J. 1996. *Getting It Right: Markets and Choices in a Free Society.* Cambridge: MIT Press.

Bates, Robert H., Avner Greif, Margaret Levi, Jean-Laurent Rosenthal, and Barry R. Weingast. 1998. *Analytical Narratives.* Princeton: Princeton University Press.

Baum, Warren. 1958. *French Economy and the State.* Princeton: Princeton University Press.

Baumol, William J., Robert E. Litan, and Carl J. Schramm. 2007. *Good Capitalism, Bad Capitalism and the Economics of Growth and Prosperity.* New Haven: Yale University Press.

BDA (Bundesvereinigung der Deutschen Arbeitgeberverbände). 1989. *Jahresbericht.* Cologne: BDA.

BDA (Bundesvereinigung der Deutschen Arbeitgeberverbände), and BDI (Bundesverband der Deutschen Industrie). 2001. *Kernforderungen der deutschen Wirtschaft für eine handlungs- und wettbewerbsfähige Europäische Union.* Berlin (December).

BdB (Bundesverband deutscher Banken). 2003. *Position zur Aktionsplan Gesellschaftsrecht.* Berlin: BdB.

BDI (Bundesverband der Deutschen Industrie). 1958. *Jahrbuch.* Bonn: BDI.

———. 1959. *Jahrbuch.* Bonn: BDI.

———. 1970. *Jahrbuch.* Bonn: BDI.

———. 1971a. Stellungnahme zur Kartellgesetznovelle. *BDI-Mitteilungen* 19 (10):1–2.

———. 1971b. Die deutsche Industrie und die Weltwährungslage. *BDI-Mitteilungen* 19 (9):1–2.

———. 1971c. Floating und Kostenexplosion: Die Hauptgefahren. *BDI-Mitteilungen* 19 (10):1.

———. 1972. Stellungnahme zum Vorschlag einer Verordnung des Rates der Europäische Gemeinschaften über das Statut für Europäische Aktiengesellschaft. *BDI-Mitteilungen* 20 (1):3–5.

———. 1988. *Stellungnahme zur Europäischen Binnenmarkt.* Bonn.

———. 1996. Interview with senior staff, Trade and Industry Section (May). Bonn.

———. 2001c. *Corporate Governance in Deutschland.* Berlin (January).

———. 2004. *Für en attraktives Deutschland: Freiheit wagen, Fesseln Sprengen. BDI-Gesamtreformkonzept.* Berlin: BDI.

———. 2005. *i2010: Eine Europäische Informationsgesellschaft für Wachstum und Beschäftigung.* Berlin: BDI.

———. 2006. Interview with senior staff, Trade and Industry Section (June). Berlin.

———. 2008. *Systemkopf Deutschland Plus: Die Zukunft der Wertschöpfung am Standort Deutschland.* Berlin.

BDI (Bundesverband der Deutschen Industrie), and BDA (Bundesvereinigung der Deutschen Arbeitgeberverbände). 2004. *Mitbestimmung modernisieren.* Berlin (November).

BDI (Bundesverband der Deutschen Industrie), BdB (Bundesverband deutscher Banken), BDA (Bundesvereinigung der Deutschen Arbeitgeberverbände), DIHK (Deutschen Industri- und Handelstag), and GDV (Gesamtverband der Deutschen Versicherungswirtschaft). 2001. *Stellungsnahme zum Nizza-Kompromiss über die Europäische Aktiengesellschaft.* Berlin (19 March).

Beaver, Sir Hugh. 1959. Address to Annual General Meeting, Federation of British Industries. Modern Records Centre (200/F/3/P5/4/1), Warwick.

Bebchuk, Lucian, and Mark Roe. 1999. A Theory of Path Dependence in Corporate Ownership and Governance. *Stanford Law Review* 52:127–170.

Becker, Gary. 1976. Introduction. In *The Economic Approach to Human Behavior.* Chicago: Chicago University Press.

Beer, Samuel H. 1982. *Britain against Itself: The Political Contradictions of Collectivism.* New York: W. W. Norton.

Berg, Fritz. 1959. Zehn Jahre Bundesverband der Deutschen Industrie: Rede des Herrn Präsident Fritz Berg. *Mitteilungen des BDI* 7 (11/12).

——. 1960. Möglichkeiten und Grenzen der europäischen Integration. *Mitteilungen des BDI* 8 (8/9).

Berger, Suzanne. 1981. Lame Ducks and National Champions: Industrial Policy in the Fifth Republic. In *The Fifth Republic at Twenty*, edited by W. Andrews and S. Hoffmann. Albany: State University of New York Press.

——. 2000. Globalization and Politics. *Annual Review of Political Science* 3 (1):43–62.

Berger, Suzanne, and Ronald Dore, eds. 1996. *National Diversity and Global Capitalism.* Ithaca: Cornell University Press.

Berghahn, Volker. 1985. *Unternehmer und Politik in der Bundesrepublik.* Frankfurt am Main: Suhrkamp.

Berghahn, Volker, and Sigurt Vitols, eds. 2006. *Gibt es einen deutschen Kapitalismus? Tradition und globale Perspektiven der sozialen Marktwirtschaft.* Frankfurt am Main: Campus.

Beyer, Jürgen, and Martin Höpner. 2003. The Disintegration of Organised Capitalism: German Corporate Governance in the 1990s. *West European Politics* 26 (4):179–198.

Bhagwati, Jagdish N. 2008. *Termites in the Trading System: How Preferential Agreements Undermine Free Trade.* New York: Oxford University Press.

Blair, Tony. 1996. *New Britain.* London: Westview Press.

——. 1997. Prime Minister's Speech to the CBI Conference. November 11. Available at http://www.number10.gov.uk/output/Page1072.asp.

——. 2000. Prime Minister's Speech to the Global Borrowers and Investors Forum Conference. 22 June. Available at http://www.number10.gov.uk/output/Page1528.asp.

——. 2001. Britain's Role in Europe. Prime Minister's Speech to the European Research Institute. 23 November. Available at http://www.number10.gov.uk/output/Page1673.asp.

——. 2006a. Speech on the Future of Europe. Available at http://www.number10.gov.uk/output/Page9003.asp.

——. 2006b. Speech to the CBI Annual Dinner. 16 May. Available at http://www.number10.gov.uk/output/Page9470.asp.

Blank, Stephen. 1973. *Industry and Government in Britain: The Federation of British Industries in Politics, 1945–65.* Lexington: Saxon House and Lexington Books.

Blyth, Mark. 2002. *Great Transformations: Economic Ideas and Institutional Change in the Twentieth Century.* New York: Cambridge University Press.

Blüm, Norbert. 1989. Mitbestimmung unvezichtbar. *Bundesarbeitsblatt* 6:12–14.

BMBF (Bundesministerium für Bildung und Forschung). 2000. *Bundesbericht Forschung 2000.* Berlin: BMBF.

BMF (Bundesministerium der Finanzen). 1979. Grundsatzfragen der Kreditwirtschaft. *Schriftenreihe des Bundesministerium der Finanzen* 28 (Bonn).

——. 1999. *Bericht der Bunderegierung über die Entwicklung der Finanzhilfe des Bundes und der Steuervergünstigung.* Berlin: BMF.

BMWi (Bundesministerium für Wirtschaft und Technologie). 1956. Frage der Harmonisierung der sozialen Belastungen in den 6 Staaten. Bundesarchiv (B 102), Koblenz.

——. 1986. *Stellungnahme zum Weißbuch der EG-Kommission über den Binnenmarkt.* Bonn: BMWi.

——. 1988. *Wirtschaftspolitische Konsequenzen aus den außenwirtschaftlichen Ungleichgewichten der großen Industrieländer.* Bonn: BMWi.

——. 2000. *Economic Report.* Berlin: BMWi.

——. 2006. Interview with senior staff, Section for Europe. Berlin (May).

——. 2008. *Jahreswirtschaftsbericht 2008: Kurs Halten!* Berlin: BMWi.

Boltho, Andrea. 1996. Has France Converged on Germany? Policies and Institutions since 1958. In *National Diversity and Global Capitalism,* edited by S. Berger and R. Dore. Ithaca: Cornell University Press.

Börzel, Tanja A., and Thomas Risse. 2003. Conceptualizing the Domestic Impact of Europe. In *The Politics of Europeanization,* edited by Kevin Featherstone and Claudio M. Radelli. Oxford: Oxford University Press.

Boswell, Jonathan, and James Peters. 1997. *Capitalism in Contention: Business Leaders and Political Economy in Modern Britain.* Cambridge: Cambridge University Press.

Boyer, Robert. 1997. French Statism at the Crossroads. In *Political Economy of Modern Capitalism: Mapping Convergence and Diversity,* edited by C. Crouch and W. Streeck. London: Sage.

Brenke, Gabriele. 1994. Europakonzeptionen im Widerstreit: Die Freihandelszonen-Verhandlungen 1956–1958. *Vierteljahrshefte für Zeitgeschichte* 42 (4):595–633.

Broadberry, Stephen N. 1997. *The Productivity Race: British Manufacturing in International Perspective, 1850–1990.* Cambridge: Cambridge University Press.

Broadberry, Stephen N., and Nicholas F. R. Crafts. 1996. British Economic Policy and Industrial Performance in the Early Post-War Period. *Business History* 38 (4):65–91.

Bromund, Theodore R. 1999. *From Empire to Europe: Material Interests, National Identities, and British Policies Towards European Integration, 1956–1963.* Ph.D. dissertation, Yale University, New Haven.

Brown, Gordon. 2009. Press Conference Ahead of the EU Council Meeting. Brussels (18 June).

Buchanan, James. 1998. Opportunity Costs. In *The New Palgrave Dictionary of Economics.* London: Macmillan.

Buchanan, James M., and Yong J. Yoon, eds. 2001. *The Return to Increasing Returns.* Ann Arbor: University of Michigan Press.

Bulmer, Simon, and William Patterson. 1987. *The Federal Republic of Germany and the European Community.* Boston: Allen & Unwin.

BIRP (Business International Research Report). 1983. *Socialist France: The New Business Environment.* New York: Business International.

Bührer, Werner. 1992. Der BDI und die Aussenpolitik der Bundesrepublik in den Fünfziger Jahren. *Vierteljahrshefte für Zeitgeschichte* 40 (2):241–261.

Callaghan, Helen. 2007. Convergence? Divergence? Hybridization? Transnational Law-Making and the Clash of Capitalisms. Paper presented at the SASE Conference, Copenhagen, 26–28 June.

———. 2008. How Multilevel Governance Affects the Clash of Capitalisms. MPIfG Discussion Paper 08 (5), Max Planck Institute for the Study of Societies, Cologne.

Callaghan, Helen, and Martin Höpner. 2005. European Integration and the Clash of Capitalisms: Political Cleavages over Takeover Liberalization. *Comparative European Politics* 3:307–332.

Calmfors, Lars, and John Driffill. 1988. Bargaining Structure, Corporatism and Macroeconomic Performance. *Economic Policy* 3:13–61.

Calvert, Randall. 1995. Rational Actors, Equilibrium, and Social Institutions. *In Explaining Social Institution*, edited by J. Knight and I. Sened. Ann Arbor: Michigan University Press.

Campbell, John L., and Ove K. Pedersen. 2007. The Varieties of Capitalism and Hybrid Success: Denmark in the Global Economy. *Comparative Political Studies* 40 (3):307–332.

Capoccia, Giovanni, and R. Daniel Kelemen. 2007. The Study of Critical Junctures: Theory, Narrative, and Counterfactuals in Historical Institutionalism. *World Politics* 59 (3):341–369.

Caporaso, James A. 2003. International Relations Theory and Multilateralism: The Search for Foundations. In *Multilateralism Matters: The Theory and Praxis of an Institutional Form*, edited by J. G. Ruggie. New York: Columbia University Press.

Caporaso, James A., and Sidney Tarrow. 2009. Polanyi in Brussels: Supranational Institutions and the Transnational Embedding of Markets. *International Organization* 63:593–620.

Carnevali, Francesca. 2005. *Europe's Advantage: Banks and Small Firms in Britain, France, Germany and Italy since 1918*. Oxford: Oxford University Press.

Caron, François. 1979. *An Economic History of Modern France*. New York: Columbia University Press.

Casper, Steven. 2001. The Legal Framework of Corporate Governance: The Influence of Contract Law on Company Strategies in Germany and the United States. In *Varieties of Capitalism: The Institutional Foundation of Competitive Advantage*, edited by P. A. Hall and D. Soskice. New York: Oxford University Press.

———. 2007. *Creating Silicon Valley in Europe: Public Policy Towards New Technology Industries*. Oxford: Oxford University Press.

CBI (Confederation of British Industry). 1966. *Britain in Europe*. London.

———. 1967a. *Britain and Europe, Volume 2* (Supporting papers). London.

———. 1967b. *Britain and Europe, Volume 3*. London.

———. 1967c. Memo. Britain and Europe: Consultations with Industry. Views of Trade Associations and Employer's Associations. July.

———. 1975. To the Council: Industry's Future in Europe (Confidential). June. Modern Records Centre (MSS 200/C/3/ECO/G/1), Warwick.

———. 1980. The Impact of EEC Legislation on British Business. 5 November. Modern Records Centre (MSS 200/C/3/ECO/6/2), Warwick.

———. 1984. *The European Community and "Social Engineering": A CBI Memorandum*. London: CBI.

———. 1985. *A Europe for Business*. London: CBI.

———. 1988a. *Maintaining the Momentum of Economic Recovery*. London: CBI.

———. 1988b. Memorandum: Harmonisation of Company Law. London: CBI.

——. 2006. Interview with staff, Corporate Governance Section, Confederation of British Industry. May 30. London.

Checkel, Jeffrey, and Peter J. Katzenstein. 2009. *European Identity*. New York: Cambridge University Press.

Cioffi, John W. 2002. Restructuring "Germany Inc." The Politics of Company and Takeover Law Reform in Germany and the European Union. *Law and Politics* 24 (4):355–402.

Citi, Manuele, and Martin Rhodes. 2007. New Modes of Governance in the EU: Common Objectives versus National Preferences. *European Governance Papers* (07–01).

Clift, Ben. 2007. French Corporate Governance in the New Global Economy: Mechanisms of Change and Hybridisation within Models of Capitalism. *Political Studies* 55:546–567.

——. 2009. The Second Time as Farce? The EU Takeover Directive, the Clash of Capitalisms and the Hamstrung Harmonisation of European (and French) Corporate Governance. *Journal of Common Market Studies* 47 (1):55–79.

CNPF (Conseil National du Patronat Français). 1965. *Declaration*. Paris.

——. 1987. Rapport de la commission sociale. *Revue des entreprises* (16 June).

——. 1990. Observations dur la proposition modifiée de la 13ieme directive. Paris.

Coase, Ronald. 1937. The Nature of the Firm. *Economica* 4 (November): 386–405.

Coates, David. 2000. *Models of Capitalism: Growth and Stagnation in the Modern Era*. Cambridge: Polity Press.

Coen, David, Wyn Grant, and Graham Wilson. 2010. Political Science: Perspectives on Business and Government. In *Oxford Handbook of Business and Government*, edited by David Coen, Wyn Grant, and Graham Wilson. Oxford: Oxford University Press.

Coffineau, Michel. 1993. *Les lois Auroux, dix ans aprés*. Paris: La Documentation Française.

Cohen, Élie. 1996. *Le tentation hexagonale: La souveraineté à l'épreuve de la mondialisation*. Paris: Fayard.

Cohen, Stephen S. 1977. *Modern Capitalist Planning: The French Model*. Berkeley: University of California Press.

Cohen, Stephen S., James Galbraith, and John Zysman. 1982. Rebuilding the Labyrinth: The Financial System and Industrial Policy in France. In *France in the Troubled World Economy*, edited by S. S. Cohen and P. A. Gourevitch. London: Butterworth Scientific.

Commissariat Général du Plan. 1992. *France: le choix de la performance globale*. Paris: La Documentation Française.

Commission of the European Communities. 2007. *Impact Assessment on the Proportionality between Capital and Control in Listed Companies*. Brussels.

Conseil d'Etat. 2007. *L'administration française et l'Union européenne: Quelles influences? Quelles stratégies?* Paris: La Documentation Française.

Council of Economic Experts. 2004. *Jahresgutachten 2004–05: Erfolge im Ausland, Herausforderungen im Inland*. Wiesbaden: Statistiches Bundesamt.

——. 2006. Deutschland in der Währungsunion. In *Jahresgutachten 2005–06*. Wiesbaden: Statistiches Bundesamt.

Cowles, Maria. 1994. *The Politics of Big Business and Brussels: Setting the Agenda for a New Europe*. Ph.D. dissertation, American University, Washington, DC.

——. 1996. German Big Business and Brussels: Learning to Play the European Game. *German Politics and Society* 14 (3):73–107.

Cowles, Maria Green, James Caporaso, and Thomas Risse, eds. 2001. *Transforming Europe: Europeanization and Domestic Change*. Ithaca: Cornell University Press.

Crafts, Nicholas F. R. 1994. Industry. In *The Major Effect*, edited by D. Kavanagh and A. Seldon. London: Macmillan.

Crespy, Cecile, Jean-Alain Heraud, and Beth Perry. 2007. Multi-Level Governance, Regions and Science in France: Between Competition and Equality. *Regional Studies* 41 (8):1069–1084.

Crouch, Colin. 2005. *Capitalist Diversity and Change: Recombinant Governance and Institutional Entrepreneurs*. New York: Oxford University Press.

Crouch, Colin, Wolfgang Streeck, Robert Boyer, Bruno Amable, Peter A. Hall, and Gregory Jackson. 2005. Dialogue on "Institutional Complementarity and Political Economy." *Socio-Economic Review* 3 (2):359–382.

CSO (Central Statistical Office). 1960–1962. *Annual Abstracts of Statistics*. London: HMSO.

———. 1969–1970. *Annual Abstracts of Statistics*. London: HMSO.

Culpepper, Pepper. 2003. *Creating Cooperation: How States Develop Human Capital in Europe*. Ithaca: Cornell University Press.

———. 2005. Institutional Change in Contemporary Capitalism: Coordinated Financial Systems since 1990. *World Politics* 57 (2):173–199.

———. 2006. Capitalism, Coordination, and Economic Change: The French Political Economy since 1985. In *Changing France: The Politics That Markets Make*, edited by P. D. Culpepper, P. A. Hall, and B. Palier. Houndmills, Basingstoke: Palgrave.

Darden, Keith. 2009. *Economic Liberalism and Its Rivals*. New York: Cambridge University Press.

David, Paul A. 1985. Clio and the Economics of QWERTY. *American Economic Review* 75 (2):332–337.

de Boissieu, Christian, and Marie-Hélène Duprat. 1990. French Monetary Policy on the Light of European Monetary and Financial Integration. In *Monetary Implications of the 1992 Process*, edited by H. Sherman. New York: St. Martin's Press.

DeBondt, Werner F., and Richard Thaler. 1994. Financial Decision-Making in Markets and Firms: A Behavioral Perspective. NBER Working Paper no. W4777.

de Gaulle, Charles. 1970. *Memoirs of Hope: Renewal and Endeavor*. New York: Simon and Schuster.

Deeg, Richard E. 1997. Banks and Industrial Finance in the 1990s. *Industry and Innovation* 4 (1):53–73.

———. 1999. *Finance Capitalism Unveiled: Banks and the German Political Economy*. Ann Arbor: University of Michigan Press.

———. 2005. Change from Within: German and Italian Finance in the 1990s. In *Beyond Continuity: Institutional Change in Advanced Political Economies*, edited by W. Streeck and T. Kathleen. New York: Oxford University Press.

Demmler, Gertrud. 1995. Europäische Sozialpolitik aus Sicht der Wirtschaft. *Forum* 44 (27).

Deregulierungskommission. 1991. *Marktöffnung und Wettbewerb*. Stuttgart: C. E. Poeschel Verlag.

Deubner, Christian. 1984. Change and Internationalization in Industry: Toward a Sectoral Interpretation of West German Politics. *International Organization* 38 (3):501–535.

DIHK (Deutscher Industrie- und Handelskammertag). 1988. *Den Gemeinsamen Markt stärken, den Binnenmarkt vollenden*. Bonn: DIHK.

———. 2005. *Going International: Erfolgsfaktoren im Auslandsgeschäft*. Berlin: DIHK.

———. 2006. *Going International 2006*. Belen: DIHK.

———. 2007. Wir fahren mit dem Euro immer noch besser als mit der D-mark. *Meldung*, 27 November.

Doremus, Paul N., William W. Keller, Louis W. Pauly, and Simon Reich. 1998. *The Myth of the Global Corporation*. Princeton: Princeton University Press.

Dorey, Peter. 1991. Corporatism in the United Kingdom. *Politics Review* 3 (2):24–37.

Drezner, Daniel. 2001. Globalization and Policy Convergence. *International Studies Review* 3 (1):53–78.

———. 2007. *All Politics Is Global: Explaining International Regulatory Regimes*. Princeton: Princeton University Press.

DTI (Department of Trade and Industry). 1996. Author's interview with Director of EU Internal, Trade Policy, and Europe Directorates. London (June).

Duina, Francesco. 1999. *Harmonizing Europe: Nation-States within the Common Market*. New York: State University of New York Press.

Dyson, Kenneth. 2001. The German Model Revisited: From Schmidt to Schröder. *German Politics* 10 (2):135–154.

Dyson, Kenneth, and Kevin Featherstone. 1999. *The Road to Maastricht: Negotiating Economic and Monetary Union*. Oxford: Oxford University Press.

Edwards, Jeremy, and Klaus Fischer. 1994. *Banks, Finance and Investment in Germany*. Cambridge: Cambridge University Press.

Ehrmann, Henry W. 1957. *Organized Business in France*. Princeton: Princeton University Press.

Eichengreen, Barry. 1993. *Reconstructing Europe's Trade and Payments: The European Payments Union*. Ann Arbor: University of Michigan Press.

———. 2007. *The European Economy since 1945: Coordinated Capitalism and Beyond*. Princeton: Princeton University Press.

EIRO (European Industrial Relations Observatory). 1998. 35-hour Working Week Adopted.

EIU (Economist Intelligence Unit). 1957. *Britain and Europe: A Study of the Effects on British Manufacturing Industry of a Free Trade Area and the Common Market*. London: Economist Intelligence Unit.

Elbaum, Bernard, and William Lazonick. 1987. *The Decline of the British Economy*. Oxford: Clarendon Press.

Elms, Deborah Kay. 2004. Large Costs, Small Benefits: Explaining Trade Dispute Outcomes. *Political Psychology* 25 (4):241–270.

———. 2008. New Directions for IPE: Drawing From Behavioral Economics. *International Studies Review* 10:239–265.

Elster, Jon. 1979. *Ulysses and the Sirens: Studies in Rationality and Irrationality*. Cambridge: Cambridge University Press.

Enriques, Luca, and Paolo Volpin. 2007. Corporate Governance Reforms in Continental Europe. *Journal of Economic Perspectives* 21 (1):117–140.

Epstein, Rachel A. 2008. *In Pursuit of Liberalism: International Institutions in Postcommunist Europe*. Baltimore: Johns Hopkins University Press.

Erhard, Ludwig. 1954. *Germany's Comeback in the World Market*. London: George Allen & Unwin.

———. 1957. *Wohlstand für Alle*. Düsseldorf: Econ Verlag.

———. 1966. *Wirken und Reden*. Ludwigsburg: Martin Hoch.

———. [1965] 1988. Formierte Gesellschaft. Rede vor dem 13. Bundesparteitag der CDU. In *Ludwig Erhard: Gedanken aus fünf Jahrzehnten*, edited by K. Hohmann. Düsseldorf: Econ Verlag.

Eur-Lex. 2009. *Legislation in Force*. Available at http://eur-lex.europa.eu/en/legis/index.htm.

Falkner, Gerda, Oliver Treib, Miriam Hartlapp, and Simone Leiber, eds. 2005. *Complying with Europe: EU Harmonisation and Soft Law in the Member States*. Cambridge: Cambridge University Press.

Fanto, James A. 1998. The Role of Corporate Law in French Corporate Governance. *Cornell International Law Journal* 31:31–91.

Farrell, Henry. 2009. *The Political Economy of Trust: Institutions, Interests, and Inter-Firm Cooperation in Italy and Germany.* New York: Cambridge University Press.

FBI (Federation of British Industries). 1961. *British Industry and Europe.* London.

Featherstone, Kevin, and Claudio M. Radelli. 2003. *The Politics of Europeanization.* Oxford: Oxford University Press.

Fernez-Walch, Sandrine, and François Romon. 2006. *Management de l'innovation: De la stratégie aux projets.* Paris: Vuibert.

Finegold, David, and David Soskice. 1988. The Failure of Training in Britain: Analysis and Prescription. *Oxford Review of Economic Policy* 4 (3):21–53.

Fioretos, Orfeo. 2001. The Domestic Sources of Multilateral Preferences: Varieties of Capitalism in the European Community. In *Varieties of Capitalism: The Institutional Foundation of Competitive Advantage,* edited by P. A. Hall and D. Soskice. New York: Oxford University Press.

——. 2009. The Regulation of Transnational Corporate Identity in Europe. *Comparative Political Studies* 42 (9):1167–1192.

——. 2011. Historical Institutionalism in International Relations. *International Organization* 65 (2):367–399.

Fohlin, Caroline. 2007. *Finance Capitalism and Germany's Rise to Industrial Power.* Cambridge: Cambridge University Press.

Foreign and Commonwealth Office. 1996. Author's interview with Head of Section, European Union Internal, Foreign and Commonwealth Office. London (25 June).

Fourastié, Jean. 1979. *Les Trente Glorieuses ou la Révolution invisible de 1946 á 1975.* Paris: Fayard.

French Presidency of the European Union. 2000. *Programme of the French Presidency of the European Union.* Brussels (1 July).

Frey, Frederick W. 1985. The Problem of Actor Designation in Political Analysis. *Comparative Politics* 17 (2):127–152.

Frieden, Jeffry A. 1999. Actors and Preferences in International Relations. In *Strategic Choice and International Relations,* edited by D. A. Lake and R. Powell. Princeton: Princeton University Press.

——. 2001. Making Commitments: France and Italy in the European Monetary System, 1979–1985. In *The Political Economy of European Monetary Unification,* edited by B. Eichengreen and J. A. Frieden. Boulder, CO: Westview Press.

Frieden, Jeffry A., and Lisa L. Martin. 2002. International Political Economy: Global and Domestic Interactions. In *Political Science: State of the Discipline,* edited by I. Katznelson and H. V. Milner. New York: W. W. Norton.

Frieden, Jeffry A., and Ronald Rogowski. 1996. The Impact of the International Economy on National Policies: An Analytical Overview. In *Internationalization and Domestic Politics,* edited by Robert O. Keohane and Helen V. Milner. New York: Cambridge University Press.

Furubotn, Eirik G., and Rudolf Richter. 2000. *Institutions and Economic Theory: The Contribution of the New Institutional Economics.* Ann Arbor: University of Michigan Press.

Garrett, Geoffrey, and Peter Lange. 1996. Internationalization, Institutions, and Political Change. In *Internationalization and Domestic Politics,* edited by Robert O. Keohane and Helen V. Milner. New York: Cambridge University Press.

George, Alexander, and Andrew Bennett. 2005. *Case Studies and Theory Development in the Social Sciences.* Cambridge: MIT Press.

George, Stephen. 1998. *An Awkward Partner: Britain in the European Community*. Oxford: Oxford University Press.

Gerber, David J. 1998. *Law and Competition in Twentieth Century Europe: Protecting Prometheus*. Oxford: Clarendon.

Giersch, Herbert, Karl-Heinz Paqué, and Holger Schmiedling. 1992. *The Fading Miracle: Four Decades of Market Economy in Germany*. New York: Cambridge University Press.

Gilpin, Robert. 2001. *Global Political Economy: Understanding the International Economic Order*. Princeton: Princeton University Press.

Goergen, Marc, Miguel C. Manjon, and Luc Renneboog. 2005. Corporate Governance in Germany. In *Corporate Governance: Accountability, Enterprise and International Comparisons*, edited by K. Keasey, S. Thompson and M. Wright. Chichester: Wiley.

Goergen, Marc, Marina Martynova, and Luc Renneboog. 2005. Corporate Governance Convergence: Evidence from Takeover Regulation Reforms in Europe. *Oxford Review of Economic Policy* 21 (2):243–268.

Goodin, Robert E. 1996. Institutions and Their Design. In *The Theory of Institutional Design*, edited by R. E. Goodin. New York: Cambridge University Press.

Gourevitch, Peter Alexis. 1986. *Politics in Hard Times: Comparative Responses to International Economic Crises*. Ithaca: Cornell University Press.

———. 1996. Squaring the Circle: The Domestic Sources of International Cooperation. *International Organization* 50 (2):349–373.

Goyer, Michel. 2001. Corporate Governance and the Innovation System in France, 1985–2000. *Industry and Innovation* 8 (2):135–158.

———. 2003. Corporate Governance, Employees, and the Focus on Core Competencies in France and Germany. In *Global Markets, Domestic Institutions: Corporate Law and Governance in a New Era of Cross-Border Deals*, edited by C. Millhaupt. New York: Columbia University Press.

———. 2006. Varieties of Institutional Investors and National Models of Capitalism: The Transformation of Corporate Governance in France and Germany. *Politics & Society* 34 (3):399–430.

Granovetter, Mark. 1985. Economic Action and Social Structure: The Problem of Embeddedness. *American Journal of Sociology* 91 (3):481–510.

Green, Diana. 1984. Industrial Policy and Policy-Making, 1974–82. In *Continuity and Change in France*, edited by V. Wright. Boston: Allen and Unwin.

Green, Donald, and Ian Shapiro. 1996. *Pathologies of Rational Choice: A Critique of Applications in Political Science*. New Haven: Yale University Press.

Greenwood, Justin, and Lara Stancich. 1998. British Business: Managing Complexity. In *Britain for and against Europe: British Policies and the Question of European Integration*, edited by D. Baker and D. Seawright. Oxford: Clarendon Press.

Greif, Avner. 1998. Historical and Comparative Institutional Analysis. *American Economic Review* 88 (2):80–84.

———. 2000. The Fundamental Problem of Exchange: A Research Agenda in Historical Institutional Analysis. *European Review of Economic History* 4:251–284.

———. 2006. *Institutions and the Path of the Modern Economy: Lessons from Medieval Trade*. New York: Cambridge University Press.

Groupe de réflexion sur les stratégies industrielles. 1974. *Problématique d'une stratégie industrielle*. Paris: La Documentation Française.

Guillén, Mauro F. 2001. *The Limits of Convergence: Globalization and Organizational Change in Argentina, South Korea, and Spain*. Princeton: Princeton University Press.

Hacker, Jacob, and Paul Pierson. 2002. Business Power and Social Policy: Employers and the Formation of the America Welfare State. *Politics and Society* 30 (2):277–325.

Hall, Peter A. 1986. *Governing the Economy: The Politics of State Intervention in Britain and France.* New York: Oxford University Press.

———. 1987. The Evolution of Economic Policy under Mitterrand. In *The Mitterrand Experiment: Continuity and Change in Modern France,* edited by G. Ross, S. Hoffmann, and S. Malzacher. New York: Oxford University Press.

———, ed. 1989. *The Political Power of Economic Ideas: Keynesianism across Nations.* Princeton: Princeton University Press.

———. 2003. Aligning Ontology and Methodology in Comparative Research. In *Comparative Historical Analysis in the Social Sciences,* edited by James Mahoney and Dietrich Rueschemeyer. New York: Cambridge University Press.

———. 2008. Systematic Process Analysis: When and How to Use It. *European Political Science* 7 (3):304–317.

———. 2010. Historical Institutionalism in Rationalist and Sociological Perspective. In *Explaining Institutional Change: Ambiguity, Agency, and Power,* edited by James Mahoney and Kathleen Thelen. New York: Cambridge University Press.

Hall, Peter A., and Daniel Gingerich. 2009. Varieties of Capitalism and Institutional Complementarities in the Political Economy: An Empirical Analysis. *British Journal of Political Science* 39 (3):449–482.

Hall, Peter A., and David Soskice, eds. 2001a. *Varieties of Capitalism: The Institutional Foundation of Competitive Advantage.* New York: Oxford University Press.

———. 2001b. Introduction. In *Varieties of Capitalism: The Institutional Foundation of Competitive Advantage,* edited by P. A. Hall and D. Soskice. New York: Oxford University Press.

Hall, Peter A., and Rosemary Taylor. 1996. Political Science and the Three New Institutionalisms. *Political Studies* 44 (5):936–957.

Hall, Peter A., and Kathleen Thelen. 2009. Institutional Change in Varieties of Capitalism. *Socio-Economic Review* 7:7–34.

Hancké, Bob. 2002. *Large Firms and Institutional Change: Industrial Renewal and Economic Restructuring in France.* Oxford: Oxford University Press.

———. ed. 2009. *Debating Varieties of Capitalism: A Reader.* Oxford: Oxford University Press.

———. 2010. Varieties of Capitalism and Business. In *Oxford Handbook of Business and Government,* edited by. David Coen, Wyn Grant, and Graham Wilson. Oxford: Oxford University Press.

Hancké, Bob, and Andrea Monika Hermann. 2007. Wage Bargaining and Comparative Advantage in EMU. In *Beyond Varieties of Capitalism: Conflict, Contradictions, and Complementarities in the European Economy,* edited by B. Hancké, M. Rhodes and M. Thatcher. New York: Oxford University Press.

Hardin, Russell. 1998. Institutional Commitment: Values or Incentives? In *Economics, Values, and Organization,* edited by A. Ben-Ner and L. Putterman. New York: Cambridge University Press.

Harrison Papers. 1961–1963. Papers of President Cyril Harrison. MSS200/F/3/E3/40/8ff and MSS200/F/3/E3/40/9, Modern Records Centre, Warwick.

Hart, Jeffrey A. 1992. *Rival Capitalists: International Competitiveness in the United States, Japan, and Western Europe.* Ithaca: Cornell University Press.

Hart, Oliver. 1995. *Firms, Contracts, and Financial Structure.* Oxford: Clarendon Press.

Hassel, Anke. 2006. *Wage Setting, Social Pacts and the Euro: A New Role for the State.* Amsterdam: Amsterdam University Press.

———. 2007. What Does Business Want? Labour Market Reforms in CMEs and Its Problems. In *Beyond Varieties of Capitalism: Conflict, Contradictions, and Complementarities in the European Economy,* edited by B. Hancké, M. Rhodes and M. Thatcher. New York: Oxford University Press.

Haverland, Markus. 2000. National Adaptation to European Integration: The Importance of Institutional Veto Points. *Journal of Public Policy* 20:83–103.

Hay, Colin. 2001. The "Crisis" of Keynesianism and the Rise of Neoliberalism in Britain: An Ideational Institutionalist Approach. In *The Rise of Neoliberalism and Institutional Analysis.* Princeton: Princeton University Press.

Hayden, Anders. 2006. France's 35-Hour Week: Attack on Business? Win-Win Reform? Or Betrayal of Disadvantaged Workers. *Politics & Society* 34 (4):503–542.

Hayek, Friedrich. 1945. The Uses of Knowledge in Society. *American Economic Review* 35 (4):519–530.

Hayward, Jack. 1984. From Planning the French Economy to Planning the French State: The Theory and Practice of the Priority Action Programmes. In *Continuity and Change in France,* edited by V. Wright. Boston: Allen and Unwin.

Heinze, Roland G. 1998. *Die Blockierte Gesellschaft: Sozioökonomischer Wandel und die Krise des "Modell Deutschland."* Opladen: Westdeutscher Verlag.

Heinzemann, Bernd. 1994. Annäherung—Nicht Harmonisierung. *Arbeitgeber* 46 (1):16–17.

Henkel, Hans-Olaf. 2000. *Die Macht der Freiheit.* Berlin: Econ.

Heston, Alan, Robert Summers, and Bettina Aten. 2006. *Penn World Table, Version 6.2.* Center for International Comparisons of Production, Income and Prices, University of Pennsylvania.

Hirschman, Albert O. 1970. *Exit, Voice, and Loyalty: Responses to Decline in Firms, Organizations, and States.* Cambridge: Harvard University Press.

Hitchcock, William I. 1998. *France Restored: Cold War Diplomacy and the Quest for Leadership in Europe, 1944–1954.* Chapel Hill: University of North Carolina Press.

Hix, Simon. 2005. *The Political System of the European Union,* 2nd ed. London: Palgrave.

HM Treasury. 1996. Interview with senior staff, Section on Europe and International Trade. April.

———. 2002. *Reforming Britain's Economic and Financial Policy: Towards Greater Economic Stability,* edited by Ed Balls and Gus O'Donnell. Houndmills: Palgrave.

HM Treasury, Financial Services Authority, and Bank of England. 2003. *The Financial Services Action Plan.* London.

HMSO (Her Majesty's stationary office). 1959. *Committee on the Working of the Monetary System.* Cmnd. 827. London.

———. 1970. *Britain and the European Communities: An Economic Assessment.* Cmnd. 4289. London.

———. 1971a. *Report of the Committee of Inquiry on Small Firms.* Cmd. 4811. London.

———. 1971b. *The United Kingdom and the European Communities.* Cmnd. 4715. London.

———. 1973. *The Future of London as an International Finance Centre: A Report by Inter-Bank Research Organisation.* London: HMSO.

———. 1994. *Competitiveness: Helping Business to Win.* London: HMSO.

———. 1995. *Competitiveness: Forging Ahead.* London: HMSO.

———. 1996. *Competitiveness: Creating the Enterprise Centre of Europe.* London: HMSO.

Hobsbawn, Eric J. 1968. *Industry and Empire: The Making of Modern British Society, 1950 to the Present Day.* London: Penguin.

Holliday, Ian. 1993. Organised Interests after Thatcher. In *Development in British Politics 4,* edited by A. Gamble, I. Holliday, and G. Peele. London: Macmillan.

Hooghe, Liesbet, and Gary Marks. 1999. The Making of a Polity: The Struggle over European Integration. In *Continuity and Change in Contemporary Capitalism,* edited by H. Kitschelt, P. Lange, G. Marks, and J. D. Stephens. New York: Cambridge University Press.

———. 2001. *Multi-level Governance and European Integration.* Oxford: Rowman and Littlefield.

Höpner, Martin. 2005. What Connects Industrial Relations and Corporate Governance? Explaining Institutional Complementarity. *Socio-Economic Review* 3 (2):331–358.

Höpner, Martin, and Gregory Jackson. 2001. An Emerging Market for Corporate Control? The Mannesmann Takeover and German Corporate Governance. MPIfG Discussion Paper (04/01), Max Planck Institute for the Study of Societies, Cologne.

Höpner, Martin, and Armin Schäfer. 2010. A New Phase of European Integration: Organised Capitalisms in Post-Ricardian Europe. *West European Politics* 33 (2):344–368.

Hopt, Klaus J. 2002. Takeover Regulation in Europe: The Battle for the 13th Directive on Takeovers. *Australian Journal of Corporate Law* 15:1–18.

House of Commons. 1991–1992. *Parliamentary Debates* 201 (Sixth Series).

Howe, Geoffrey, Keith Joseph, James Prior, and David Howell. 1977. *The Right Approach to the Economy: An Outline of the Economic Strategy of the Next Conservative Government.* 17 August. Margaret Thatcher Foundation.

Howell, Chris. 1992. *Regulating Labor: The State and Industrial Relations Reform in Postwar France.* Princeton: Princeton University Press.

———. 2005. *Trade Unions and the State: The Construction of Industrial Relations Institutions in Britain, 1890–2000.* Princeton: Princeton University Press.

———. 2009. The Transformation of French Industrial Relations: Labor Representation and the State in a Post-*Dirigiste* Era. *Politics & Society* 37 (2):229–256.

Huelshoff, Michael G. 1993. German and European Integration: Understanding the Relationship. In *From Bundesrepublik to Deutschland: German Politics after Unification,* edited by M. G. Huelshoff, A. S. Markovits, and S. Reich. Ann Arbor: University of Michigan Press.

Hundt, Dieter. 2007. Speech at Europatag der Deutschen Wirtschaft. Berlin, 20 January.

Hutton, Will. 1995. *The State We're In.* London: Jonathan Cape.

Institut der deutschen Industrie. 1980. *Standort Bundesrepublik Deutschland: Wirtschaftliche Position und internationale Verflechtung.* Köln: Deutscher Instituts-Verlag.

Jackson, Gregory, and Richard Deeg. 2006. How Many Varieties of Capitalism? Comparing the Comparative Institutional Analyses of Capitalist Diversity. MPIfG Discussion Paper (06/2), Max Planck Institute for the Study of Societies, Cologne.

Jacoby, Wade. 2006. *The Enlargement of the European Union and NATO: Ordering from the Menu in Central Europe.* New York: Cambridge University Press.

Kahneman, Daniel, Jack L. Knetsch, and Richard H. Thaler. 1991. Anomalies: The Endowment Effect, Loss Aversion, and Status Quo Bias. *Journal of Economic Perspectives* 5 (1):193–206.

———. 2000. Experimental Tests of the Endowment Effect and the Coase Theorem. In *Behavioral Law and Economics,* edited by Cass R. Sunstein. New York: Cambridge University Press.

Kahneman, Daniel, and Amos Tversky. 1979. Prospect Theory: An Analysis of Decision under Risk. *Econometrica* 47:263–291.

———. 1984. Choices, Values, and Frames. *American Psychologist* 39 (4):341–350.

——, eds. 2000. *Choices, Values, and Frames.* New York: Cambridge University Press.

Katzenstein, Peter J., ed. 1978. *Between Power and Plenty: Foreign Economic Policies of Advanced Industrial States.* Madison: University of Wisconsin Press.

——. 1985. *Small States in World Markets: Industrial Policy in Europe.* Ithaca: Cornell University Press.

——. 1987. *Policy and Politics in West Germany: The Growth of a Semi-Sovereign State.* Philadelphia: Temple University Press.

——. 1997. United Germany in an Integrating Europe. In *Tamed Power: Germany in Europe,* edited by P. J. Katzenstein. Ithaca: Cornell University Press.

Katzenstein, Peter J., Robert O. Keohane, and Stephen D. Krasner. 1998. International Organization and the Study of World Politics. *International Organization* 52 (4):645–685.

Katznelson, Ira. 2003. Periodization and Preferences. Reflections on Purposive Action in Comparative Historical Social Science. In *Comparative Historical Analysis in the Social Sciences,* edited by J. Mahoney and D. Rueschemeyer. New York: Cambridge University Press.

Katznelson, Ira, and Barry R. Weingast. eds. 2005a. *Preferences and Situations: Points of Intersection Between Historical and Rational Choice Institutionalism.* New York: Russell Sage Foundation.

——. 2005b. Interactions between Historical and Rational Choice Institutionalism. In *Preferences and Situations: Points of Intersection between Historical and Rational Choice Institutionalism,* edited by I. Katznelson and B. R. Weingast. New York: Russell Sage Foundation.

Keasey, Kevin, Helen Short, and Mike Wright. 2005. The Development of Corporate Governance Codes in the UK. In *Corporate Governance: Accountability, Enterprise and International Comparisons,* edited by K. Keasey, S. Thompson and M. Wright. Chichester: Wiley.

Keegan, William. 1984. *Mrs. Thatcher's Economic Experiment.* London: Penguin.

Keohane, Robert O., and Helen V. Milner, eds. 1996. *Internationalization and Domestic Politics.* New York: Cambridge University Press.

Kern, Horst, and M. Schumann. 1984. *Das Ende der Arbeitsteilung? Rationalisierung in der industriellen Produktion.* München: Verlag C. H. Beck.

Kindleberger, Charles. 1963. The Postwar Resurgence of the French Economy. In *In Search of France,* edited by S. Hoffmann, C. P. Kindleberger, L. Wylie, J. R. Pitts, J.-B. Duroselle, and F. Goguel. New York: Harper & Row.

Kitschelt, Herbert, and Wolfgang Streeck. 2003. From Stability to Stagnation: Germany at the Beginning of the Twenty-First Century. *West European Politics* 26 (4):1–34.

Knight, Arthur. 1982. Statement at the ICC Symposium on Structural Adjustment. 10–11 June. Modern Records Centre (MSS200/C/Box 7732), Warwick.

Knight, Jack. 1992. *Institutions and Social Conflict.* New York: Cambridge University Press.

Kohl, Helmut. 1982. Regierungserklärung von Bundeskanzler: 13 Oktober. Dokumente, Deutsches Historisches Museum Berlin.

Kohler-Koch, Beate, ed. 2003. *Linking EU and National Governance.* Oxford: Oxford University Press.

Kohler-Koch, Beate, and Rainar Eising. 2002. *The Transformation of Governance in Europe.* London: Routledge.

Koremenos, Barbara, Charles Lipson, and Duncan Snidal. 2001. The Rational Design of International Institutions. *International Organization* 55 (4):761–799.

Kreile, Michael. 1978. West Germany: The Dynamics of Expansion. In *Between Power and Plenty: Foreign Economic Policies of Advanced Industrial States,* edited by P. J. Katzenstein. Madison: University of Wisconsin Press.

Kuisel, Richard F. 1981. *Capitalism and the State in Modern France: Renovation and Economic Management in the Twentieth Century.* Cambridge: Cambridge University Press.

La Porta, Rafael, Florencio Lopez-de-Silanes, Andrei Shleifer, and Robert Vishney. 2000. Investor Protection and Corporate Governance. *Journal of Financial Economics* 58 (1–2):3–27.

Labour Party. 1997. *Because Britain Deserves Better: The Labour Manifesto.* London: Labour Party.

Lake, David. 2002. Progress in International Relations: Beyond Paradigms in the Study of International Institutions. In *Millennial Reflections on International Studies,* edited by Michael Brecher and Frank P. Harvey. Ann Arbor: University of Michigan Press.

——. 2006. International Political Economy: A Maturing Interdiscipline. In *The Oxford Handbook of Political Economy,* edited by B. R. Weingast and D. Wittman. New York: Oxford University Press.

——. 2009. Open Economy Politics: A Critical Review. *Review of International Organization* 4 (3):219–244.

Lallement, Michel. 2006. New Patterns of Industrial Relations and Political Action since the 1980s. In *Changing France: The Politics that Markets Make,* edited by P. D. Culpepper, P. A. Hall, and B. Palier. Houndmills, Basingstoke: Palgrave.

Lawson, George. 2006. The Promise of Historical Sociology in International Relations. *International Studies Review* 8 (3):397–423.

Lee, Frank. 1960. The Six and the Seven: Long Term Arrangements ("The Lee Report"). 25 May. Public Records Office (CAB 134/1852), Kew Gardens.

Levy, Jack. 1992. Prospect Theory and International Relations: Theoretical Applications and Analytical Problems. *Political Psychology* 13 (2):283–310.

——. 1997. Prospect Theory, Rational Choice, and International Relations. *International Studies Quarterly* 41:87–112.

Jonah Levy, Robert A. Kagan, and John Zysman. 1998. The Twin Restorations: The Political Economy of the Reagan and Thatcher Revolutions. In *Ten Paradigms of Market Economies.* Seoul: Research Institute for Human Settlements.

Levy, Jonah. 1999. *Tocqueville's Revenge: State, Society, and Economy in Contemporary France.* Cambridge: Harvard University Press.

——. 2005. Redeploying the State: Liberalization and Social Policy in France. In *Beyond Continuity: Institutional Change in Advanced Political Economies,* edited by W. Streeck and K. Thelen. New York: Oxford University Press.

Lieber, Robert J. 1970. *British Politics and European Unity: Parties, Elites and Pressure Groups.* Berkeley: University of California Press.

Lindblom, Charles E. 1977. *Politics and Markets: The World's Political-Economic Systems.* New York: Basic Books.

Lloyd, Selwyn. 1961. Revised Draft of Letter from the Chancellor of the Exchequer to the Two Sides of Industry. 16 September. Public Records Office (CAB 129/136), Kew Gardens.

Loriaux, Michael. 1991. *France After Hegemony: International Change and Financial Reform.* Ithaca: Cornell University Press.

——. 2003. A New "Capitalism of Voice"? In *Bringing Domestic Institutions Back In,* edited by L. Weiss. Cambridge: Cambridge University Press.

Lynch, Frances M. B. 1984. Resolving the Paradox of the Monnet Plan: National and International Planning in French Reconstruction. *Economic History Review* 37 (2):229–243.

——. 1997. *France and the International Economy: From Vichy to the Treaty of Rome.* London: Routledge.

Lütz, Susanne. 2000. From Managed to Market Capitalism? German Finance in Transition. *German Politics* 69 (2):149–170.

Maclean, Mairi, Charles Harvey, and Jon Press. 2006. *Business Elites and Corporate Governance in France and the UK.* Houndmills: Palgrave.

MacLennan, Malcolm C. 1964. The Common Market and French Planning. *Journal of Common Market Studies* 3 (1):23–46.

Macmillan, Harold. 1960. Conclusions. 14 July. Public Records Office (CAB 128/34), Kew Gardens.

———. 1961. Economic Planning: Memo by the Prime Minister. 16 September. Public Records Office (CAB 129/136), Kew Gardens.

———. 1973. *At the End of the Day.* London: Macmillan.

Mahoney, James. 2000. Path Dependence in Historical Sociology. *Theory and Society* 29:507–548.

Mahoney, James, and Kathleen Thelen. 2009. A Theory of Gradual Institutional Change. In *Explaining Institutional Change: Ambiguity, Agency, and Power,* edited by J. Mahoney and K. Thelen. New York: Cambridge University Press.

Maier, Charles S. 1987. *In Search of Stability: Explorations in Historical Political Economy.* Cambridge: Cambridge University Press.

Majone, Giandomenico. 1996. *Regulating Europe.* London: Routledge.

March, James G., and Johan P. Olsen. 1984. The New Institutionalism: Organizational Factors in Political Life. *American Political Science Review* 78:734–749.

Mares, Isabela. 2003. *The Politics of Social Risk: Business and Welfare State Development.* New York: Cambridge University Press.

Markovits, Andrei S., and Simon Reich. 1997. *The German Predicament: Memory and Power in the New Europe.* Ithaca: Cornell University Press.

Martynova, Marina. 2006. *The Market for Corporate Control and Corporate Governance in Europe.* Ph.D. dissertation, University of Tilburg.

Mazower, Mark. 2000. *Dark Continent: Europe's Twentieth Century.* New York: Vintage.

McCreevy, Charlie. 2005. *Future of the Company Law Action Plan.* Brussels: European Commission.

McDermott, Rose. 2004. Prospect Theory in Political Science: Gains and Losses from the First Decade. *Political Psychology* 25 (2):289.

McKinlay, Alan, Helen Mercer, and Neil Rollings. 2000. Reluctant Europeans? The Federation of British Industries and European Integration, 1945–63. *Business History* 42 (4):91–116.

McNamara, Kathleen R. 1998. *The Currency of Ideas: Monetary Policy in Europe.* Ithaca: Cornell University Press.

Menz, Georg. 2005. *Varieties of Capitalism and Europeanization: National Response Strategies to the Single European Market.* Oxford: Oxford University Press.

Mercer, Jonathan. 2005. Prospect Theory and Political Science. *Annual Review of Political Science* 8:1–21.

Meunier, Sophie. 2004. Globalization and Europeanization: A Challenge to French Politics. *French Politics* 2:125–150.

Michalet, Charles-Albert. 1974. France. In *Big Business and the State: Changing Relations in Western Europe,* edited by R. Vernon. Cambridge: Harvard University Press.

Middlemas, Keith. 1986a. *Power, Competition and the State. Volume 1: Britain in Search of Balance, 1940–61.* Houndmills: Macmillan.

———. 1986b. *Power, Competition and the State. Volume 2: Threats to the Postwar Settlement: Britain, 1961–74.* Houndmills: Macmillan.

Middleton, Roger. 1996. *Government Versus the Market: The Growth of the Public Sector, Economic Management and British Economic Performance, c. 1980–1979.* Cheltenham: Edward Elgar.

Milgrom, Paul, and John Roberts. 1992. *Economics, Organization, and Management.* Upper Saddle River, NJ: Prentice Hall.

Millington, Andrew I., and Brian T. Bayliss. 1991. Non-Tariff Barriers and U.K. Investment in the European Community. *Journal of International Business Studies* 22 (4):695–710.

Milward, Alan S. 1992. *The European Rescue of the Nation-State.* London: Routledge.

———. 2002. *The UK and the European Community: The Rise and Fall of a National Strategy, 1945–63.* London: Frank Cass.

Minc, Alain. 2000a. *La France de l'an 2000: Rapport au Premier Ministre de la Commission Prësidée Alain Minc.* Paris.

———. 2000b. *www.capitalisme.fr.* Paris: Grasset.

Ministère de la Recherche et de l'Industrie. 1982. *Une Politique Industrielle pour la France.* Paris: La Documentation Française.

Ministère de l'Industrie, and Ministère de l'Économie. 1995. *Rapport de la Mission sur le Financement des Entreprises de Haute Technologie.* Paris: La Documentation Française.

Monnet, Jean. 1978. *Memoirs.* Doubleday: Garden City.

Moravcsik, Andrew. 1998. *The Choice for Europe: Social Purpose and State Power From Messina to Maastricht.* Ithaca: Cornell University Press.

Morin, François. 2000. A Transformation in the French Model of Shareholding and Management. *Economy and Society* 29 (1):36–53.

Mouvement des Entreprises de France (MEDEF). 2002. Encourager l'innovation dans les PME françaises: Propositions du Groupe Projet PME et Innovation. Paris.

———. 2006. Position du MEDEF sur le marché intérieur européen. Paris.

Moynot, Jean-Louis. 1987. The Left, Industrial Policy and Filiére Électronique. In *The Mitterrand Experiment: Continuity and Change in Modern France,* edited by G. Ross, S. Hoffmann, and S. Malzacher. New York: Oxford University Press.

Müller-Armack, Alfred. 1947. *Wirtschaftslenkung und Marktwirtschaft.* Hamburg: Verlag für Wirtschaft und Sozialpolitik.

———. 1948a. Soziale Irenik. *Weltwirtschaftliches Archiv* 64:181–203.

———. 1948b. Die Wirtschaftsordnung soizial gesehen. *ORDO* 1:125–154.

Müller-Hennberg, Hans, and Gustav Schwartz. 1963. *Gesetz gegen Wettbewerbbeschränkungen und Europäische Kartellrecht.* Cologne: Heymann.

Mustar, Philippe, and Philippe Larédo. 2002. Innovation and Research Policy in France (1980–2000), Or the Disappearance of the Colbertist State. *Research Policy* 31 (1):55–72.

Necker, Tyll. 1988. Die Bundesrepublik Deutschland im industriellen Standortwettbewerb. *Markenartikel* 6:246, 250–253.

Neebe, Reinhard. 2004. *Weichenstellung für die Globalisierung: Deutsche Weltmarktpolitik, Europa und Amerika in der Ära Ludwig Erhard.* Köln: Böhlau Verlag.

Newton, Scott, and Dilwyn Porter. 1988. *Modernization Frustrated: The Politics of Industrial Decline in Britain since 1900.* London: Unwin Hyman.

Nichols, A. J. 1994. *Freedom with Responsibility: The Social Market Economy in Germany, 1918–1963.* Oxford: Clarendon Press.

Niederleithinger, Ernst. 1990. Das Verhältnis nationaler und europäischer Kontrolle von Zusammenschlüssel. *Wirtschaft und Wettbewerb*: 721–730.

North, Douglass C. 1990. *Institutions, Institutional Change and Economic Performance.* New York: Cambridge University Press.

——. 1991. Institutions. *Journal of Economic Perspectives* 5 (1):97–112.

——. 1993. Institutions and Credible Commitment. *Journal of Institutional and Theoretical Economics* 149 (1):11–23.

Nölke, Andreas, and Arjan Vliegenthart. 2009. Enlarging the Varieties of Capitalism: The Emergence of Dependent Market Economies in East Central Europe. *World Politics* 62:670–702.

OECD. 1997. *Historical Statistics, 1960–1995.* Paris: Organisation for Economic Cooperationand Development.

——. 1999. *OECD Economic Surveys: France.* Paris: OECD.

——. 2004. *International Direct Investment Statistics Yearbook, 1992–2003.* Paris: Organisation for Economic Cooperation and Development.

Official Committee on Europe. 1966. Future Relations With Europe. 26 May. Public Records Office (CAB 134.2757 (E1241)), Kew Gardens.

Olson, Mancur. 1982. *The Rise and Decline of Nations: Economic Growth, Stagflation, and Social Rigidities.* New Haven: Yale University Press.

Orenstein, Mitchell A. 2001. *Out of the Red: Building Capitalism and Democracy in Postcommunist Europe.* Ann Arbor: University of Michigan Press.

O'Sullivan, Mary. 2000. *Contests for Corporate Control: Corporate Governance and Economic Performance in the United States and Germany.* Oxford: Oxford University Press.

——. 2005. Analysing Change in Corporate Governance: The Example of France. In *Corporate Governance: Accountability, Enterprise and International Comparisons,* edited by K. Keasey, S. Thompson, and M. Wright. Chichester: Wiley.

Owen, Geoffrey. 1999. *From Empire to Europe: The Decline and Revival of British Industry Since the Second World War.* London: HarperCollins.

Palmade, Guy P. 1972. *French Capitalism in the Nineteenth Century.* Newton Abbot: David & Charles.

Parsons, Craig. 2005. *A Certain Idea of Europe.* Ithaca: Cornell University Press.

Parsons, Nick. 2005. *French Industrial Relations in the New World Economy.* London: Routledge.

Pernod-Ricard. 2006. Response to the Consultation on Future Priorities for the Action Plan on Modernising Company Law and Enhancing Corporate Governance in the European Union. Brussels.

Peterson, John. 1996. Research and Development Policy. In *The European Union and National Industrial Policy,* edited by H. Kassim and A. Menon. London: Routledge.

Phelps, Edmund. 2007. The Economic Performance of Nations: Prosperity Depends on Dynamism, Dynamism on Institutions. In *Entrepreneurship, Innovation, and the Growth Mechanism of the Free-Enterprise Economies,* edited by E. Sheshinski, R. J. Strom, and W. J. Baumol. Princeton: Princeton University Press.

Pierson, Paul. 1995. The Scope and Nature of Business Power: Employers and the Development of the American Welfare State, 1900–1935. Paper presented at the American Political Science Association, August.

——. 2000. Increasing Returns, Path Dependence and the Study of Politics. *American Political Science Review* 94 (2):251–267.

——. 2004. *Politics in Time: History, Institutions, and Social Analysis.* Princeton: Princeton University Press.

Piore, Michael J., and Charles F. Sabel. 1984. *The Second Industrial Divide: Possibilities for Prosperity.* New York: Basic Books.

Pitman, Paul Marsh. 1997. *France's European Choices: The Political Economy of European Integration in the 1950s*. Ph.D. dissertation, Columbia University, New York.

Polanyi, Karl. 1944. *The Great Transformation: The Political and Economic Origins of Our Time*. Boston: Beacon.

Pollack, Mark A. 2000. A Blairite Treaty: Neo-liberalism and Regulated Capitalism in the Treaty of Amsterdam. In *European Integration after Amsterdam: Institutional Dynamics and Prospects for Democracy*, edited by K. Neunreither and A. Wiener. New York: Oxford University Press.

Pontusson, Jonas. 2005. *Inequality and Prosperity: Social Europe vs. Liberal America*. Ithaca: Cornell University Press.

Pontusson, Jonas, and Peter Swenson. 1996. Labor Markets, Production Strategies, and Wage Bargaining Institutions: The Swedish Employer Offensive in Comparative Perspective. *Comparative Political Studies* 29 (April): 223–250.

Porter, Michael E. 1990. *The Competitive Advantage of Nations*. New York: Free Press.

Portes, Alejandro, and Julia Sensenbrenner. 1993. Embeddedness and Immigration: Notes on the Social Determinants of Economic Action. *American Journal of Sociology* 98 (6):1320–1350.

Ragin, Charles, and David Zaret. 1983. Theory and Method in Comparative Research: Two Strategies. *Social Forces* 61:731–754.

Rajan, Rughuram G., and Luigi Zingales. 2001. The Great Reversals: The Politics of Financial Development in the 20th Century. NBER Working Paper no. 8178.

Reddaway, William B. 1968. *Effects of U.K. Direct Investment Overseas*. Cambridge: Cambridge University Press.

Reich, Simon. 1990. *The Fruits of Fascism: Postwar Prosperity in Historical Perspective*. Ithaca: Cornell University Press.

Riddell, Peter. 1989. *The Thatcher Decade: How Britain Has Changed During the 1980s*. Oxford: Basil Blackwell.

Risse, Thomas, Maria Green Cowles, and James Caporaso. 2001. Europeanization and Domestic Change: Introduction. In *Transforming Europe: Europeanization and Domestic Change*, edited by M. G. Cowles, J. Caporaso, and T. Risse. Ithaca: Cornell University Press.

Robert, Rüdiger. 1976. *Konzentrationspolitik in der Bundesrepublik: Das Beispiel der Entstehung des Gesetzes gegen Wettbewerbsbeschränkungen*. Berlin: Duncker & Humboldt.

Roberts, John. 2004. *The Modern Firm: Organizational Design for Performance and Growth*. New York: Oxford University Press.

Rodrik, Dani. 2007a. *One Economics, Many Recipes: Globalization, Institutions, and Economic Growth*. Princeton: Princeton University Press.

———. 2007b. Cheerleaders Threat to World Trade. *Financial Times* (26 March).

Rollings, Neil. 1998. British Industry and European Integration 1961–73: From First Application to Final Membership. *Business and Economic History* 27 (2):444–454.

Ruggie, John Gerard. 1982. International Regimes, Transactions, and Change: Embedded Liberalism in the Postwar Economic Order. *International Organization* 36 (2):379–415.

———. 1993. Multilateralism: The Anatomy of an Institution. In *Multilateralism Matters: The Theory and Praxis of an Institutional Form*, edited by J. G. Ruggie. New York: Columbia University Press.

Sandholtz, Wayne, and Neil Fligstein, eds. 2001. *The Institutionalization of Europe*. New York: Oxford University Press.

Scharpf, Fritz. 2010. The Asymmetry of European Integration, or Why the EU Cannot Be a "Social Market Economy." *Socio-Economic Review* 8 (2):211–250.

Schmidt, Helmut. 1974. Regierungserklärung: Kontinuität und Konzentration. Dokumente, Deutsches Historisches Museeum (17 May), Berlin.

Schmidt, Vivien. 1996. *From State to Market? The Transformation of French Business and Government.* Cambridge: Cambridge University Press.

———. 2002. *The Futures of European Capitalism.* Oxford: Oxford University Press.

———. 2003. French Capitalism Transformed, Yet Still a Third Variety of Capitalism. *Economy and Society* 32 (4):526–554.

Schumpeter, Joseph A. 1942. The Process of Creative Destruction. In *Capitalism, Socialism, and Democracy.* New York: Harper and Row.

———. 1950. The March into Socialism. *American Economic Review* 40 (2):446–456.

Schwartz, Herman. 2001. The Danish "Miracle": Luck, Pluck, or Stuck? *Comparative Political Studies* 34 (2):131–155.

Seillière, Ernest-Antoine. 2005. *Qu'est-ce que le MEDEF.* Paris: L'Archipel.

Serra, Narcis, and Joseph E. Stiglitz. 2008. *The Washington Consensus Reconsidered: Towards a New Global Governance.* Oxford: Oxford University Press.

Seyppel, Marcel, and Saskia Sell. 2001. The Takeovers Directive Has Failed: What Will Follow the National Solution? *Finanzplatz* 1 (August):6–9.

Sheahan, John. 1963. *Promotion and Control of Industry in Postwar France.* Cambridge: Harvard University Press.

Shelley, John. 2000. French Forced into U-turn on Social Policy. *European Voice,* 23 November 2000.

Shennan, Andrew. 1989. *Rethinking France: Plans for Renewal, 1940–1946.* Oxford: Clarendon Press.

Shepsle, Kenneth A. 1986. Institutional Equilibrium and Equilibrium Institutions. In *Political Science: The Science of Politics,* edited by H. F. Weisberg. New York: Agathon Press.

———. 1991. Discretion, Institutions, and the Problem of Government Commitment. In *Social Theory for a Changing Society,* edited by P. Bourdieu and J. Coleman. Boulder, CO: Westview Press.

Sherwen, T. 1970. British Business Attitudes to E.F.T.A. In *Europe's Free Trade Area Experiment: E.F.T.A. and European Economic Integration,* edited by H. Corbet and D. Robertson. Oxford: Pergamon Press.

Shlaes, Amity. 1994. Germany's Chained Economy. *Foreign Affairs* 73 (5):109–124.

Shonfield, Andrew. 1965. *Modern Capitalism: The Changing Balance of Public and Private Power.* Oxford: Oxford University Press.

———. 1972. *Europe: Journey to an Unknown Destination.* Harmondsworth: Penguin.

———, ed. 1976. *International Economic Relations of the Western World, 1959–1971. Volume 1: Politics and Trade.* London: Oxford University Press.

Siebert, Horst. 2005. *The German Economy: Beyond the Social Market.* Princeton: Princeton University Press.

Silvia, Stephen J. 1997. German Unification and Emerging Divisions within German Employers' Associations. *Comparative Politics* 29 (2):187–208.

Simon, Herbert A. 1955. A Behavioral Model of Rational Choice. *Quarterly Journal of Economics* 69 (1):99–118.

———. 1957. *Models of Man: Social and Rational.* New York: Wiley.

———. 1976. *Administrative Behavior: A Study in Decision-Making in Administrative Organizations* (3rd ed.). New York: Free Press.

———. 1978. Rationality as Process and as a Product of Thought. *American Economic Review* 68 (May):1–16.

——.1997. *An Empirically-Based Microeconomics: Raffaele Mattioli Lectures.* Cambridge: Cambridge University Press.

Sinn, Hans-Werner. 1999. *The German State Banks: Global Players in International Financial Markets.* Cheltenham: Edward Elgar.

——. 2003. *The New Systems Competition.* London: Blackwell.

——. 2004. *Ist Deutschland noch zu retten?* Düsseldorf: Econ.

Skocpol, Theda. 2003. Doubly Engaged Social Science: The Promise of Comparative Historical Analysis. In *Comparative Historical Analysis in the Social Sciences,* edited by James Mahoney and Dietrich Rueschemeyer. New York: Cambridge University Press.

Smith, Mitchell. 2001. In Pursuit of Selective Liberalization: Single Market Competition and Its Limits. *Journal of European Public Policy* 8 (4):519–540.

Soskice, David. 1990. Wage Determination: The Changing Role of Institutions in Advanced Industrialized Countries. *Oxford Review of Economic Policy* 6 (4):36–61.

——. 1991. The Institutional Infrastructure for International Competitiveness: A Comparative Analysis of the UK and Germany. In *Economics for the New Europe,* edited by A. B. Atkinson and R. Brunetta. New York: New York University Press.

——. 1994. Innovation Strategies of Companies: A Comparative Institutional Approach of Some Cross-Country Differences. In *Institutionenvergleich und Institutionendynamik,* edited by W. Zapf and M. Dierkes. Berlin: WZB.

——. 1997. German Technology Policy, Innovation, and National Institutional Frameworks. *Industry and Innovation* 4 (1):75–96.

——. 1999. Divergent Production Regimes: Coordinated and Uncoordinated Market Economies in the 1980s and 1990s. In *Continuity and Change in Contemporary Capitalism,* edited by H. Kitschelt, P. Lange, G. Marks, and J. D. Stephens. New York: Cambridge University Press.

Spivey, W. Allen. 1982. *Economic Policies in France, 1976–1981: The Barre Program in a West European Perspective.* Ann Arbor: University of Michigan, Graduate School of Business Administration.

Springer, Beverly. 1992. *The Social Dimension of 1992: Europe Faces a New EC.* Westport, CT: Praeger.

Stark, David, and Laszlo Bruszt. 1998. *Postsocialist Pathways: Transforming Politics and Property in East Central Europe.* Cambridge: Cambridge University Press.

Steil, Benn, David G. Victor, and Richard R. Nelson. 2002. *Technological Innovation and Economic Performance.* Princeton: Princeton University Press.

Stein, Arthur. 2208. Neoliberal Institutionalism. In *The Oxford Handbook of International Relations,* edited by C. Reus-Smit and D. Snidal. Oxford: Oxford University Press.

Story, Jonathan, and Ingo Walter. 1997. *Political Economy of Financial Integration in Europe: The Battle of the Systems.* Cambridge: MIT Press.

Streeck, Wolfgang. 1989. Successful Adjustment to Turbulent Markets: The Automobile Industry. In *Industry and Politics in West Germany: Toward the Third Republic,* edited by P. J. Katzenstein. Ithaca: Cornell University Press.

——. 1992. Productive Constraints: On the Institutional Preconditions of Diversified Quality Production. In *Social Institutions and Economic Performance.* London: Sage.

——. 1997. German Capitalism: Does It Exist? Can It Survive? In *Political Economy of Modern Capitalism: Mapping Convergence and Diversity,* edited by C. Crouch and W. Streeck. London: Sage.

——. 2009. *Re-Forming Capitalism: Institutional Change in the German Political Economy.* London: Oxford University Press.

Streeck, Wolfgang, and Anke Hassel. 2003. The Crumbling Pillars of Social Partnership. *West European Politics* 26 (4):101–124.

Streeck, Wolfgang, and Kathleen Thelen, eds. 2005a. *Beyond Continuity: Institutional Change in Advanced Political Economies.* New York: Oxford University Press.

———. 2005b. Introduction: Institutional Change in Advanced Political Economies. In *Beyond Continuity: Institutional Change in Advanced Political Economies,* edited by W. Streeck and K. Thelen. New York: Oxford University Press.

Streit, Manfred E., and Werner Mussler. 1995. The Economic Constitution of the European Community: From Rome to Maastricht. *European Law Journal* 1 (1):5–30.

Swenson, Peter A. 2002. *Capitalists against Markets: The Making of Labor Markets and Welfare States in the United States and Sweden.* Oxford; New York: Oxford University Press.

Takeover Panel. 2004. *Report on the Year Ended 31 March 2004.* London: The Panel on Takeovers and Mergers.

Tetlock, Philip, and Aron Belkin, eds. 1996. *Counterfactual Thought Experiments in World Politics: Logical, Methodological, and Psychological Perspectives.* Princeton: Princeton University Press.

Thaler, Richard. 1980. Toward a Positive Theory of Consumer Choice. *Journal of Economic Behavior and Organization* 1:39–60.

———. 1992. *The Winner's Curse: Paradoxes and Anomalies of Economic Life.* Princeton: Princeton University Press.

———, ed. 1993. *Advances in Behavioral Finance.* New York: Russell Sage.

———. 2004. Mental Accounting Matters. In *Advances in Behavioral Economics,* edited by Colin E. Camerer, George Loewenstein, and Mathew Rabin. Princeton: Princeton University Press.

Thaler, Richard, and H. M. Shefrin. 1981. An Economic Theory of Self-Control. *The Journal of Political Economy* 89 (2):392–406.

Thatcher, Margaret. 1988. Speech to the College of Europe. 20 September.

———. 1993. *The Downing Street Years.* New York: HarperCollins.

———. 2002. *Statecraft: Strategies for a Changing World.* New York: HarperCollins.

Thelen, Kathleen. 1991. *Union of Parts: Labor Politics in Postwar Germany.* Ithaca: Cornell University Press.

———. 1999. Historical Institutionalism in Comparative Politics. *Annual Review of Political Science* 2:369–404.

———. 2000. Why German Employers Cannot Bring Themselves to Abandon the German Model. In *Unions, Employers, and Central Banks: Wage Bargaining and Macroeconomic Regimes in an Integrated Europe,* edited by T. Iversen, J. Pontusson, and D. Soskice. New York: Cambridge University Press.

———. 2004. *How Institutions Evolve: The Political Economy of Skills in Germany, Britain, the United States, and Japan.* New York: Cambridge University Press.

Thelen, Kathleen, and Ikuo Kume. 2005. Coordination as a Political Problem in Coordinated Market Economies. *Governance* 19 (1):11–42.

Tietmeyer, Hans. 1999. *The Social Market Economy and Monetary Stability.* London: Economica.

Tilly, Charles. 2009. Europe Transformed, 1945–2000. In *The SAGE Handbook of European Studies,* edited by Chris Rumford. London: Sage.

Tomilson, Jim. 1990. *Public Policy and the Economy since 1900.* Oxford: Clarendon.

Trumbull, Gunnar. 2004. *Silicon and the State: French Innovation Policy in the Internet Age.* Washington, DC: Brookings Institution Press.

Tsebelis, George. 1990. *Rational Choice in Comparative Politics.* Berkeley: University of California Press.

Tuppen, John. 1988. *France under Recession, 1981–86.* Houndmills: Macmillan.

Tversky, Amos, and Daniel Kahneman. 1991. Loss Aversion in Riskless Choice: A Reference-Dependent Model. *Quarterly Journal of Economics* 106 (4):1039–1061.

Tzeng, Rueyling, and Brian Uzzi, eds. 2000. *Embeddedness and Corporate Change in a Global Economy.* New York: P. Lang.

United States Department of Labor. 2008. Productivity and Unit Costs in Manufacturing. In *International Labor Comparisons.* Available at http://stats.bls.gov/fls/#productivity.

Vachudova, Milada Anna. 2005. *Europe Undivided: Democracy, Leverage, and Integration after Communism.* Oxford: Oxford University Press.

Vedrine, Hubert. 2001. *France in an Age of Globalization.* Washington, DC: Brookings Institution Press.

Vitols, Sigurt. 1995. The German Industrial Strategy: An Overview. Manuscript, Wissenschaftszentrum Berlin für Sozialforschung, Berlin.

——. 2001a. Varieties of Corporate Governance: Comparing Germany and the UK. In *Varieties of Capitalism: The Institutional Foundation of Competitive Advantage,* edited by P. A. Hall and D. Soskice. New York: Oxford University Press.

——. 2001b. Frankfurt's *Neuer Markt* and the IPO Explosion: Germany on the Read to Silicon Valley? *Economy and Society* 30 (4):553–564.

——. 2005. Changes in Germany's Bank-Based Financial System: Implications for Corporate Governance. *Corporate Governance: An International Review* 13 (3):386–396.

Vogel, Steven K. 1996. *Freer Markets, More Rules: Regulatory Reform in Advanced Industrialized Countries.* Ithaca: Cornell University Press.

von Wartenberg, Ludolf. 2004. Deutschland im strukturellen Wandel: Herausforderungen für die Wirtschaftspolitik. 22 October. Speech delivered in Halle.

Weber, Steven, ed. 2001. *Globalization and the European Political Economy.* New York: Columbia University Press.

Wendt, Alexander. 1999. *Social Theory of International Politics.* New York: Cambridge University Press,

Wessels, Wolfgang. 1996. Introduction. In *The European Union and the Member States: Toward Institutional Fusion?* edited by D. Rometsch and W. Wessels. Manchester: Manchester University Press.

Wessels, Wolfgang, and Dieter Rometsch. 1996. Conclusion. In *The European Union and Member States: Toward Institutional Fusion?* edited by D. Rometsch and W. Wessels. Manchester: Manchester University Press.

Weyland, Kurt. 1996. Risk Taking in Latin American Economic Restructuring: Lessons from Prospect Theory. *International Studies Quarterly* 40:185–208.

——. 2002. *The Politics of Market Reform in Fragile Democracies: Argentina, Brazil, Peru, and Venezuela.* Princeton: Princeton University Press.

——, ed. 2004. *Learning from Foreign Models in Latin American Policy Reform.* Baltimore: Johns Hopkins University Press.

——. 2008. Toward a New Theory of Institutional Change. *World Politics* 60 (2):281–314.

Whitley, Richard. 1999. *Divergent Capitalisms: The Social Structuring and Change of Business Systems.* Oxford; New York: Oxford University Press.

Wiedeking, Wendelin. 2001. Nein. *Finanzplatz* 1 (August).

Wiener, Martin J. 1981. *English Culture and the Decline of the Industrial Spirit, 1850–1980.* New York: Cambridge University Press.

Williamson, Oliver E. 1985. *The Economic Institutions of Capitalism: Firms, Markets, Relational Contracting.* New York: Free Press.

——. 1991. Comparative Economic Organization: The Analysis of Discrete Structural Alternatives. *Administrative Science Quarterly* 36 (2):269–296.

——. 1996a. *Mechanisms of Governance.* New York: Oxford University Press.

——. 1996b. Prologue: The Mechanisms of Governance. In *Mechanisms of Governance.* New York: Oxford University Press.

Woll, Cornelia. 2006. National Business Associations under Stress: Lessons from the French Case. *West European Politics* 29 (3):489–512.

——. 2008. *Firm Interests: How Governments Shape Business Lobbying on Global Trade.* Ithaca: Cornell University Press.

Wood, Stewart. 2000. Why "Indicative Planning" Failed: British Industry and the Formation of the National Economic Development Council (1960–64). *Twentieth Century British History* 11 (4):431–459.

——. 2001. Business, Government, and Patterns of Labor Market Policy in Britain and the Federal Republic of Germany. In *Varieties of Capitalism: The Institutional Foundation of Competitive Advantage,* edited by P. A. Hall and D. Soskice. New York: Oxford University Press.

Woolcock, Stephen. 1997. Competition among Rules in the European Union. In *The Evolution of the Single European Market,* edited by David G. Mayes. Cheltenham: Edward Elgar.

Zaharidis, Nikolaos. 1995. *Markets, States, and Public Policy: Privatization in Britain and France.* Ann Arbor: University of Michigan Press.

Zeitlin, Jonathan, and Philippe Pochet. 2005. *The Open Method of Coordination in Action: The European Employment and Social Inclusion Strategies.* Brussels: Peter Lang.

Zysman, John. 1977. *Political Strategies for Industrial Order: State, Market, and Industry in France.* Berkeley: University of California Press.

——. 1978. The French State in the International Economy. In *Between Power and Plenty: Foreign Economic Policies of Advanced Industrial States,* edited by P. J. Katzenstein. Madison: University of Wisconsin Press.

——. 1983. *Governments, Markets, and Growth: Financial Systems and the Politics of Industrial Change.* Ithaca: Cornell University Press.

——. 1994. How Institutions Create Historically Rooted Trajectories of Growth. *Industrial and Corporate Change* 3 (1):243–283.

Zysman, John, and Abraham Newman. 2006. *How Revolutionary Was the Digital Revolution? National Responses, Market Transitions, and Global Technology.* Stanford: Stanford Business Books.

Additional Sources

A number of archives and individuals were consulted during the completion of this book. Specific documents from archives that are referenced in this volume are found in the general reference section. The list below provides names of archives and organizations at the time research was conducted, with clarifications where names and locations have changed. Individuals were granted anonymity. Quotes from such exchanges identify only the office and organization and appear in the general reference section.

Archives

Politisches Archiv, Auswärtiges Amt (Foreign Ministry), Berlin
Bundesarchiv (Federal Archive), Koblenz
Historical Archive of the European Union, Florence
Modern Records Office, Warwick
Public Record Office (National Archives), Kew Gardens, Great Britain

Individuals

European Commission

DIRECTORATE GENERAL FOR COMPETITION

Section on State Aids, June 1996 and June 2006
Section on Mergers, June 1996

DIRECTORATE GENERAL FOR ECONOMIC AND FINANCIAL AFFAIRS

Economic Services and Structural Reforms, September 2009

DIRECTORATE GENERAL FOR EMPLOYMENT, SOCIAL AFFAIRS AND EQUAL OPPORTUNITIES

Policy and Perspectives Group, June 1996
Section on Employment and International Affairs, June 2006
Section on Labour Law, June 2006

DIRECTORATE GENERAL FOR INDUSTRY/ENTERPRISE

Sections on Competitiveness and General Industrial and Technology Policy, June 1996, June 2006
Section on SMEs and Innovation, June 2006

DIRECTORATE GENERAL FOR INTERNAL MARKET AND (FINANCIAL) SERVICES

Section on Internal Market, June 1996, June 2006
Section on Financial Services, June 2006
Section on Capital, Company Law and Corporate Governance, June 2006, September 2009

COMPETITIVENESS ADVISORY GROUP

Senior staff member, June 1996

Britain

CABINET OFFICE

Office of Public Service, June 1996
Staff responsible for Competitiveness Reports, June 1996
Economic and Domestic Affairs, April 2008
European and International Issues, May 2007

FOREIGN AND COMMONWEALTH OFFICE

European Union Internal, Foreign, and Commonwealth Office, June 1996
European Union, June 2006
International Trade, June 2006

DEPARTMENT OF TRADE AND INDUSTRY

EU Internal, Trade Policy and Europe Directorates, June 1996
Industrial Relations Division, June 1996
EC and International Competition Policy, June 1996
Single Market/European Union Section, June 1996, June 2006
International Trade Policy Division, June 1996, June 2006

HER MAJESTY'S TREASURY

Europe and International Trade, June 1996, July 2006

CONFEDERATION OF BRITISH INDUSTRY

Manufacturing and International Markets, June 1996
Brussels Office, July 1996
Corporate Governance, May 2006
Financial Services, May 2006

France

PERMANENT REPRESENTATION OF FRANCE TO THE EUROPEAN UNION

Political Affairs, June 1996, May 2006

MINISTRY OF FINANCE

Section on Internal Market, April 2008

CONSEIL NATIONAL DU PATRONAT FRANÇAIS (CNPF)

Brussels Advisor, June 1996

MOUVEMENT DES ENTREPRISES DE FRANCE (MEDEF)

Brussels Representative, June 2006
Section on Corporate Governance, May 2006

Germany

FOREIGN MINISTRY

European Union Affairs, June 2001, May 2006

MINISTRY OF ECONOMICS AND TECHNOLOGY

Europe Section, April 1996, May 2006
Industrial Support Section, April 1996

MINISTRY OF FINANCE

Europe Section, May 2006

MINISTRY OF SOCIAL POLICY AND WORK

Section on European and International Social Policy, April 1996

FEDERATION OF GERMAN INDUSTRY (BDI), BONN/BERLIN

Trade and Industry Section, May 1996, June 2006
Brussels Office, June 1996
Company Law, Corporate Governance May 2006

GERMAN FEDERATION OF EMPLOYERS' ASSOCIATIONS (BDA), BONN/BERLIN

Section for European and International Social Policy, April 1996, May 2006
Brussels Office, June 1996
Section for Wages and Compensation, May 2006

GERMAN CHAMBERS OF INDUSTRY AND COMMERCE (DIHK) BERLIN

Section on International Issues, May 2006
Section on Competition Law, May 2006

Bund deutscher Banken

Section on International Commercial and EU Issues, May 2006
Section on Competitiveness, May 2006

Other

Union of Industrial and Employers' Confederations (UNICE), Brussels

Economic and Financial Affairs, June 1996, June 2006
Social Affairs, June 1996

Index

adaptation benefits, 27, 36, 82, 84, 148, 167, 174, 198

adaptation losses
    definition, 30
    directives, role of, 32–33
    external, 31–32, 84–85, 98, 154, 161, 181
    firms, effect on, 31–34, 47, 55, 70, 82
    government, role of, 29–37, 41, 173–74, 180–81, 183
    maladaptation costs, relationship to, 30–31, 197
    preference transformations, role of, 29–30, 55

Adenauer, Konrad, 145–46

adjustment benefits, 27–29, 36–37, 61, 174

adjustment costs, 31, 197
    See also adaptation losses; maladaptation costs

Advisory Council of the Economics Ministry (Germany), 151

Allied powers, 137, 138, 140, 143

Alternative Economic Strategy, 89

analytical narratives tradition, 13, 101

Association of German Banks (BdB), 160

Aubry laws, 129–31

Auroux laws, 129–30

balance of payments, 72, 74, 107, 116, 118–21, 124

Bank of England, 88–89

Bardhan, Pranab, 183

Barre, Raymond, 114–17

Beaver, Hugh, 73, 75

behavioral economics, 12–13, 39–41, 45, 49–51, 176–79, 199

behavioral institutionalism
    contributions, 13–14, 39–41, 81
    credible commitments, 13, 95–96
    variant of historical institutionalism, 13, 176–79

behavioral rationality models, 14, 42, 45, 49–51, 55–57, 62–67, 185–87

bilateralism, 108, 119, 144–45, 181, 195

biotechnology industries, 28, 90, 157

Blair, Tony, 87–91, 93–96

blockholding arrangements, 18, 25, 102, 123–25, 139, 143, 161, 162

Bretton Woods, 76, 151

Britain
    adaptation benefits, 82, 84
    adaptation losses, 32, 84–85, 91–98
    corporate governance system, 68, 71, 80, 86, 89, 95
    domestic reforms, 3–4, 68–69, 73–75, 78–81, 84–87, 173
    economic models, 19, 24, 68–74, 80, 94–98
    exports, 72, 75–78, 83
    financial services industries, 36, 68, 71, 73, 77, 82, 84, 86, 89
    financial system 73, 78, 80–82, 84–86, 88–91
    firms, role of, 69, 73–77, 81–83, 86, 93
    industrial relations system, 68, 71, 73, 78, 80, 86, 89, 175
    industrialization, 7, 74–76
    innovation system, 68, 71, 80, 87, 89
    institutional consolidation, 69, 80, 86–87
    institutional specialization, 87–96
    institutional trajectory, 3–4, 68–69, 87, 96–97
    institutional transformation, 70–74, 79–80
    investment patterns, 73–82, 84–85, 88–91, 94–97
    maladaptation costs, 83
    manufacturing industries, 72–77, 81, 86
    modernization, 79–82
    multilateralism, effect of, 75–78, 82–86, 90–95
    social contracts, 68, 87

Brown, Gordon, 89, 205
Bundesbank, 151
business
    coalitions, within, 20–22, 26, 35, 44, 58, 82,
        98, 100, 148
    political actor, as, 43, 45, 196
    See also firms

capitalism
    diversity, 5–8, 48
    evolution, 6–7, 9, 14
    historical legacies, 6, 69, 135, 176
    laissez faire, 70, 75, 96
    liberal model, 19
    multilateralism, effect of, 8–11, 14, 172–73
    varieties of, 5–7, 13, 17–18, 41, 45, 98, 176–77
    See also economic models
cartels, 80, 108, 114, 141
centralized market economy, 1, 17–18, 23–24, 29,
    52–53, 57–61, 64–66, 71–73, 99–112, 120
Chirac, Jacques, 121
coalitions
    business, 20–22, 26, 35, 44, 58, 82, 98, 100,
        148, 173–74
    domestic, 60, 172–73
Coase, Ronald, 52
codetermination, 18, 30, 142–43, 149, 154–55,
    162, 168, 209
Colbert, Jean-Baptiste, 101
collective bargaining, 17–18, 71, 103, 106,
    129–30, 142, 163–64
common minimum standards, 35, 85, 122,
    154–56, 181, 198
Community Charter on the Fundamental Social
    Rights of Workers, 85
Companies Act, 95
comparative institutional advantages, 21, 25–26,
    32–33, 35–36, 73, 81–88, 91–93, 97, 107,
    125, 137, 142–43, 148, 156, 166, 181, 197,
    201–2, 204
comparative institutional disadvantages, 2, 26, 87,
    90, 166, 197
competition law
    Britain, 89, 205
    France, 110, 128, 134
    Germany, 141, 146–49, 155–56, 160
Confederation of British Industry (CBI), 80
Confederation of German Employers'
    Associations (BDA), 163–64
Conservative Party (Britain), 68, 72, 79, 81,
    86–88, 94
Conservative Party (France), 113–14, 116–17,
    119–20, 124, 131

Conservative Party (Germany), 140, 153
constructivism, 11
coordinated market economy, 1, 4, 6, 17–19,
    25, 52–53, 57, 59–61, 65–67, 69, 71, 81,
    120–23, 132, 138–42, 148–49, 152, 167
core competencies, 26, 28, 98, 125, 128, 160, 166,
    197, 201–2
Corporate Sector Supervision and Transparency
    Act, 160
Council of Economic Experts (Germany),
    166
Council of Ministers (Britain), 84
credible commitments
    imperative means, 23–24, 48
    motivational means, 23, 25
    preferences, role of, 37
    theories, of, 11–13
    See also governments, relationship with
        firms
credit controls, 17–18, 23, 114–16, 121, 142,
    162
currency values, 25, 75, 88, 107, 116, 120,
    123–24, 152, 155, 159

de Gaulle, Charles, 104
Deeg, Richard, 9
design problem
    adaptation benefits, 36–37
    adaptation losses, 31–33
    British resolution, 86, 93, 95–96, 173
    definition of, 10, 30–31
    embedded rationality model, 49
    French resolution, 112, 126–27, 132
    German resolution, 137, 148, 154–56, 161,
        165, 174
    global rationality model, 46
    maladaptation costs, 33–35
    open governance, 60–61
discretion
    credible commitments, 23–24, 199
    disabled, 29–30
    European Commission, 92
    governments, 32, 132, 155
    macroeconomic policy, 88
    national, 94–95, 110, 117, 122–23, 127, 131,
        146–47, 151, 156, 165, 170, 174, 180–82
    multilateral institutions, 35, 154
directives (European Union), 32–34, 86, 93–95,
    122–23, 127, 161–62, 180, 193
discrete structural analysis, 44, 53–54
distributional conflict, 25–30, 35, 149–50, 158,
    166, 173, 176
Drezner, Daniel, 34

East Asia, 150, 152, 155

Economic and Monetary Union (EMU), 37, 91–94, 124–25, 128, 130, 132–33, 157, 159, 164–65, 175

economic models
business, role of, 20–25
centralized market economy, 1, 17–18, 23–24, 29, 52–53, 57–61, 64–66, 69, 71–73, 99–112, 120
consolidation, 8, 17, 19
coordinated market economy, 1, 4, 6, 17–19, 25, 52–53, 57, 59–61, 65–67, 69, 71, 81, 120–23, 132, 148–49, 152, 167
disaggregation of, 8, 16–17
government, role of, 1–2, 19–25, 59–67, 100
hybrid market economy, 7–8, 19, 59, 99–100
imperfect alternatives, choice of, 26
internal coherence, 4, 28, 90, 136–37, 149, 156, 167, 174, 177
liberal market economy, 17–19, 24–25, 28, 33, 52–53, 57–61, 64, 66, 69–71, 81, 85–86, 94–98, 174
open systems of governance, 10, 16, 181
specialization, 8, 17, 19
transformation, in, 19, 22

Eichengreen, Barry, 36

embedded rationality models, 42, 47–49, 54–55, 62, 185–87

embeddedness hypothesis, 48, 55

employment contracts, 10, 17–18, 28, 33, 129, 142, 158

endowment effects, 40–41, 49–50, 55–56, 62, 202

endowment premium, 50, 56–57, 62, 177, 200, 202

equity markets, 18, 24–27, 71, 80, 82, 89, 102, 114, 123, 162

Erhard, Ludwig, 140–41, 144–46

Euro, 159, 164

European Coal and Steel Community (ECSC), 108, 111, 133, 145–46

European Commission, 85, 92, 126–27, 147, 155, 180

European Company Statute (ECS), 85–86, 122, 154–56, 162

European Council, 85, 131

European Court of Justice (ECJ), 32, 83, 94, 160

European Economic Community (EEC), 9, 36, 70, 76–78, 83–84, 86, 97, 101, 110–12, 134, 145–47, 173

European Employment Strategy (EES), 165

European Free Trade Association (EFTA), 76

European Monetary System (EMS), 117, 121, 152

European Parliament, 94, 161

European Payments Union (EPU), 144

European Union (EU), 7, 9, 11, 31–33, 47, 92, 93, 95, 131, 137, 165, 168, 171, 175–76, 181–83, 194

European Works Council Directive, 162

exchange rates, 92, 114, 116, 151–52, 172

Federal Cartel Office (Germany), 141

Federal Constitutional Court (Germany), 149

Federation of British Industries (FBI), 73

Federation of German Industry (BDI), 147–48, 153

feedback effects
positive, 6, 27–28, 36, 38, 41, 48–50, 90, 177
negative, 29, 115, 119, 134

Financial Services Act (Britain), 89

Financial Services Action Plan (Britain), 94

Financial Services Authority (Britain), 88

firms
adaptation losses, effect of, 31–34, 47, 55, 70, 82
behavioral rationality model, 49–51, 55–57, 62–67, 185–87
Britain, government and, 69, 73–77, 81–83, 86, 93
distributional conflict, 25–30, 35, 149–50, 158, 166, 173, 176
embedded rationality models, 42, 47–49, 54–55, 62, 185–87
endowment effects, 40–41, 49–50, 55–56, 62
France, government and, 104–6, 109–10, 114–23, 128–31
Germany, government and, 140–44, 149, 153–54, 161–67
global rationality models, 12, 13, 38–41, 46–48, 54–57, 62–63, 185–87
government, relationship with, 11–12, 16–30, 36–37, 42, 50–54, 59–67, 128–29, 141
loyalty, 13, 20, 24, 31, 33, 51, 54–55
market economies, role in, 12, 20–21, 45
market integration, 54–59, 66–67
multilateralism, 10–11, 67, 95–96
pivots, as, 20–23, 28–29, 65
preferences, theories of, 45–51
social investments, 51–54, 62–63

framing, 12–13, 27–30, 39–40, 45, 50, 175

Franc Zone, 109, 111

France
adaptation losses, 109–10, 123, 126–29
banking, 29, 102, 114–15, 118, 121

France (continued)
  blockholding arrangements, 102, 123–25
  centralized market economy, 6, 22, 23, 30, 99–112, 120
  coordinated market economy, 120–23, 132
  corporate governance system, 33, 100, 102, 105, 117, 126
  credit controls, 114–16, 121
  domestic reforms, 3–4, 30, 99, 101, 104–5, 110, 113–23, 134
  economic models, 6, 22, 23, 99–112, 120–23, 133–35
  equity markets, 123
  exports, 107, 111, 115, 118–19
  financial services industries, 102, 105, 117, 118, 127
  financial system, 100, 105, 113–15, 117–24, 132–33
  firms, role of, 104–6, 109–10, 114–23, 128–31
  hybrid governance system, 99–100, 123–24, 131–33, 181
  industrial relations system, 100, 103, 106, 117, 129–31, 175
  industrialization, 7, 22, 104–5, 108–9, 118, 124
  innovation system, 100, 103, 106, 113, 117, 121, 123, 127–28
  institutional consolidation, 101–04, 111–12
  institutional recombination, 123–33
  institutional specialization, 117–19
  institutional trajectory, 3–4, 101, 132
  institutional transformation, 114–17, 133
  investment patterns, 105–6, 109, 112, 116–19, 132
  maladaptation costs, 110, 122, 125, 129, 131–34
  manufacturing industries, 99–100, 105, 107–15, 126–27
  multilateralism, effect of, 107–12, 129, 134–35, 173–74
  natural resources, 107–8
  pointillist character, 99
  unemployment, 117, 119, 122–23, 127, 130–31
Frankfurt, 159
free trade agreements, 110, 145
French Business Federation (MEDEF), 131, 132
French Overseas Union, 111
Frieden, Jeffry, 10

General Agreement on Tariffs and Trade (GATT), 9, 76, 145, 151, 153
German Democratic Republic, 140
Germany
  adaptation losses, 32, 146–48, 154–56, 165
  banking, 29, 32, 139, 142–43, 150, 159–60
  blockholding arrangements, 139, 143, 161, 162
  codetermination, 142–43, 149, 154–55, 162, 168
  coordinated market economy, 6, 24, 138–40, 148–49, 152, 167
  corporate governance system, 139, 143–44, 150, 155, 157–58
  domestic reforms, 3–4, 26–27, 136–38, 142, 147–49, 158–65, 168–69, 174
  economic models, 19, 24, 136
  exports, 148, 152–53
  financial services industries, 139, 162–63
  financial system, 138, 142–44, 150, 157, 157–60, 162–63, 167–69
  firms, role of, 140–44, 149, 153–54, 161–67
  hybrid governance system, 138, 158–59, 167–69, 181
  industrial relations system, 37, 139, 142, 150, 155, 157–58, 168, 175
  industrialization, 7, 149
  innovation system, 137, 139, 157, 165–67
  institutional consolidation, 138–48
  institutional recombination, 157–68
  institutional specialization, 137, 148–51
  institutional trajectory, 3–4, 35, 149
  institutional transformation, 167–68
  investment patterns, 136, 143, 152, 166
  maladaptation costs, 154, 158, 161, 161–65, 167–68
  manufacturing industries, 140–44, 150, 162, 166
  multilateralism, effect of, 136–37, 144–48, 153, 155, 165–71, 174
  social market economy, 140–45, 151, 168, 171, 207
Gilpin, Robert, 178
Giscard d'Estaing, Valery, 114, 117
global rationality models, 12, 13, 38–41, 46–48, 54–57, 62–63, 185–87, 198–99
Goodin, Robert, 31, 36
governance costs, 51–57, 185–87, 201
governments
  adaptation losses, 29–37, 41, 173–74, 180–81, 183
  designs, role in, 9–11, 14, 16–17, 20, 24, 30–37
  distributional conflict, 25–30, 35, 149–50, 158, 166, 173, 176
  domestic status quo, 33–36
  economic models, role in, 1–2, 19–26, 59–67, 100
  firms, relationship with, 11–12, 16–30, 36–37, 42, 50–54, 59–67, 128–29, 141

historical legacies, role of, 5–7, 12, 38, 40
maladaptation costs, 29–37, 40, 173–75, 180–81
multilateralism, effect of, 8–11, 14, 16, 29, 46, 60–62, 173, 178
open governance, 59–61, 105, 135, 179
reform programs, 2–3, 7, 10–14, 20, 23, 27–30, 74
See also Britain, France, and Germany
Granovetter, Mark, 200

Hall, Peter A., 38, 81
Hardin, Russell, 23
harmonization
    adaptation losses, 33
    European Commission, 180
    financial services, 94
    maladaptation costs, 34, 133
    social standards, 122, 131, 134, 146, 153–54,
    workplace conditions, 85, 110–11
Hirschman, Albert O., 20, 54, 202
historical institutionalism, 5–7, 12–13, 30, 38–41, 45, 48–51, 176–77, 194–95
    See also behavioral institutionalism
historical legacies, 5–7, 12, 38, 40, 69, 135, 176
Hobsbawn, Eric, 70
hostile takeovers, 30, 33, 90, 95, 123, 126–27, 143, 160
    hybrid governance, 7–8, 19, 22, 41, 59, 99–101, 131–32, 158, 167–68, 181

incentive compatibility, 14, 28, 37, 60–62, 67, 87, 172–73, 186
industrial innovation, 3, 28–29, 100, 166
inflation, 25, 75, 79, 81, 88, 109, 113, 116, 119, 124, 151
information technology industries, 90, 123, 127, 159, 166
institutional analysis
    behavioral, 11–14, 39–41, 81, 95–96, 176–83
    discrete structural analysis, 44, 53–54
    firm-centric, 20–22
    general equilibrium analysis, 10, 193
    historical, 5–7, 12–13, 30, 38–41, 45, 48–51, 176–77
    pivots, role of, 17, 20–23, 29
    rational choice, 6–7, 12, 38–39, 46
    systematic process analysis, 13, 37–43, 198
institutional arbitrage
    behavioral rationality model, 57
    exit option, 54–55, 201–2
    practice, 54–55, 57, 201

institutional complementarities, 27–29, 41, 48–49, 167, 197
institutional development
    consolidation, 7–8, 17–19, 21, 37, 65–67, 69–70, 80, 101–12, 138–48, 173, 175
    market integration, and, 7–8
    patterns, 8, 17–19, 87, 100–103, 170
    preferences, role of, 11–12
    recombination, 4, 8, 19, 22, 65–66, 123–33, 138, 157–68, 181
    specialization, 7–8, 17–19, 57–59, 64–67, 87–96, 101, 137, 148–51
    transformation, 7–8, 19, 22, 64–65, 70–87, 114–17, 159–63
institutional differentials, 27–31, 34–35, 41, 50–51, 54, 60
institutional innovation 1–2, 87, 113, 121
institutions
    definition, 20, 195
    innovation, 1–2, 87, 113, 121
    radical change, definition, 19, 196
    self-enforcing, definition, 17, 195
    self-reinforcing, definition, 27, 195
    self-undermining, definition, 22, 29, 55, 78
    social contracts, and, 20–21, 44, 51, 54, 62, 65, 68, 88, 152, 162, 169, 185–87, 201–2
interaction intensity, 60–61, 67, 187
internal market (European Union)
    Britain, 36, 83–85, 91
    effects, varied, 10
    France, 101, 121–23, 125, 128, 132, 134, 206
    Germany, 32, 137, 151, 153, 155–56, 159, 167–68
    Single European Act, 198
International Monetary Fund (IMF), 9, 181
International Trade Organization, 76, 145

Jackson, Gregory, 9
Jospin, Lionel, 130–31

Katzenstein, Peter, 171
Katznelson, Ira, 37

labor markets, 21–22, 25, 28, 32, 69, 80, 82, 88–89, 130–31, 161, 164
Labour Party (Britain), 68, 70, 72, 87–89, 93–95
Law against Restraints on Competition (GWB), 141, 147, 149, 155
liberal market economy, 17–19, 24–25, 28, 33, 52–53, 57–61, 64, 66, 69–71, 81, 85–86, 94–98, 174
loyalty, 13, 20, 22–24, 31, 33, 51, 54–55
Luxembourg Process, 165

Maastricht Treaty
   See Treaty on European Union
Macmillan, Harold, 76–77
Major, John, 87–93, 95–96
maladaptation costs
   adaptation losses, relationship to, 30–31
   definition, 29, 197
   directives, role of, 34, 131
   external, 33–35, 46, 61, 83, 134, 161, 169
   government, role of, 29–37, 41, 173–75,
      180–81
   preference transformations, role of, 47, 55,
      57, 158
March, James, 38
Marshall Plan, 109, 144
Martin, Lisa, 10
mental accounting, 41, 167
mergers, 30, 90, 100, 105, 110, 118, 128, 141,
   147, 149, 155
Ministry of Finance (France), 106
Mitterrand, François, 117, 119
Monetary Policy Committee, 88
Monnet, Jean, 108
monopolies, 104, 147
multilateralism
   Britain, in, 75–78, 82–86, 90–95
   capitalism, effect on, 8–11, 14, 172–73
   comparative capitalism literature, 9, 172
   constraint on domestic reform, as, 35, 91
   definition, 194–95
   domestic reforms, 8–11, 16, 83–84, 107
   external adaptation benefits, 36
   external adaptation losses, 31–32, 91, 93
   firm strategies, 10–11, 95–96
   forms, 59–61
   France, in, 107–12, 129, 134–35, 173–74
   Germany, in, 136–37, 144–48, 153, 155,
      165–71, 174
   government, effect on, 8–11, 14, 16, 29, 46,
      60–62, 173, 178
   institutional differentials, and, 60
   preference transformations, 34
multilateralism null hypothesis, 46, 61–62, 64,
   202–3
mutual recognition, 83, 122, 153, 180–81

National Enterprise Board (Britain), 86
National Plan (Britain), 89
natural resources, 107–8
non-tariff barriers (NTBs), 83

Olsen, Johan, 38
Olson, Mancur, 4

open governance, 59–61, 105, 135, 179
open method of coordination, 165, 180–81
open system of governance, 10, 16, 30, 105, 135,
   172, 181
open systems analysis, 10, 179
opportunity costs, 12–13, 26, 29, 34–35, 38, 40,
   46–50, 55, 61–62, 72, 74, 110–12, 125, 132,
   175, 182, 197, 202
opt-outs, 33, 63, 70, 92–94, 175, 181, 205
Organization for Economic Co-operation and
   Development (OECD), 119
Organization for European Economic
   Cooperation, 76

Parliament (Britain), 84, 93
path dependence, 6, 31, 38, 69
pharmaceutical industries, 82, 90
poison pills, 126, 127
Polanyi, Karl, 96
political economy null hypothesis, 46, 54–58
Portes, Alejandro, 42
preferences
   business coalitions, structure of, 44, 86
   institutional, 11–12, 45, 64, 86, 159, 164
   institutional development, role in, 11, 86
   transformations, 12, 29, 34, 47, 55, 57
price stability, 136, 140, 151

reciprocity clauses, 127
reference points, 12, 39–41, 50, 56–57, 120, 164,
   167, 177, 200
regulations (European Union), 32, 180, 193
research and development (R&D) spending, 21,
   23, 77, 90–92, 128, 166, 176
risk capital, 17–18, 20, 71, 90, 102, 129, 139,
   157–58
Rodrik, Dani, 182
Ruggie, John, 36

Schuman, Robert, 108
Schumpeter, Joseph A., 2, 179
Sensenbrenner, Julia, 42
shareholder arrangements, 17–18, 20–21, 28, 71,
   160, 162
Shonfield, Andrew, 8–9
Single European Act (SEA), 84, 204–5
Smithsonian agreement, 152
social contracts, 20–22, 44, 51, 54, 62, 68, 87,
   142, 152
Social Democratic Party (Germany), 140, 153,
   161
Socialist Party (France), 113, 117–20, 124,
   130–31

software industries, 82, 157
Soviet Union, 140
Spain, 127
Stability and Growth Pact, 124
Sterling Area, 72, 77
stock markets, 84, 90, 104, 125, 132, 159
Streeck, Wolfgang, 143
sunk costs, 46, 48, 55
Sweden, 126–27
structural reform, 1, 16–17, 20–30, 34–35, 68, 196
systematic process analysis, 13, 37–43, 198

Takeover Directive, 95, 122–23, 126–27, 161–62
tariffs, 9, 31, 75, 83, 110, 145, 154
taxation, 79–80, 82, 131, 154, 161
technology industries, 17, 22, 28, 81, 118, 157, 163, 176
Thatcher, Margaret, 79–86, 88–89, 94, 97
transaction costs, 52–53, 125, 153
Treaty of Rome, 110–11, 146–47
Treaty on European Union, 33, 91–93, 193

unemployment, 80, 117, 119, 122–23, 127, 130–31, 157, 163, 165
United States, 104, 108, 109, 125, 128, 138, 141, 145

variable geometry, 180–81
varieties of capitalism, 5–7, 13, 17–18, 41, 45, 98, 176–77
    See also capitalism
    See also economic models
Vogel, Steve, 96
Vredeling Directive, 84–86

Washington Consensus, 181
Weber, Max, 53
Williamson, Oliver, 52–53, 200
Working Time Directive, 86, 93
World Bank, 181
World Trade Organization (WTO), 128, 183
World War I, 104
World War II, 2, 5, 15, 69, 96, 104, 136, 145

Zysman, John, 107, 112

1